THE ETHICS OF HISTORY

Northwestern University

Topics in Historical Philosophy

General Editors   David Kolb
                   John McCumber

Associate Editor   Anthony J. Steinbock

THE ETHICS
OF HISTORY

Edited by David Carr, Thomas R. Flynn,
and Rudolf A. Makkreel

Northwestern University Press
Evanston, Illinois

Northwestern University Press
Evanston, Illinois 60208–4170

Copyright © 2004 by Northwestern University Press.
Published 2004. All rights reserved.

Printed in the United States of America

10 9 8 7 6 5 4 3 2 1

ISBN 0–8101–2026–7 (cloth)
ISBN 0–8101–2027–5 (paper)

Library of Congress Cataloging-in-Publication data are available from the
Library of Congress.

Contents

Introduction

The "Ethics of History"—what is implied by this phrase? What questions does it evoke? The term "history" is notoriously ambiguous, of course, since it refers both to the historical process itself and to the knowledge we have of that process—or rather to the inquiry or discipline of acquiring such knowledge. The historical process itself consists in large part of the actions and sufferings of persons and groups, and ethics concerns human action, so presumably the whole historical process could be seen as subject to ethical constraint. Historical inquiry explores that process in hindsight, and if we are all inclined to judge ethically the actions of people around us, will historians not inevitably bring the same kind of moral judgment to bear on the past actions and human sufferings they learn about? Some historians have followed Ranke in claiming neutrality, but many others have rejected this posture. This raises the further question whether the ways in which historians present their subject matter is not itself subject to moral scrutiny.

These are some of the questions that motivated the editors of this volume to conceive of an interdisciplinary conference devoted to the Ethics of History. We are philosophers with a shared interest in the philosophy of history, even though we have come to this shared interest from different backgrounds and points of view. It occurred to us that the juxtaposition of ethics and history, in all its novelty and ambiguity, might serve to stimulate the interest of a number of researchers in such fields as literary studies and religion as well as history and philosophy. We wanted to bring people together to exchange their ideas on this topic, and see where it would lead us. This volume is the result.

We proposed the idea of the conference to the Department of Philosophy of Emory University, which was about to embark on a series of biennial conferences honoring the late Leroy E. Loemker. Loemker was a noted historian of philosophy—his edition of the Leibniz correspondence is perhaps his best-known legacy as a scholar—who taught at Emory from 1929 to 1969, and who served as chair of the Philosophy Department and dean of the Graduate School of Arts and Sciences. Above all, he was an influential teacher and mentor to several generations of students, and the conferences will be a testimony to that influence. Years ago a group of his students and friends set up a fund to sponsor lectures in his honor. Through the continued generosity of the donors, it has become possible to envisage a more ambitious commemoration. This is how the idea of the conferences was born. The department decided to support our proposed topic, and we received further financial support from the deans of Emory College and of the Graduate School of Arts and Sciences. The conference was held at the Emory Conference Center on April 17–19, 1998, and two others have occurred since then.

We think the present topic is an appropriate one to inaugurate the series of publications of the papers from the Emory Loemker Conferences. One aspect of the ethics of history which is dealt with in the papers that follow is our sense of obligation to our predecessors and our moral need to preserve their memory. In a way the entire series has its origin in the conviction of some students that they had an obligation to their teacher and a need to commemorate him.

The conference itself was a rare occasion of insightful reflection, eloquence, and respectful and valuable exchange of ideas. The participants came from different countries, different disciplines, and different philosophical directions, and without any prior coaching each person approached the topic in his or her own way. The results could have been very disjointed; anyone who attends academic conferences knows that some simply do not come together. There seemed to be general agreement that this one did. We hope that this collection will have something of the same coherence for the reader that the conference had for its participants.

One especially poignant moment deserves mention. Jean-François Lyotard, who was the Woodruff Professor of French and Philosophy at Emory, and had taught there since 1992, was a friend, colleague, or teacher of many who attended the conference. Though he was seriously ill, we hoped until quite late that he could be present. He had prepared a particularly striking English text for presentation, but in the event it was read by his colleague in the Emory French Department, Professor Dalia Judovitz. He died two days later in Paris.

The twelve authors in this collection exploit the ambiguity of their common topic, the ethics of history. And yet in the resultant space several issues emerge on which nearly all of them agree. The first is their critique of representation in the standard sense that historians should "represent" the past as it actually happened. All reject the flat-footed correspondence theory of historical truth that this sense presumes, as well as the implicit obligation of the historian to be dispassionate and value-free in his or her account of the past. Explicitly or implicitly, each accepts Michel de Certeau's thesis of an unbridgeable gap between the past and the historian's present account. Secondly, they are nearly unanimous in their call for a revision of the popular appeal to historical *objectivity*. While none settles for an epistemic anarchism or wishes that arbitrariness hold sway in the domain of historical inquiry and writing, most remind us of the need to respect the role of the subject in history, both as historian and as historical agent. Each author agrees that objectivity and respect for the subject are not incompatible, indeed that they demand each other. Most introduce an *aesthetic* component into historical discourse, whether by way of a reformed concept of representation or an appeal to the likely story. While none articulates an explicit ethical position, each acknowledges an *ethical dimension* to the historical enterprise and views that dimension as integral to what history is. In other words, the positivist model, with its appeal to covering laws and its ideal of value-free historiography, is dead as far as these authors are concerned. Curiously, the most commonly cited philosopher is Nietzsche, a sign that the post-structuralist canon of his opinion is respected even by its critics.

But if these authors share several theses in common, each does so in a distinctive manner, reflecting both their larger philosophical interests and their respective epistemic and ethical perspectives. Though the ensuing discussion of each paper in a conference is not recorded here, the fact that such focused conversation occurred is reflected in all but the essay by Lyotard. This includes the three conveners who, though their essays were prepared after the debates, participated fully in each session.

F. R. Ankersmit sets the tone for the discussion with his rehabilitation of subjectivity in historical discourse. He is critical of several traditional views on the subjectivity/objectivity problem because "these views fail to recognize that the problem arises from the logical proximity of truth and value." He assures those who sense a kind of nihilism afoot here that, in his view, "'truth' determines 'value' and not vice versa." His argument turns on aesthetic and political uses of "representation" that are more functional than substitutional in nature. If epistemology ties words to things, he insists, "representation ties *things* to *things*" in the sense that it is futile to seek a one-to-one correspondence between a representation and the "thing" it represents. The relevance of this claim to historical epistemology is apparent: absent a simple referent for historical discourse in the world, we are counseled to view historical representations of part of the past "as *proposals* for what specific piece of language could best be tied to a specific part of the past" rather than as epistemic propositions about its precise identity. This entails the choice of relevance and insight over precision and accuracy in constructing one's account. Because of the gap between the two domains, "either we will go to the heart of reality with representation, but then we will inevitably be vague and imprecise, or we shall have to sacrifice relevance and insight to the precision and accuracy of the true statement." Ankersmit sees this as an unfortunate but necessary feature of language itself. It follows, he argues, that from a logical point of view representation is prior to the true statement, aesthetics precedes epistemology (the very antithesis of what Allan Megill will claim). Indeed, it takes logical precedence over normative discourse as well, for ethical rules and values, he argues, are ingredients in the "circumstances" under which the historian presents his or her proposals. Moreover, just as historical discourse is our best source for information about what moral and political standards we should adopt, he claims, so we should "prefer the political and moral values that have inspired the strongest and most successful representations of the past." By appeal to the aesthetic criteria of *representational success* and specifically to what he calls the greatest "*scope*" of a representation in subsuming the greatest part of reality, Ankersmit hopes that aesthetics can keep at bay the twin threats of relativism and irrationality that stalk a position such as his.

If Ankersmit revises representation, Edith Wyschogrod rejects it entirely. She insists that the "original" and the "narrated" events are heterogenous. The past is to be re-figured, not represented, by the historian, whose twin personae of "lover of the past" and "one who promises" are combined in what she calls the "heterological historian." She credits Foucault for "initiating discursive practices that make possible the genre of heterological history" in which the other is positioned between words and things. It is the excluded other to whom the heterological historian gives voice in what Wyschogrod describes as "passionate disinterestedness." This oxymoron denotes the impossibility of the historian to absent herself from her work. What appear at first to be purely epistemic questions about truth and evidence get rephrased under this description as, in Foucault's words, "whose truth is being told, to whom, by whom and to what end?"

As if to stem the tide of aestheticism that he sees rising from the representationalist model of historical understanding, Allan Megill insists on the primacy of epistemological considerations in the historian's craft. The historian, he claims, ought to model truth-telling; this veridical responsibility is the primary source of whatever ethical considerations enter the historian's discipline. Acknowledging the dark, traumatic side of history to which Wyschogrod refers, he recommends that the historian employ a form of Peircean "abduction" to deal with such areas, resting content with possibility, not certainty or even probability in this domain. He believes one can thereby reserve a place for the speculative and the fictive within historiography itself while tempering potential excess by the epistemological commitment that he takes to be essential to the discipline. For the historian, he argues, ought to be a judge rather than an advocate. His obligation is to provide accounts of the past that are "maximally true and maximally illuminating."

Arthur Danto suggests addressing the topic of the conference by focusing on "something stronger than morality as a topic for history but weaker than history as a topic for morality." The former would entail little more than the analytic moves of linking historical explanation to reasons and recognizing that such reasons are often moral in content; whereas the latter approach, he thinks, would quickly slip into a kind of theodicy. He settles on Herodotus's stated aim "to preserve the memory of the past by putting on record the astonishing achievements both of our own and other people." The ethical issue arises when we ask whether we have a duty to the past itself to find out its truth: "Does history . . . exist for the sake of the past which somehow has a right correlative with our duty not to allow it to vanish from consciousness—a right not to be forgotten and a duty not to forget?" Admitting he does not have the answer, he modestly proposes reflections toward a possible response. Among these is the Nietzschean suggestion that we owe our humanity and likewise our historiality to Bad Conscience (to our inability to forget). From which it follows that morality and historical consciousness arise together, namely, through our paradigmatic power to make and keep promises (compare Wyschogrod and Caputo). Though Danto resists the temptation to read history as individual memory writ large, he admits that our status as *pour autrui* (for others) in the Sartrean sense demands that our "astonishing achievements" be preserved to future generations for their awe and admiration. But it is the truth of these achievements, not their falsehood, that deserves preservation, and he claims that it is the ethical task of the historian to sift the true from the false in critical assessment. Citing an example from the history of painting, he concludes that "history and morality, mediated by the ontological reality of other consciousness, form . . . a metaphysical knot." Though not addressing the cognate issue of *l'art pour l'art*, he does avow that "just because something is past does not remove it from moral scrutiny."

Limiting his discussion to what he calls "eschatological history," John Caputo takes up the question that Danto sets aside, namely, the one that threatens to slip into a kind of theodicy. But Caputo addresses the Achille's heel of traditional theodicy, the irrecuperable loss that is human suffering: "[There is] no theodicy to explain it which is not an obscenity." Building on the work of Levinas and Derrida, he shifts the question from matters of retribution and restitution (such loss is essentially an-economic) to that of gift and memory: "All that history has is fragile memory, which is a poor substitute for justice, but the only one available." He concludes that "historical writing begins in earnest . . . only when it experiences this impossible exigency." He parses this experience of the impossible reconciliation of physical suffering and "redemptive" memory by a Levinasian analysis of the "other" (Danto/Sartre's *autrui*) whose "appeal" frees me from the confines of my "self" and makes morality possible. "There is no justice . . . wise enough or swift enough to 'repair' the present, which has been irreparably damaged. Such 'repair' of the irreparable is the effect, not of justice, but of salvation; that is the exigency of salvation." And this is the hope against hope, the messianic hope (without a Messiah, as Derrida insists) that alone can deliver us from the depths of our solitude by splitting it in half with the other's touch. Eschatological history, far from ransoming the losses via long-term gains, lets the loss be a loss and seeks, "by an impossible gesture," to comfort it. That gesture is the historian's recounting the dead's gift of their suffering (the only pure, because unrequitable, gift) to the generation to come (*a-venir*). In sum, "the historian writes in the time between the dead and the children."

Taking Sophocles' *Antigone* as her vehicle, Joan Copjec contrasts different readings of the play, specifically those of Hegel and Lacan, to underscore the possibilities of a psychoanalytic approach to history and a secularized conception of immortality. Lacan is shown to revise Hegel's understanding of history "by (1) sexualizing work [via Freudian sublimation] and (2) debiologizing death in an effort, in both cases, to corporealize the ethical subject." Her argument turns on two axes: (a) a refinement of the popular understanding of "sublimation" that enables her to read the "immortality" at issue in Antigone's need to bury her brother as the necessary frustration (read "sublimation") of the death drive; and (b) Claude Lefort's notion of the "singular," described as "that which 'once it has come into being, bears the strange hallmark of something that *must be*' and therefore cannot die." It is through the psychoanalytic concept of sublimation, she argues, "that we will be able to clarify exactly how singularity is able to serve as the modern social bond." Whereas Hegel argues that both Antigone and Creon are guilty because each embraces one principle of the dialectic to the exclusion of another (the particular and the universal, respectively), Lacan insists that Antigone alone is the heroine of the play: her perseverance (Freud's *Haftbarkeit*) in carrying out her brother's burial is ethically different from Creon's fixation (Freud's *Fixierarbeit*) on enforcing the statist prohibition against his burial. In the course of the play, she metamorphoses herself, making the ethical decision—"in light of the partialness of every sublimation—to continue to pursue fresh sublimations," starting with the public, symbolic act that honors her brother's singularity or *ate*, while Creon chooses idealization over sublimation, submitting to the superego's imperative of repressed satisfaction.

In an essay sent to the conference shortly before his death, Jean-François Lyotard turns to the classical text of Augustine's *Confessions* to consider whether memory might be a means of distancing oneself from an event that continues to change the earlier direction of one's life. Appealing to the obviously sexual imagery of the discourse, in particular the spiritual ravishment of the experience of grace, he finds Augustine first delaying his conversion and then prolonging it in the face of what Freud characterizes as the atemporal attraction of the sexual. The mode of a "confession" constitutes the testimony to an ineffable event but also continues its effect. Rather than the report of an occurrence, Lyotard argues, Augustine's text *is* the wound, the ecchymosis, that marks the transformation of the body into soul-flesh. But the conversion is both a distancing from and a reappropriation of one's past. Focusing on his theme of "remembering amnesia," Lyotard writes: "Only after the event, when the uneasiness will have prevailed, when the worry of having gone astray concerning the direction of his life will have driven him to scrutinize the past in order to tear from its loquacious mutism what this past perhaps meant, or means for him now, only then, through memory, or rather through anamnesis, [Augustine] recomposes the hidden semiotics bestrewing his history." Lyotard sees Augustine sketching out "from below, a libidinal-ontological constitution of temporality." Though Augustine seeks wholeness in the presence that draws him on, "he is . . . duped by the repeated deception that the sexual hatches, in the very gesture of writing, postponing the instant of presence for all times." One recognizes the theological function of the "differend" at work in both accounts, Augustine's and Lyotard's.

Joseph Margolis intends to recover historical objectivity while rejecting objectivism and the various errors it presumes: correspondentism, essentialism, foundationalism, and the like. He notes the collapse of objectivism in the twentieth century as sealed by Wittgenstein's post-Tractarian writings. Arguing from the hybrid nature of the human condition (a mix of biology and culture) that extends to the self and its enabling society, he defends a social constructivism "all the way down," including the norms of rationality and legitimation for the societies we inhabit as well as the rule of objectivity itself. Wittgensteinian *Lebensformen* offer the saving context in which objectivity is preserved, though Margolis admits Wittgenstein would never have approved his relativizing use of the term. The biological dimension of our hybrid condition yields plausible needs, interests, and vulnerabilities of our selves. But "historicity," of which he lists eight basic features, is a "sufficient condition for the emergence of apt selves." He faults Kuhn, Wittgenstein, and Foucault for failing to sustain a concept of the self that is "robust enough to serve as responsible agents of history and judgment." This then is his challenge: to correct this failing of constructivism without borrowing from a discredited objectivism. In a move that reminds us just how close existentialism and pragmatism are to each other, he proceeds to spell out the implications of his appeal to *lebensformliche* practices for science, history, and ethics. In cases where ideology and doctrinal bias cannot be eliminated, he recommends "a dampened measure of what is to count as 'objective.'" And in face of conflicting principles and norms, he counsels something like Plato's "second-best conjecture," namely, one that refuses the excesses of the "best" (objectivist) solution in favor of the one that proposes plausible gains against such claims and against all other second-best alternatives.

Historical objectivity concerns Jörn Rüsen as well when he asks whether "methodological rules of research," which stand for objectivity, dissolve historical responsibility. In response he distinguishes three complementary levels of responsibility on which the historian labors: that of the needs of contemporary society for identity and orientation, that of future generations for the ethical effects of historical investigation (e.g., threatening environmental issues), and that of past generations, whose values and norms proper to their epoch must be acknowledged. Each level carries its proper form of irresponsibility. The search for identity can conflict with the value system or the collective self-esteem of one's contemporaries. The relevance of ethical considerations can be undermined by a determinist approach that fails to direct interpretation toward the spontaneity of human activity. And historians can callously or anachronistically ignore the valuational context in which their subjects acted, or, conversely, fail to respect the distance between those contexts and our own, making them our contemporaries by the worship of ancestors and/or tradition. Rüsen sees *temporal intersubjectivity* as the ground for historical responsibility. It is the factor that mediates our relation and our responsibility across the generations. Among the possibilities for responsibility toward past generations that are mediated thereby, he lists doing justice to the dead (a problematic that Wyschogrod and especially

Caputo address), accepting the normative heritage, achievements, and even crimes of past generations, and making oneself an addressee of expectations and threats of the people in the past (Benjamin's "*Wir sind erwartet worden* [We have been expected]"). Echoing Caputo's remarks but in a different key, Rüsen admits that "in its core, history has an eschatological feature. . . . But only under the condition of temporal intersubjectivity [does] this change of the past after it actually happened [have] a chance of consolidation or even reconciliation." He argues that a more than metaphorical concept of intersubjectivity would seem possible along the lines of intergenerational connection of culture and mentality. He concludes with recommendations for a hermeneutics as a broadly conceived methodological procedure to understand those normative and narrative aspects of such temporal intersubjectivity and to mediate the same with the epistemic results of traditional historical research.

It is just such a hermeneutics of history that Rudolf Makkreel discusses. Employing a distinction between the reflective and the reflexive generated by his work on Kant and Dilthey, he calls a hermeneutical interpretation "authentic" when it is not only aesthetically reflective and morally normative but also "reflexive" in the sense that the interpreter is immediately and directly aware of his or her stand toward the world (recall Ankersmit's and Rüsen's appeals to subjectivity in historical judgments). Interpretation is hermeneutical, Makkreel explains, "if what is understood requires (1) reflection on how we are related to others, (2) evaluation of what universal norms if any bind us, and (3) a reflexive sense of how this affects self-understanding." By inserting "hermeneutics" between "ethics" and "history" in the title of this conference, he hopes to expand the scope of more traditional ethical accounts of history so as to include the "other" in our midst—the misfit, the marginalized, the outcast.

Thomas Flynn takes a page from Jean-Paul Sartre's famous theory of committed literature to consider the nature and possibility of "committed history" in the Sartrean mode. He argues that the historian's account is a doing (praxis) and a kind of making (*poiēsis*) for which the doer and maker must take full moral responsibility. The primacy of praxis is the key to Sartre's existentialist approach to history. It justifies one's search for the responsible agent in any historical event or process and it carries over to the historian himself as the one whose narrative fosters certain value-laden issues while ignoring or neglecting others. It follows that the historian's craft is as close to the poetic and the moral as it is to the properly epistemic. It also espouses advocacy of certain moral values (pace Megill), particularly those of freedom and self-realization.

Its model is the extended "existential psychoanalysis" of Flaubert's life and time in *The Family Idiot*. To the charge that this is at best psychohistory and at worst propaganda, Flynn responds that the explicit fostering of freedom is precisely anti-propagandistic and that emphasis on praxis over consciousness frees one from the liabilities of subjectivism.

David Carr responds to recent moves to dilute the distinction between history and fiction, which according to him would undermine the historian's obligation to truth. He points out three presuppositions that lie behind such a tendency. The first assumes that narrative is not cognitive, the second that knowledge and imagination are distinct, separate, and unrelated faculties/functions, and the third that the only reality is physical reality. In the process of countering each of these basic claims, he points out how such "post-structuralist" assumptions share much with the discredited positivist view of reality that they are supposed to reject. Appealing to a phenomenological understanding of "lived" time as opposed to purely successive time, Carr defends the ability of historical narrative to give us a plausible account of how events in the past really happened, and consequently the ability of historians to fulfill the moral obligations of their discipline.

The editors are pleased to present here a collection of essays that, in all their variety, throw light on each other as they explore our ethical relationship to the past. They reflect on the complex intersection of the ethical dimension of life, the historical process, and the attempts of historians to know and render intelligible that process.

THE ETHICS OF HISTORY

Part 1

Historical Representation

In Praise of Subjectivity

F. R. Ankersmit

Introduction

Since antiquity historians have recognized that the historian's political and moral convictions strongly determine the nature of his accounts of the past. In the second century AD Lucian urged the historian, just as Ranke would do some two millennia later in exactly the same words, "to tell the past as it has actually been" and again, like Ranke, this primarily meant to him that the historian should write like an impartial judge and avoid all partisanship.[1] The kind of intuitions behind this recommendation to avoid political and moral partisanship are too well-known and too obvious to need further elucidation here.

However, there is a less obvious aspect to these intuitions that demands our attention. The words "subjectivity" and "objectivity" themselves will prove to be our best clue here. If we consider these terms, the suggestion clearly is that the historian should at all times be "objective," since his possible "subjectivity" would make him add to the "object" investigated by him, i.e., the past, something that belongs exclusively to the "subject," i.e., the historian himself. And in this way the historian would distort the past itself by projecting something on it that is alien to it. This, obviously, is the picture which is suggested or implied by these two words "subjectivity" and "objectivity."

When we think this over it must strike us as odd, in fact, that the historian's subjectivity has always been so exclusively linked to political and moral values. Why is this so, we may well ask ourselves. For it might be argued that the historian's subjectivity, i.e., his own presence in his writings, may just as well be due to many other factors. A historian may have a preference for a specific kind of historical topic, have a specific style of writing or argument, belong to a specific historical school, or

3

simply demonstrate in his writings a stupidity that is characteristic of his well-attested lack of intellectual capacities.

But why, again, have these other causes of subjectivity so rarely been associated with the problem of subjectivity? The explanation cannot be that the traces of these other factors would be so much less obviously present in historical writing than political and moral values. For example, one only needs to open the kind of book written some thirty years ago by a disciple of the Annales school in order to recognize immediately the scholarly affiliations of its author, whereas it would probably be hard to find any identifiable political or moral commitment in it. Nevertheless, no reviewer in his right mind would criticize the book as "subjective" merely because it so conspicuously is a product of the Annales school—even if the reviewer in question would happen to hold the Annalistes in very low esteem.

And there is more occasion for wonder. For to be the disciple of a certain historical school, to write in a certain style, to be characteristically stupid, etc., these are all things that are far less part of the historical past investigated by the historian than our political and moral values, which will almost always be most intimately tied up with the vicissitudes of the historical process itself. Political and moral values have most importantly contributed to what the past has been like; they truly are an important component of the historian's "object" of investigation. So if one were to use the term "subjectivity" in a sense close to its etymological origins, one had better call the Annaliste historian "subjective" rather than the historian whose socialist or liberal values are clearly present in his work. There truly is something "objective" about political and moral values that is wholly absent from disciplinary affiliations, historical style, or sheer personal stupidity.

But perhaps this *is* precisely why historians tend to be so extremely sensitive to the influence of political and moral values. Perhaps they intuitively feel that these influences are so much more dangerous, and a much more serious threat to historical truth because of their quasi-"*objectivity*" than these ostensibly more "*subjective*" factors. Or, to put it differently, perhaps political and moral values are perceived to be such a threat to historical truth, *not* because they are so *remote* from it and do belong to such an entirely different world, but precisely because they are, in fact, so *close* to historical truth, that the two can often hardly be distinguished from each other. Moral and political values belong to the world of the object rather than to that of the subject—and the so-called "subjective" historian therefore obeys the world of the *object* (in the way required by objectivism) rather than what constitutes his own *subjectivity* and what is personal to him. Or, to put it differently, the problem, therefore, might well be that political and moral values are a way in which historical truth may sometimes manifest itself and vice versa.

This, then, will determine the plot of my argument. I shall start with an exposition of some traditional views on the subjectivity versus objectivity problem and attempt to show that these views fail to recognize that the problem arises from the logical proximity of truth and value. After this has been established, it obviously follows that we shall have to look much harder for the exact nature of their relationship than has been done up till now. Precisely because (historical) truth and value are so extremely close to each other, we should develop the best philosophical microscope we can in order to accurately investigate the interaction of historical truth and value.

What we shall see, in the end, through our microscope will prove to be most reassuring: for it will become clear that "truth" determines "value" and not vice versa and, hence, that we need not fear value as much as we have traditionally been taught to do. On the contrary, it may be argued that value will often be a useful or even indispensable guide on our difficult way to historical truth.

Traditional Objectivist Arguments

My thesis that we should not worry so much about subjectivism as most of the handbooks advise has, admittedly, its antecedents in historical theory. A good starting point is William Walsh's observation that nothing need necessarily be wrong with the indisputable fact that different historians will always present us with different accounts even when writing about one and the same historical event, say the French Revolution. The handbooks often already saw in this an occasion for relativist despair, because the fact seemed to suggest that an intersubjective account of the past acceptable to all, or most historians, is an unattainable ideal. But Walsh points out that this is an overhasty conclusion. Relativism only becomes an option to be considered if these accounts should all be mutually incompatible and if, next, we had no means at our disposal to decide which of them is right and which is wrong. But nothing as bad as that will necessarily be the case when we are presented with different accounts of the French Revolution, for example. For most often these accounts will complement rather than contradict each other. An account focusing on the intellectual causes of the French Revolution and another on its economic causes can peacefully coexist together. It would require a most naive and unsophisticated conception of the notion of "cause" to presume incompatibility here. If you say that your car hit another one because the road was slippery, this explanation can unproblematically co-exist with the alternative one that you had been driving too fast. And to the extent that the descriptive component of historical accounts tends to outweigh their causal component, incompatibility becomes even less likely. The statement that a chair has four legs is not in the least contradicted by the statement that it was made by Hepplewhite. Similarly, a political history of France in the eighteenth century does not contradict but complement an economic history of France in that same period. And we may agree with Walsh that this simple and pedestrian observation will already solve most of the problems that so often and so needlessly have driven relativist historians to despair.[2]

Yet Walsh is prepared to admit that in some cases there may actually be incompatibility—and I note in passing the remarkable fact that it will be far from easy to find convincing examples of this, for outright conflict is astonishingly rare in the history of historical writing. But an example would be the conflict between the Marxist thesis that the French Revolution served bourgeois interests and Alfred Cobban's argument a generation ago that the Revolution was reactionary and hurt rather than furthered capitalist bourgeois interests. Here, indeed, we have a conflict and, next, the conflict undoubtedly had its origins in the fact that Cobban held other political values than the Marxists.

But Walsh remains undeterred by even this kind of example. And his argument is that even in this example conflict is merely apparent. Conflict disappears, he goes on to say, as soon as we recognize that a liberal might agree with the Marxist if he were prepared to consider the French Revolution within the framework of *Marxist* values while the Marxist, in his turn, would be ready to see Cobban's point after having embraced *his* set of moral and political values.

But I expect that most historians will find this an impossibly Arcadian view of historical debate; and they would probably object that in this way history would be emptied of meaningful discussion. For all that would now be required is the readiness of the historian to temporarily and dispassionately accept the values of his opponents—and all disagreement would disappear like snow under a hot sun. However, if debate and disagreement could really be banned in this way from historical writing, the same would be true for historical truth as such. For if there is no longer anything to disagree about, the search for historical truth would have become an illusion, and then there would be no room for truth anymore. Similarly, the search for something that is white is unworkable in a world in which everything is white.

We may observe in this later part of Walsh's argument this tendency (that I mentioned a moment ago) to so completely separate truth and value that the two could never come into real conflict with each other. And I would now agree with the historian's conviction that this would be a most naive simplification of the role of values in historical writing—though, admittedly, at this stage of my argument I am not yet in the position to present a convincing argument for my agreement with the historian. This I can only do after having shown how closely truth and value are really related in historical writing.

A similar strategy for explaining away the problem of historical subjectivity by putting truth and value miles apart can be found in the well-known "reasons versus causes" argument. The main idea in this argument is that we should always clearly distinguish between what *caused* a person to hold a certain opinion (such as his moral convictions) and the rational arguments or *reasons* that this person may have, or fail to have, in favor of this opinion. And since these are completely different things, the argument goes on to say, it may well be that certain political or moral values cause people to have certain beliefs, but this fact alone is completely irrelevant with regard to the question whether the belief in question is right or wrong. For example, three decades ago a person may have believed that Mao's China was an awful mess simply because his conservative values caused him to believe so; but nevertheless the belief was completely correct. Hence, even if we can explain what values have caused people to hold certain opinions, these opinions may well be correct and true to actual fact. Or, as Arthur Danto once so succinctly put it: "there are few more pernicious beliefs than the one which suggests that we have cast serious doubts upon an opinion by explaining why someone came to hold it."[3]

This surely is a most effective way of dealing with the problem of subjectivism; but it shares with most knockdown arguments of this type the disadvantage of being, in practice, a bit too effective. For, as each historian will be able to tell you, this philosophically neat and convincing distinction between causes and reasons will simply not work in practice. In actual historical debate, the arguments in favor of or against certain views of part of the past cannot be carved up into what belongs to the world of political and moral values on the one hand, and what belongs to the world of fact and of rational argument on the other. What is objective truth to one historian may well be a mere value judgment in the eyes of another historian. Hence, as was already the case in Walsh's argument, the fatal weakness of the reasons versus causes argument is that it fails to take into account how close historical truth and political and moral values actually are to each other.

Historical Representation

For a more detailed exploration of the interconnections between historical truth on the one hand and political and moral values on the other, it will be necessary to start with a few general observations on the nature of historical representation. I am intentionally using here the term "historical representation" instead of alternative terms like "historical interpretation," "description," "explanation," "historical narrative," etc. For as will become clear in a moment, the relevant secrets of the nature of historical writing can only be discerned if we see the historical text as a *representation* of the past in much the same way that the work of art is a representation of what it depicts—or, for that matter, in the way that Parliament or Congress is a representation of the electorate.

The most widely accepted theory of aesthetic representation presently is the so-called "substitution theory of representation."[4] According to this theory—and in agreement with the etymology of the word "representation"—a representation essentially is a substitute or replacement of something else which is absent. And, obviously, precisely because of the latter's absence we may be in need of the substitute "representing it." To take the example made famous by Ernst Gombrich— who was one of the most influential proponents of the substitution theory—a hobby horse may be a representation of a real horse for a child, because it may function in the child's eyes as a substitute or replacement of a real horse. Similarly, because the past is past—and therefore no longer present—we are in need of representations of the past; and we have the discipline of history in order to avail ourselves of those representations of the past that may best function as a textual substitute for the actual, but absent, past.

There is one feature, or implication, of this account of aesthetic and historical representation that especially deserves our attention within the present context. Namely, that a representation aims at being, from a certain perspective, just as good as the original that it represents. To be more precise: in the first place, the representation attempts to be such a believable and effective substitute or replacement of what it represents that differences between the represented and its representation can safely be disregarded. Yet, in the second place, there *will* and always *must* be such differences. For as Virginia Woolf so aptly summarized the nature of artistic representation: "art is not a copy of the world, one of the damn things is enough." So the paradox about representation is that it combines a resistance to difference with a love of it. A paradox that can be solved as soon as we recognize the logical affinities between the notions of representation and identity: for just like representation, identity somehow attempts to reconcile sameness and difference (by change through time) and is expected to do just that.[5]

Three conclusions follow from these considerations. In the first place, though language may be used for representing reality (as will typically be the case with the historical text), the opposition between the represented and its representation by no means coincides with the opposition between reality and language. Even more so, if we think of works of art, of political representation, of representation in legal contexts, the represented and its representation will share the same ontological status. For both will belong to the world, both will unproblematically be part of the inventory of reality. And, as I have argued elsewhere, language when used for representing historical reality also takes on the logical features that we normally attribute to things (in objective reality) and withhold from the language we use for making true statements about things. If, then, we conventionally define epistemology as the philosophical subdiscipline that investigates the relationship between cognitive language and reality, it follows that nothing is to be expected from epistemology, if we wish to know more about the relationship between the represented and its representation. Epistemology ties *words* to *things*, whereas representation ties *things* to *things*. And it follows that historical theorists, attempting to develop a brand of *historical epistemology* that will explain to us how historical narrative and historical reality are or should be related to each other, are like those philistines who try to explain artistic merit in terms of photographic precision. In both cases the merits of relevance and importance are recklessly sacrificed to those of precision and accuracy. History cannot be understood on cognitivist assumptions only—though undoubtedly these will always be involved in any account of the past. Cognitivism undoubtedly gives us access to part of the historian's intellectual activities, but the nature of these activities could never completely be reduced to it.

Secondly, and most importantly, an explanation can be given for why representation is so little inclined to satisfy the cognitive desires of the epistemologist. The crucial insight here is, as Arthur Danto has shown, that the represented only comes into being, or to be more precise, only gains its contours, thanks to its being represented by a representation.[6] An example from the writing of history may be helpful here. Suppose a historian is writing a history of the labor movement. This phrase "a history of the labor movement" suggests that there exists in historical reality some unambiguously identifiable thing like Karl Marx or Friedrich Engels and that something is named, or can be referred to, by the phrase "the labor movement"—and whose history we can subsequently describe by following it on its, albeit complex, path through space and time. And this picture suggests, furthermore, that when historians disagree about the history of the labor movement, they will be in the fortunate position to settle their disagreements by simply looking at the labor movement's path through space and time, in order to establish who is right and who is wrong. But then we should ask ourselves, what exactly *is* this labor movement whose history the historian wishes to write? In the case of a historical individual such as Marx the answer is simple enough. But what *exactly* is the thing in historical reality that *this* phrase purportedly refers to?

Indeed, in a case such as Marx's you will have, on the one hand, the *individual human being* who lived from 1818 to 1883, while, on the other, you will have the *histories* that have been written about him by historians such as Franz Mehring or Isaiah Berlin. But when we consider the labor movement, we shall make the rather amazing discovery that discussions about what the labor movement *is*, or *was*, and what the phrase may be thought to *refer* to, will prove to be completely identical with the kind of discussions that historians have about its *history*. Disagreements about what the labor movement is or was will be settled in terms of accounts of its history and vice versa. Things (that are represented) seem to coincide here with their histories (i.e., with representations)—as nineteenth-century historicists such as Ranke and Humboldt had already taught us.[7] And this is where things like the labor movement will differ essentially from less problematic things such as Karl Marx or Friedrich Engels. So we must recognize that we actually have *two* categories of things in past reality: on the one hand, there are things that we can unproblematically identify without taking their history into account, such as Karl Marx, but on the other there are things where identification depends on the histories or the historical representations that we have of these things. And of this latter category of representable things in the past we can therefore truly say that they have no contours in the absence of the representation that has been proposed of them. In such cases, if we have no representation, then we will have no represented either. Self-evidently, in the case of cognitive language, the situation is a completely different one, for here things exist independently of the true statements that we can make about them.

It might be objected now that this is true only of historical representation and that things will be different already in the case of the artistic, pictorial representation of reality. Think, for example, of the portrait painter. Is the represented, the sitter, not unproblematically given to us first, so that only at a later stage his portrait, i.e., the representation of the represented, can be painted? But this objection fails to do justice to the challenges of portrait painting, since it identifies the represented exclusively with those physical features of the sitter that may correspond to a good and clear photograph. However, if we think of Titian's famous portrait of the Holy Roman emperor Charles V, it is not photographic precision that makes us admire this representation of the emperor. We admire Titian's portrait because it so strikingly presents us with the emperor's personality and his state of mind after the immense political struggle that had consumed so much of his energy and vitality. And *this* is a feature of the emperor that is by no means unambiguously and unproblematically given to us. This is a feature of the emperor as elusive and as impossible to accurately define as those features of historical reality that the historian of the labor movement attempts to account for in his narrative. So from this point of view, the represented of the portrait painter is no less dependent on how it is represented than the past that is represented by the historian.

To put the same point differently, the physical appearance of the sitter for a portrait as presented by a photograph corresponds to a mere "shadow," a mere "abstraction," so to speak, which is constructed out of all the "representeds" having their counterpart in the representations of the sitter produced by portrait painters (or even by all those people in his entourage knowing him sufficiently well to have formed for themselves an opinion about him). This is where the objectivity of so-called objective reality may so dangerously deceive us. For representations are truly basic, whereas the things of "objective reality" are mere constructions, abstract truncations of concrete representations. Hence, as in the case of the narrative representation of the past, pictorial representation and what it represents logically depend upon each other and owe their existence to each other.[8]

Thirdly, it follows that precision, in the sense of an exact match of words and things, will never be attainable in representation in the arts or historical writing—nor, for that matter, in how in politics the state represents the electorate. Precision can only be achieved if we have at our disposal some generally accepted standard or scheme determining how words are or ought to be related to things. But such epistemological standards or schemes will typically be absent in the case of representation. At most each representation could be seen as a *proposal* for such a rule to be generally accepted—I shall return to this in the next section. And this should not be interpreted as some regrettable shortcoming of representation, if compared to situations in which such standards *are* available—as paradigmatically will be the case with singular true statements such as "the cat lies on the mat." For the absence of such epistemological standards is precisely what makes representation so useful, if not positively indispensable to us. Here we are still at liberty to make our *choice* of those standards, and this will most rigorously be applied at a later stage, when strict conventions are needed for meaningful and effective communication. Put differently, representation offers us language in its presocialized or natural state, so to speak; in its representational use, language essentially still is a "private" language. And those eighteenth-century philosophers, such as Rousseau, who were so passionately interested in the origins of language would have been well-advised to focus on language in its representational use, instead of on the socializing dimension of language. For from a logical point of view this Rousseauistic dimension of language really belongs to a later stage.

Hence, the indeterminacy of the relationship between words and things is not a defect but the supreme virtue of all representational use of language. And those historians who regret the lack of precision of their discipline distrust their discipline precisely for what is its greatest merit and its greatest interest. For here language is born from what was *not yet* language.

Narrative versus Cognitive and Normative Discourse

In the previous section we discussed some logical features of representation in general and applied our conclusions to the historian's representation of the past. Put differently, we moved from a variant of representation that is not necessarily linguistic to a variant of representation that is exclusively so. One aspect of this transition deserves our special attention. Namely, that precisely this strategy will permit us to attribute to the narrative use of language properties that have no necessary connection with language as such. For from the present perspective, (narrative) language is just one more variant of the representation of reality. Here we are not relying upon previously observed properties of language in order to derive from these properties knowledge about its narrative or representational use—our strategy has been exactly the reverse: here insight into the nature of representation is the basis for a clarification of (the narrativist use of) language. Language here is the dependent variable, so to speak, instead of being the origin and source of all true philosophical insight—as ordinarily has been the case in most of twentieth-century philosophy.

The important insight to be gained from this can be summarized in the following paradox. On the one hand, there are no independent standards on the basis of which the link between the represented and its representation can be justified, explained, or verified—and from this perspective we may observe here an indeterminacy in the relationship between language and reality not having its counterpart in the uses of language that have customarily been investigated by epistemologists. But on the other hand, the relationship between language and the world is, in the case of representation, far more intimate and direct since *this* narrative representation has with the utmost care specifically been devised by the historian in order to most convincingly account for *this* represented part of the past. So there are two different ways in which language and the world may be connected; and, moreover, where the one is strong the other is weak, and vice versa. Representation is strong in the sense that it most intimately and exclusively connects one representation to one represented only, but weak in the sense that no formal epistemological schemes can be relied upon to justify this special and unique connection, schemes that could demonstrate that this really is the "correct" connection. The relationship between the singular true statement and reality, on the other hand, is weak in that many other true statements may connect language to this specific part or aspect of reality; but it is strong in the sense that formal epistemological schemes will successfully decide about the truth or falsehood of any of those statements. So either we will go to the heart of reality with representation, but then we will inevitably be vague and imprecise, or we shall have to sacrifice relevance and insight to the precision and accuracy of the true statement. It is between these two extremes that all our use of language must inevitably oscillate—and never will we succeed in combining relevance with precision, or insight with accuracy. This, alas, is our predicament as language users.

What has been said just now about the difference between representations and true statements can be rephrased in terms of the difference between proposals and rules. For think of the following. We may make a proposal for a specific action under a specific set of circumstances; and although the proposal in question may be as specific and as well adapted to these specific circumstances as you like, alternative proposals will nevertheless always be conceivable. Thus proposals share with representation this peculiar combination of uniqueness or specificity with a tolerance of alternatives. Because of this shared feature, we may well see historical representations of part of the past, essentially, as *proposals* for what specific piece of language could best be tied to a specific part of the past. And other historians may then disagree with this proposal and present, in their turn, other proposals for how best to link language and historical reality for this specific case. But none of these proposals for how best to represent the past could ever be justified by an appeal to some specific general rule for how language and reality are to be related. Nevertheless, life tends to repeat itself, and the contexts in which we have to think and act may be often sufficiently similar to allow of generalization. If this happens, the same proposal we made on previous occasions may be considered to be the appropriate one for other, similar occasions as well. And in this way what originally has been a mere *proposal* intended for a particular occasion may become a general *rule* for a certain type of situational context. Representation is then reduced to the level of language use that is investigated by epistemologists—in so far as epistemology attempts to formulate general rules for how words and things are related.

Two remarks are relevant at this stage. In the first place, against the background of the notion of representation we will now recognize that the attempt to formulate such a general account of the relationship between words and things may take two different forms. For such a general account may focus primarily *either* on the nature of the relationship itself *or* on what is most generally true of the things that are related by the relationship. And these focuses should be distinguished. For if x is in the relation R to y, an investigation of R is not necessarily identical to an investigation of what makes x and y stand in this relationship R to each other. The former investigation is *internal* to R, so to speak, whereas the latter is *external* to it. And we may say that aesthetics, as a general theory of *representation,* focuses preferably on the internalist aspects of this relationship, whereas epistemology as a general theory about *how things are related to words* has almost exclusively been interested in its externalist aspects. Hence, it has been the perennial myopia of epistemology to believe that only the latter investigation can help us to further philosophical insight into the relationship between language and the world.

A second and more important remark concerns the *logical hierarchy* between these two accounts of the relationship between words and things. When considering the issue of this hierarchy we should notice that without there first being *proposals* for how to relate words to things, these proposals could never crystallize out into *rules* for this relationship. And this justifies the inference that from a logical point of view representation is prior to the true statement. Or, to put it differently, aesthetics precedes epistemology and it is only against the background of aesthetics that we may discern what is, and what is not, of value in epistemology. We may therefore well agree with the postmodernist attack on epistemology that was inaugurated by Rorty's *Philosophy and the Mirror of Nature* two decades ago, but with the all-important qualification that aesthetics, i.e., a theory of representation, should guide us in this attack and show us, firstly, what precedes epistemology and, secondly, what parts of episte- mology can be rescued (or how it should be supplemented) after we have learned to see it as a mere offshoot of representation.

This latter remark is all the more important since it has its coun- terpart in ethical discourse. For ethics attempts to present us with *general* rules for action given certain types of circumstances. Ethical discourse will typically have the nature of statements such as "given a situation of the type S, one ought to perform an action of the type A." This is where ethical discourse differs from political discourse: political decisions ordi- narily concern issues for which no general rules are, as yet, available. In this way there is, as has often been observed, a truly intimate and direct relationship between history and politics. And the notion of the pro- posal may help us to explain this relationship. The historian will make a proposal to us for how best to see part of the past, whereas the politician will do much the same with regard to an aspect of contemporary politi- cal reality and for how to act accordingly. And such proposals may in- deed result at a later stage in general rules for how to relate language to words, or for how to act under a certain general type of circumstances, but in neither case are such general rules presupposed.

Here, then, may we discern the wisdom of Machiavelli when he so strongly opposed politics to ethics and when he warned us against the now so-popular fallacy which derives politics from ethics. For *if* there is any relationship between the two at all, this relationship is precisely the reverse.[9] Political decisions should not be based on ethical consid- erations, but just as representation may ultimately become codified in epistemological rules for how to relate things to words, so political expe- rience may ultimately become codified into ethical rules. And, surely, there is an interesting historical connection between the origins and the claims of epistemology on the one hand and those of ethics on the other. For both came into being after Descartes withdrew the self from the complexities of the real world into the quiet sanctuary of a Cartesian *forum internum*—thus dealing the death-blow to the Aristotelian "Weltan- schauung" that was still shared by Machiavelli and his humanistic con- temporaries. This Cartesian self was henceforth considered to be both the source of all true knowledge of the world and of an exact science of morals—as most paradigmatically would be the case within the architec- ture of Kant's first two *Critiques*. After the withdrawal of the Machiavel- lian human individual from all the complexities of social and political life into this cognitive and normative *forum internum*, history and politics were automatically and inevitably reduced to the lowly status of being mere impure, tainted, and uncertain derivatives of epistemology and morals, instead of being recognized as logically prior to these.

This is why a high prestige was granted to both cognitive and moral discourse in most of Western intellectual history, whereas history and politics have had to pay dearly for the triumphant successes of their rivals over the last few centuries.

Truth and Value in Historical Writing

On the basis of the foregoing, a preliminary account can be given of the relationship of fact and value in the narrative representation of the past (in the next section we shall see how the account given in this one has to be supplemented or corrected). We have seen that narrative representations should be conceived of as proposals of what could be seen as the best (textual) substitute or replacement of part of the past. And then the decisive question will be—as Gombrich's theory of representation indicates—what could best *function* as such a textual substitute. But if we wish to come to a decision about this question, much, if not all, will depend on the kind of circumstances within which we shall have to consider our decision. We can only adequately evaluate proposals when taking into account the specific kind of circumstances to which the proposal is related. The proposal to put up an umbrella obviously makes sense if it is raining, but, equally obviously, not if the sun is shining. An important consideration is directly connected with this. Proposals can be neither true nor false in the way that statements can be so: the proposal to put up an umbrella when the sun is shining is "stupid," "silly," or "inappropriate" (or whatever other adjective one might prefer), but could not possibly be said to be "false." However, the fact that proposals cannot properly be said to be either true or false does not in the least exclude the possibility of rationally discussing the merits of proposals. Hence, the fact that narrative representations of the past are, from a logical point of view, proposals does not automatically place historical writing outside the reach of rational debate. On the contrary.

When discussing the rationality of narrative representations, two sets of circumstances will primarily demand the historian's attention. In the first place, each proposal made by a historian in order to account for part of the past will have to be compared to other, rival proposals that historians have already made for that specific purpose or that could be sketched, or roughly outlined, on the basis of already existing knowledge of the past. Here the "circumstances" under which the historian presents his proposals can be identified with the present state of the art in historical writing about some historical topic. And, self-evidently, when thinking of *this* kind of circumstances, we evaluate historical representations from a perspective where normative, ethical, or political considerations need not necessarily play a role. For example, the debate about the contribution made by the Dutch state to the economic and political success of the Dutch Republic in the seventeenth century would involve no obvious or necessary commitment to the historian's moral or political standards.

But in the second place, these circumstances may (also) include the social and political realities of the historian's world. For example, the discussion of the totalitarian state during the Cold War period, and the proposals made by historians for how best to see this regrettable phenomenon, cannot possibly be isolated from the East/West conflict of that time. And this is not merely because of the difficulty of distinguishing between the purely historical and the political dimensions of the debate, but because these proposals were simply *intended* to be both a historical account *and* suggestions for a purely political standpoint. Furthermore, think of histories of the Holocaust. Obviously such histories would fail to meet even the most elementary standards of taste and appropriateness if they were to observe a complete moral neutrality and impartiality with regards to the unspeakable atrocities that had been committed against the Jews.[10]

When considering these two types of circumstances under which the historian may formulate his proposals for how to see the past, we will agree that a clear distinction between the two will be difficult to make in the practice of historical writing. Most if not all of historical writing will have to be located somewhere between the situation in which only the former set of circumstances or only the latter set will have to be taken into account. Next, most often each individual work of history will in certain stages of its argument move closer to one set and further from the other—or vice versa. The history dealing with the state of the seventeenth-century Dutch Republic that I mentioned a moment ago may in certain stages of its argument, either explicitly or implicitly, express or imply a political philosophy about what the relationship between the state and civil society ought to be like. Next, a history of the Holocaust will always require a basis in solid documentary research. So even the extremes presented in the previous paragraph will ordinarily already present us with a mixture of fact and value. And the attempt to completely separate the two is unrealistic because no historian can completely abstract from one set of circumstances in favor of the other. The belief that such a clean separation is or ought to be possible has its only basis in our post-Humean and post-Kantian conviction that fact and value are logically distinct domains, but decidedly not in the actual realities of historical writing (or of human life in general, for that matter).

A theoretical explanation can even be given of this continuity between fact and value. For consider the following. A historical representation of the past may contain only true statements about the past, yet these statements may have been selected and arranged by the historian in such a way that it strongly suggests a certain (political) course of action. For example, nineteenth-century nationalist historical writing may occasionally have been wholly unobjectionable from a purely factual point of view, and yet have functioned in contemporary political discussion as a historical justification of expansionist purposes. In this way historical representation truly presents us with the much sought after *trait d'union* between the "is" and the "ought." We begin with merely a set of true statements and move then, automatically and naturally, to an answer to the question of how to act in the future. It may well be true that a dissociation between the "is" and the "ought" will make sense if we ask ourselves how we ought to act given a certain *type* of situation. But as soon as as we have to do with the unicity and the concreteness of individual historical contexts, this continuity between fact and norm immediately takes over, and then the distinction between the "is" and the "ought" will have become a wholly artificial and unrealistic construction.

These considerations may explain why truth and value can come so infinitesimally close to each other in the practice of historical writing—as we had already observed at the beginning of this chapter. Another conclusion would be that all these traditional and well-known worries about the historian as the helpless victim of moral and political standards are justified after all. For if there is this continuity between facts and value, if these two come so close to each other, and even shade off into each other to such an extent that we cannot say whether we have to do with fact rather than with values (or vice versa), what resources would then be left to the historian in order to successfully resist the political and moral prejudices of the day?

But, as we shall see in the remainder of this essay, there is no occasion for despair about the rationality of historical writing and historical debate. For we shall discover that aesthetics will provide us with the means for rescuing historical writing from the twin threat of relativism and irrationality.

In Praise of Subjectivity

This brings me to the last stage of my argument. There will be general agreement that we may discern in the historian's narrative of the past all of the three variants of discourse that were mentioned above. Firstly, it presents us with a *representation* of the past, in the second place this representation will consist of *true statements* embodying its cognitive pretensions and, thirdly, though this may take different forms, and though it may be more prominent in some cases than in others, *ethical rules and values* will co-determine the historian's account of the past.[11]

Most accounts of historical writing (and of its "subjectivity") up till now have focused on the interaction of the cognitive and the moral dimensions of historical writing and on how the two might get in each other's way. That these two should ordinarily obstruct each other need not surprise us. For the same philosophical regime that reversed the Machiavellian relationship between historical and political discourse on the one hand and cognitive and moral discourse on the other also gave us the distinction between the "is" and the "ought." The intimate interaction of thought and action, of what was to become at a later phase the cognitive and the normative, now broke apart. Their unity now gave way to one formal and epistemological scheme for thought, and quite another one for the science of ethical action. Even for Kant the distinction between the "is" and the "ought" was an indisputable truth, although his love of philosophical symmetry inspired him more than any philosopher living either before or after him to discover as many parallels as possible between the two schemes. The realm shared by history and politics was now divided between the social sciences on the one hand and ethics on the other.[12] So for the post-Kantian philosopher the potential conflict between cognitive and normative discourse had to be the most obvious source of worries as soon as he started thinking about historical writing. And indeed, as we all know, the neo-Kantians of the end of the nineteenth and the beginning of the twentieth century saw in this potential conflict the single most important and most urgent problem of all historical theory. In this way, this reversal of the Machiavellian relationship between historical and political discourse on the one hand and cognitive and normative discourse on the other has strongly contributed to the low esteem of historical and political discourse in the modernist intellectual climate. Just as Belgium was the hapless terrain where France and Germany used to fight their wars, so history now came to be seen as the domain where the never-ending war between fact and value was preferably fought. Obviously a place where nobody in his right senses would wish to live. So much the worse, then, for the poor historian who unsuspectingly built his home in this strife-ridden area.

But this perception self-evidently requires us to set matters straight again. That is, we should realize that narrative discourse and its representational proposals have a logical priority over cognitive and normative discourse. Consequently, against this background, this private war going on between cognitive and normative discourse—which so much interested the neo-Kantians—is of a mere subsidiary significance. What truly counts is that the aesthetic criteria that enable us to evaluate historical representations logically precede the criteria we apply for evaluating cognitive and normative discourse. Narrative representation should not be evaluated by an appeal to these criteria of cognitive and normative discourse—on the contrary, the aesthetic criteria of representational success will enable us to evaluate the contribution of cognitive and normative discourse to historical representations. Elsewhere I have tried to define the nature of these aesthetic criteria. First, there is no a priori scheme in terms of which the representational success of individual narrative representations can be established; representational success always is a matter of a decision between rival narrative representations. It is a matter of comparison of narrative representations of the past with *each other* and not of a comparison of individual narrative representations with *the past itself* (i.e., the kind of situation that the singular true statement presents us with). An implication is that the more representations we have, the more successfully can they be compared to each other and the better we will be equipped to assess their relative merits. If we were to possess only *one* representation of part of the past, we would be completely helpless to decide about its scope. Next, when comparing such a set of comparable narrative representations of the past the decisive question to ask will be which one has the largest scope, is capable of subsuming the greatest part of reality. And second, the narrative representation that is most risky, most hazardous, and most unlikely to be the right one on the basis of existing historical knowledge, but that can nevertheless *not* be refuted on that same basis, is this representation with the largest scope. I emphasize that this set of criteria for the evaluation of historical representations contains no *normative* elements: in no way is an appeal made to ethical norms or standards.

Next, it must strike the reader to what extent these aesthetic criteria resemble Popper's view of how to evaluate scientific theories. Popper convincingly attacked the logical positivist view that the best scientific theory is the one that is most likely to be true, the one with the greatest probability. This would promote statements such as "tomorrow it will rain, or not rain" into the very ideal of scientific truth.[13] However, precisely because of its probability, precisely because it could not possibly be refuted by whatever the facts tomorrow will prove to be like, this "theory" lacks all "empirical content" and gives us no useful information whatever about the world. Hence, only if one is prepared to take risks with one's theories, to move *away* from probability, only then can "empirical content" be maximalized and meaningful information about the nature of empirical reality be gained. "Hypotheses are nets: only he who casts will catch," as Popper quotes Novalis in the epigraph of his famous study. Obviously, then, much that Popper has written about how scientific theories may succeed in maximalizing their empirical content can also be said to be true of how we should evaluate historical representation of the past.[14]

So from this perspective the criteria of representational success in the writing of history may seem at first sight to be closer to those of cognitive truth than to those of aesthetic perfection (or of ethical rightness). But since even in the sciences we move at this level beyond the sphere of cognitive truth in the proper and original sense of the word—since scientific theories cannot properly be said to be "true," but "plausible," or "better than rival theories," or, at most, to "approximate the Truth"—one might surmise that an account of the evaluation of scientific theories as proposed by Popper belongs to the realm of aesthetics rather than to that of cognitive certainty. But in the end it would, in all likelihood, be a matter of philosophical strategy rather than of ineluctable philosophical truth how we should decide about this. Indeed, one may decide to move from (the) cognitive truth (of the singular true statement) as far as possible in the direction of scientific plausibility—and this is the strategy that has almost universally been adopted in both the philosophy of science and in historical theory. But one may just as well try the opposite track that is advocated here, and see how far we may get in the attempt to account for both the plausibility of scientific theories and for representational success in the writing of history from the perspective of aesthetics. To see aesthetics with just a little more respect than we are accustomed to do is all that would be needed to make the latter strategy worth trying. And if we embrace this strategy, it might well prove to be a plausible assumption that it is in the realm of aesthetics that science and history do finally meet each other.

However this may be, within the context of the present chapter I shall refrain from a further discussion of the aesthetic criteria of representational success that I mentioned a moment ago. It is of more interest for my argument here to recognize that these criteria (however defined and spelled out in detail) logically precede the criteria we might adopt for the evaluation of cognitive and normative discourse and that they do not depend on these. And this brings me to the main thesis that I wish to defend in this chapter, namely the uncommon thesis that narrative or historical discourse is what we had best rely upon when we wish to decide what moral and political standards we had best adopt. To put it differently, we can decide about the important question of what politics and ethics we should accept by establishing, first, what historical representations of the past we think best and, next, seeing what political and moral standards are exemplified by them. And we should then prefer the political and moral values that have inspired the strongest and most successful representations of the past. For example, few historians will doubt that Tocqueville's account of the French Revolution is superior to the one that was presented by Michelet. In precisely this datum we may see a strong argument in favor of the liberal-individualist values present in Tocqueville's account and against the values of leftist liberalism as exemplified by Michelet's *Histoire de la Révolution Française*. And, next, if the comparison of other historical accounts presents us with roughly the same picture, we are justified in seeing this as a convincing and even decisive argument in favor of liberal individualism and against leftist liberalism.

Hence, it is in historical writing and not in rationalist, a priorist argument of whatever variant that we will find our most reliable instrument for deciding about what our most recommendable political and moral values are. Historical writing is, so to speak, the experimental garden where we may try out different political and moral values and where the overarching aesthetic criteria of representational success will allow us to assess their respective merits and shortcomings. And we should be most grateful that the writing of history provides us with this experimental garden, since it will enable us to avoid the disasters that we may expect when we would have to try out in actual social and political reality the merits and shortcomings of different ethical and political standards. Before starting a revolution in the name of some political ideal, one had best begin with assessing as accurately and as dispassionately as possible the merits and shortcomings of the kind of historical writing inspired by this political ideal. A striking illustration of how history may confirm or refute ethical or political standards would be the anti-Americanism of the so-called revisionist account of the Cold War. A revisionist such as Gabriel Kolko finally decided to abandon his revisionist anti-Americanism because, however unwillingly, he had to acknowledge that the traditional view of the Cold War proved in the end to be the more convincing one, the one with the greater scope. Here we may see, as embodied in the thought of one and the same historian, how aesthetic criteria of representational success necessitated the abandonment of one set of political standards in favor of an alternative set. Here, clearly, aesthetics triumphed over ethics.

This is, lastly, why we should praise subjectivity and not demand of the historian that he should lay aside all his moral and political commitments when starting to write history. In the first place, such a commitment to moral and political values will often give the kind of a historical writing that is of greatest use to us for our orientation in the present and towards the future. We need only think of, for example, the histories written by authors like Jakob Talmon, Isaiah Berlin, or Carl Friedrich, which were so obviously inspired by a devotion to liberal democracy and by an uncompromising rejection of totalitarianism, in order to see that subjectivity is not in the least under all circumstances a fatal shortcoming of historical writing. It may equally well be that all truly important historical writing will require the adoption of certain moral and political standards. "No bias, no book," as the British historian Michael Howard so forcefully put it.[15]

But even more important is the fact that a historical writing that has successfully eliminated all traces of moral and political standards from itself can no longer be of any help to us in our crucial effort to distinguish between good and bad moral and political values. Having knowledge of the past surely is one thing; but it is perhaps no less important to know what ethical and political values we should cherish. So both our insight into the past and our orientation in the present and towards the future would be most seriously impaired by a historical writing which tries (however vainly) to avoid all moral and political standards. And, thus, instead of fearing subjectivity as the historian's mortal sin, we should welcome subjectivity as an indispensable contribution to both our knowledge of the past *and* to contemporary and future politics.

I end this section with a final note on politics as defined in the previous sections and the political values that were discussed in this one. In the previous section politics was closely related to history, for as we have seen, what both share is that they are essentially proposals, from a logical point of view. On the other hand, I have been speaking fairly indiscriminately of moral and political standards in this section, thereby suggesting that political discourse should rather be associated with the kind of cognitive and moral discourse that I had previously opposed to history and politics. The explanation of this ambiguity is that politics combines an affinity with the discourse of history to an affinity with ethics. For on the one hand, the politician has to find his way in a complex political reality in much the same way that the historian has to look for the best grasp of the complexities of some part of the past. And the kind of representational synthesis that the historian aims for is also the necessary prerequisite of all meaningful political action. Without such a minimally adequate grasp of the historical context in which the politician has to act, political action can only result in utter disaster.[16] But on the other hand, the politician will observe or apply certain moral values in political action as inspired by political ideology. For example, the value that he should further the cause of political equality or the interests of a certain segment of civil society may govern much of his behavior and most of his individual decisions as a politician.

Now, these ideologically inspired political and moral values may, as we all know, also play an important role in the writing of history. Think for example of socioeconomic history as inspired by Marxist or socialist ideologies. But whereas such values will be used *normatively* by the politician, the historian will make a *cognitive* use of them—he will discern in them an additional instrument for understanding the past. Once again socioeconomic history (or the history of one's nation, to take another example) may exemplify how such values can cognitively be exploited by the historian. Hence, when the role of cognitive discourse was discussed above, we associated cognitive discourse here primarily with how political ideologies suggest how historical realities should be tied to historical narrative. For this is the way in which the epistemological concern of how to tie things to words will customarily present itself when we investigate the writing of history.

But, obviously, this does not substantially alter the picture given in this section of the logical hierarchy of narrative or representational discourse versus normative discourse and the specific variant of political discourse discussed just now. Narrative representational discourse, and the aesthetic criteria we rely upon for its evaluation, may be expected to be just as successful in assessing this variant of political values as they have been seen to be in the case of ethical discourse in the strict sense.

Conclusion

I come to a conclusion. At the beginning of this essay we established what the real problem with historical subjectivity is. The problem is not, as is ordinarily believed, that the introduction of ethical and political standards in the historian's narrative amounts to the introduction of something that is wholly alien to his subject matter and thus can only occasion a gross distortion of what the past has actually been like. The real problem is precisely the reverse: historical reality and the historian's ethical and political values may often come so extremely close to each other as to be virtually indistinguishable. Two conclusions follow from this. In the first place, just as a construction line in geometry, after having deliberately been made into a part of the geometrical problem itself, may well help us to solve it, so ethical and political standards, because of their natural affinity with the historian's subject matter, may often prove to be a help rather than an obstacle to a better understanding of the past. I would not even hesitate to say that all real progress that has been made in the history of historical writing in the course of the centuries, somehow or somewhere had its origins in the ethical or political standards that were, either knowingly or unwittingly, adopted by the great and influential historians of the past.

But, as we all know in our age of automobiles, of TV sets and of transistor radios, what may be a blessing under certain circumstances may easily be worse than a curse under others. And so it is with ethical and political values in historical writing. They may at times have contributed immeasurably to the advancement of historical learning, but on other occasions they have proven to be the most effective and insurmountable barrier to historical enlightenment. And it is precisely because ethical and political (and, even more obviously, cognitive) values are so inextricably tied up with historical writing that they could have led to what is both the best and the worst in the discipline's past. So, in order to preserve this best and discard the worst, it will be necessary (as we have argued) to develop a philosophical microscope that will enable us to see what exactly goes on where the finest ramifications of historical discourse and of ethical and political discourse meet, and where they get entangled with each other. As we have seen, a theory of the nature of historical representation will present us with the required philosophical microscope.

When looking at historical writing through this microscope of historical representation, we discovered, first, the logical priority of the aesthetic criteria of representational adequacy to criteria of what is right from an ethical and political point of view. The reassuring insight to be derived from this has been that we may trust the discipline in how it will, in the long run, succeed in dealing with ethical and political values and even in making them subservient to its own purposes.

We discovered, second, that we may safely assign to history the most important and responsible task of telling apart recommendable from objectionable moral and political values. A task, obviously, that history can only adequately perform if we are not scared off by the manifest presence of these values in historical writing. And we need not be scared off by this presence, since aesthetics is the stronger partner in the interaction between the criteria of aesthetic success and those of what is ethically, politically, or cognitively right. Though there is one all-important exception to this rule: aesthetics can only perform this function if freedom of speech and of discussion about the past are completely and unconditionally guaranteed. So *this* moral requirement is the *conditio sine qua non* of all that I have argued in this essay. But the supremely important role that is played by *this* moral value is not in contradiction with what I have been saying about the regime of the aesthetic versus the cognitive and the normative: for though this value guarantees the indispensable *multiplication* of narrative representations, it does not tell us how to *evaluate* them.

Notes

1. Quoted in F. Wagner, *Geschichtswissenschaft* (Munich: Karl Alber Verlag, 1951), 34.

2. See W. H. Walsh, *An Introduction to Philosophy of History* (London, New York: Hutchinson's University Library, 1951, 1967), 93–117.

3. Arthur Danto, *Analytical Philosophy of History* (Cambridge: Cambridge University Press, 1965), 98.

4. Its most serious rival is the resemblance theory of representation. For a discussion of the relative merits of these two theories, see the chapter "Danto on Representation, Identity and Indiscernibles" in my book *History and Theory* (forthcoming).

5. See my "Danto on Representation, Identity and Indiscernibles."

6. Arthur C. Danto, *The Transfiguration of the Commonplace* (Cambridge: Harvard University Press, 1981), 81.

7. Within the "Weltanschauung" of nineteenth-century historicism (not to be confused with Popper's historicism), the nature of a nation, a cultural or intellectual tradition, etc., lies in its history. A thing is what its history is.

8. Of course, this is not idealism. Representation does not actually create what it represents, but merely defines it or, as we shall see in a moment, is a proposal for how it *should* be defined. And this is crucial for any intellectual grasp of the world. For without such proposals, reality would remain as inaccessible to us as a well-protected strong room to the potential bank robber.

9. For this relationship between politics and ethics, see the introduction to F. R. Ankersmit, *Aesthetic Politics: Political Philosophy beyond Fact and Value* (Stanford: Stanford University Press, 1997).

10. The issue is intensively discussed in S. Friedlander, ed., *Probing the Limits of Representation: Nazism and the "Final Solution"* (Cambridge: Harvard University Press, 1992).

11. See also S. G. Crowell, "Mixed Messages: The Heterogeneity of Historical Discourse," *History and Theory* 37 (1998): "my argument is that historical narrative (as opposed to fictional narrative) *necessarily* involves links between (at least) two 'heterogeneous' language games or discourses, each with its own aim—

viz., the cognitive and the normative—and in so doing poses the difficult philosophical problem of determining, first, the 'stakes' of this sort of discourse, so that, second, we can see what a proper standard for evaluating it might be" (222).

12. Though this account is complicated by the tradition of natural law philosophy, which until the end of the eighteenth century succeeded in keeping together what was later recognized as the domain of the cognitive and that of the normative.

13. Karl R. Popper, *The Logic of Scientific Discovery* (London: Hutchinson, 1959), 4.

14. F. R. Ankersmit, *Narrative Logic* (The Hague: Reidel, 1983), 239 ff.

15. Michael Howard, "Lords of Destruction," *Times Literary Supplement,* November 12, 1981.

16. This exchange of ethics for history as our primary guide for political action was recommended already by Machiavelli. According to Machiavelli, political evil arises not only "from the weakness into which the present religion has led the world," but even more "from not having a true knowledge of histories, through not getting from reading them that sense nor tasting that flavor that they have in themselves." See Niccolò Machiavelli, *Discourses on Livy,* trans. Harvey C. Mansfield and Nathan Tarcov (Chicago: University of Chicago Press, 1996), 6.

Representation, Narrative, and the Historian's Promise

Edith Wyschogrod

ho is the historian? Perhaps she is best envisioned by way of what Gilles Deleuze called "conceptual personae."[1] The philosopher's name, Deleuze asserted—Plato, Descartes, Kant—is merely a pseudonym. The philosopher who says "I" does so in and through the concepts that she thinks. Thus "Nicholas of Cusa or even Descartes should have signed himself 'the Idiot' just as Nietzsche signed himself 'The Antichrist' or 'Dionysus Crucified,'" says Deleuze.[2] Neither a psychosocial nor a mythological type, conceptual personae are figures philosophers have propagated and into which they withdraw and, conversely, these figures transfigure them: "It is Plato who begins: he becomes Socrates at the same time that he makes Socrates become philosopher," says Deleuze.

To be sure, the historian's calling is not that of the philosopher who, in the view just stated, effects the becoming of thought through the mediation of a concept. The historian does not pluck the subjects of her narrative from a prior conceptual tradition, but rather is a passageway for the emergence of an always already partly configured past, just as for Heidegger the poet is a passageway for language. Yet the historian's account is not the outcome of an inert and lifeless relation to the past, but is rather the result of a double passion: an eros for the past and an ardor for the others in whose name there is a felt urgency to speak. To convey that-which-was in the light of these passions *is* to become a historian.

The historian has in all likelihood received academic training in the study of a period, theme, or concatenation of events within a geographical region; is the member of a profession; and, as such, is recognized as belonging to a culture of experts. Thus she is constrained by rules of evidence in the received sense of the term. It is widely assumed that statements produced by the craft of historical writing are true assertions, true in the sense that what the historian claims to have happened did happen, that the historian's assertions are as accurate as proximity to the sources—written, pictographic, or artifactual—can make them. This view presupposes a relation of similarity such that the "original" and the "narrated" events are homologous, each layer transparent towards a more primordial one until the original events or event patterns are disclosed.

In what follows, I hope to explain why this account of telling the truth about the past is viewed as naive by many post-structuralist and analytic philosophers and requires emendation while, paradoxically, the claim that the truth about the past must be told remains standing. For if, per contra, an effort were made to regenerate what might be thought of as epistemological fundamentalism—the view that historical truth is the stringing together of propositions that match words and events—the critique of this position could undermine historical claims founded upon it. Thus if the historian were to concede that the ideal of historical truth reflected a misguided hope, this view might further corrode the already frayed affective and juridical bonds that hold contemporary societies together. Is the historian then destined to be tossed between the Scylla of a naive representationalism and the Charybdis of unbridgeable difference?

In what follows, I shall rehearse briefly some arguments that have been adduced to demonstrate the epistemic difficulties to which I have alluded. I shall then try to resolve the problem of narrative truth first by invoking some novel conceptions of narration and then by appealing to Foucault, who brings the conditions of historical disclosure into the historical narrative itself. Finally, I shall try to resolve the conflict between the ethical posture of the historian and her role as narrator by appealing to the differing conceptions of time that govern each of these contexts. Although the contemporary historian works in many media, I shall confine myself to considering written narrative.

The Historian's Promise: "Je te jure"

It is a commonplace that when historians recount what has occurred in the past of nations or societies, that past may be configured as a sequence of discrete events or as exhibiting larger and more complex social, economic, political, and cultural patterns. I shall not catalogue here the types of historical writing that have been described in a historiographic tradition descended from the nineteenth century. Whatever her view of history's object, the historian is still bound to ask, "What happened? How was it *then?*" If language is understood as a system of signs, the task implied by these questions may be characterized as bringing into a system of articulated signs that which was.

Because the past is irrecoverable in the sense that it cannot be brought back and those in whose stead the historian speaks are dead, retrievable only through documents, images, and artifacts, she cannot hope that her passion for the dead other is reciprocal. To be a historian, then, is to accept as one of her conceptual personae the destiny of the spurned lover, to write, photograph, film, televise, archive in an effort to bring back, *per impossibile,* a past that is irrecoverable in its vivacity. Nietzsche may have been right in proclaiming that remembering the past is a sick passion; yet without the necrophilia of the historian who gives herself over to overcoming the past's passing into oblivion, there would be only the finality of death.

It might also be asked whether the historian is, in fact, not a spurned but a faithless lover, one who seduces with a promise yet knows all along that truth as the return of the past just as it was is a chimera. Does she lie when she avers, "I will tell the truth about the past, *je te jure*"? Although the historian's task is the re-figuration of the past, she does not create affects through the transformation of percepts; instead her primary role is an ethical one. Prior to the creation of a historical narrative, her first act is one of promising the dead others to make past events available to present and perhaps future generations. Thus she is mediator of a legacy. The twin personae "lover of the past" and "one who promises" must be brought together in her as were the Platonic Socrates and Plato and Nietzsche and Dionysus.

If promising is itself neither an analytic nor a descriptive act but an ethical one that belongs in an axiological rather than a narrative framework, then what might be called the discursive space of historical writing must be redescribed. The linguistic instruments of historical narrative, a linking of signs, are preceded by a prior de-signing, an ethical act. To be sure, a promise is made by someone to someone stating that one will believe or act in a specified way. It is as it were a note to be cashed out in the future and is often made in response to an imperative. "Promise you won't forget me," says the beloved to a departing lover. "*Jamais, je te jure,*" he or she replies. The imperative heeded by the historian is not only or even primarily the demand by a contemporary readership that she disclose something hitherto unknown or misunderstood about the past. It is rather the charge she receives from the dead for whom she is resolved to speak. Such a historian assumes liability for the Other, feels the pressure of an Ethics that is prior to the exercise of historical judgment (an Ethics of ethics, to borrow the phrase of philosopher Emmanuel Levinas) that dissolves the system of signifiers that constitute the articulation of historical narrative, one whose narrative is governed by a promise to provide voice to the dead others.[3]

"Facts Settle Matters"

In what sense is the promise of the historian related to claims of factuality? So intimate is the relation of historical discourse to the events of history that the term "history" in Hegel's account of this relation has been taken to refer both to the *res gestae,* the historical object, and to the *historia rerum gestarum,* the verbal account of these events. For Hegel, truth is not primordially a property of propositions, but rather something that comes about in and through the actualization of history's moments. The meaning of historical veracity as a recounting of the facts is perhaps first embodied in Aristotle's famous dictum: "the [historian] describes the thing that has been, the [poet] a kind of thing that might be" (*Poetics,* 1451b). The commonsense view, more or less in conformity with Aristotle, sees historical knowledge as a subset of a general theory in which knowledge is conceived as representation. Bernard Williams, an analytic philosopher who rejects this view, says in his cogent summary of it: "We can select among our beliefs and features of our world picture some that we can reasonably claim to represent the world . . . to the maximum degree independent of our perspective and its peculiarities."[4] In this commonsense view, it may be presumed that, in the absence of error or the will to lie, what is said is true.

If the question of truth conditions as understood in the context of formal logical relations is set aside, for the unamended empirical philosophies of modernity, from the seventeenth century to the present, "fact" and "truth" are virtually commutable terms. Facts are seen as the atomic constituents of our beliefs that no reasonable person could dispute, configurations of the real that brook no disagreement. This view of facts generally works from the bottom up, as it were, from part to whole. Using the same ontological presuppositions, we could however proceed from whole to part. On that view, facts are the sediment that remains after the whole that is to be studied is subjected to scrutiny. Facts can become facts by paring down a wider field through the application of criteria of relevance to a portion of it. To simplify: design a study that will take into account environmental factors, diet, and genetic mutations as possible causes of a specified form of cancer, show why the first two can be discounted but not the third, and you may conclude that this type of cancer is the result of a gene mutation.

In sum, the statements, "What is true is a fact. What is false is contrary to fact" can, on the view of truth I have described, be construed as saying the same thing. The factuality blueprint I have drawn takes for granted, first, that true beliefs are governed by a relation to things and events that enable us to distinguish these true beliefs from false ones; second, that strategies of justification (answers to questions of "why" and "how" things fall out in a given way) bind statements about things to the way things are and convert such statements into warranted beliefs; and finally, that inquiry is undertaken from a standpoint of studied neutrality, is disinterested, reflects, in Leibniz's famous dictum, the view from nowhere.

The Historian and the Linguistic Turn

Even current accounts that reflect strong, straightforwardly empiricist propensities concede the inseparability of thought from its linguistic articulation. Quine, in a by now familiar claim, maintains that what we hold to be true can be understood only within a linguistic nexus, i.e., the web of all our beliefs. An empirical constructivist view such as that of Arthur C. Danto concedes that narrativity penetrates the way we see events even as he tries to salvage the veracity of historical facts by suggesting that narrative is connected to historical events in much the same way as theory penetrates observations in science.[5] Although a chasm is often perceived between Anglo-American and Continental philosophers, metahistorian Jacques Rancière's statement applies to both factions: "Words, whatever the realists might say, are more stubborn than facts."[6]

Phenomenological views of knowledge that claim to be empirical have been modified by the linguistic turn of structuralism. In addition, classical phenomenology dethrones the view that perception is passive. Instead, knowing that-which-is is seen as the object of an intentional act which becomes manifest in language. Linguistic signs, in turn, acquire meaning by virtue of their differences from other signs and are unified into the synchronicity of a story. This amalgam is reflected in Emmanuel Levinas's claim that words do not substitute for things but rather there is a prior intention of consciousness to narrate. He concludes: "On this view, knowing is not an act of making transparent what is merely there, given, a content that is passively registered upon a receptive subject. Instead knowing is . . . an active proclaiming, declaring something as something."[7]

In a quite different vein, Donald Davidson attacks the view of knowledge as representation by focusing upon the distinction between organizing system and that which awaits organization, between scheme and content. Sentences do not mirror a referent because "Nothing . . . no thing makes sentences or theories true: Not experience, not surface irritations, not the world, can make a sentence true."[8] Elsewhere Davidson contends:

> It would be a mistake to suppose that we could first determine what a
> person believes, wants, hopes for, intends, and fears and then go on to a
> definite answer to the question what his words refer to. For the evidence
> on which all these matters depend give us no way of separating out the
> contributions of thought, action, desire and meaning one by one. . . .
> This is to state once more the thesis of the inscrutability of reference . . . [9]

In the same spirit, Richard Rorty declares, "The lines of evidential force . . . do not parallel the lines of referential direction" in that the former depends upon knowing the language in which the beliefs are expressed and the latter the rules used by speakers of the language.[10] For Derrida, cognitive acts as usually understood exhibit what might be called a moral failure. Thus the trouble with cognition is that by concealing the difference between itself and the items it links as well as the interim, however minuscule, that separates primary memory and anticipation from present perception, knowing acts are disingenuous. Thinking is a time-bound process: a before and after passes invisibly through language, a passing through that philosophy in its classical and modern versions has tried to hide. This covering over is pointed out in his influential essay "Difference," whose title is a multivalent term that refers to the interpreting of past and future as modes of the present and therefore as hiding the diffractions of time. As is the case with psychoanalytic accounts of the unconscious, these modes of "nonpresence" are constitutive of presence, cannot themselves be made present, and display themselves only as aftereffects.[11] Derrida acknowledges that temporal diffraction or difference does not eliminate the need to confer an identity, but reveals "that a lack of foundation is basic and non-empirical and that the security of presence in the metaphorical form of ideality arises and is set forth again upon this irreducible void."[12]

Replacing Narrative
as Linguistic Replica

Once the ideal of truth as linguistic replica is abandoned, does the historian as narrator of past events become de facto a writer of fiction? For if the notion of fact reflects the effort to say that which is, fiction attempts to say that which is not, to bring absence into presence, to construct a world that does not exist. If we reverse the opposition fact/fiction, the liberation of what is fictive may be freshly construed so as to generate new possibilities for the study of history. The binary opposition itself is the product of a long tradition which cannot be rehearsed here. As a genealogical note, however, it may be observed that the fact/fiction bifurcation is preceded by that of myth/logos and that Plato's account of their relation opens the way to the fact/fiction distinction of modernity. For Plato, tales about the gods are seen as handed down and as deriving their social force in part from their antiquity, whereas constructed myths are made up of preexisting units of meaning malleable enough to accommodate didactic reshaping. The genre of the constructed myth is undecidable: as didactic it is incipiently philosophical; on its narrative side it is a conscious construction by the imagination of events that are not alleged to have transpired and, as such, opens the way for fiction. More important, as fiction, such constructions do not exhibit blind error, but concessions to image-making propensities.

In Rousseau's account of fiction, the theme of the lie persists. His *Reveries of a Solitary Walker* presents a hair-splitting description of lying, perhaps an apology for his own questionable practices. Despite his purported horror of falsehood, he recalls only indifference towards his own fabrications, weaseling out of accountability by distinguishing between withholding the truth and deliberate deception. What determines whether statements contrary to fact are innocent or blameworthy is, for him, utility. That which has value is property whose value in turn is grounded in usefulness. Long before postmodern intellectual historians identified discourse as a commodity, Rousseau declared: "Truth without any possible usefulness can never be something we owe to one another; it follows therefore that anyone who conceals or disguises it is not telling a lie."[13] Rousseau judges the guilt or innocence of statements that are contrary to fact on the basis of whether they harm others. Rousseau concludes, "To lie to one's own advantage is an imposture, to lie to the advantage of others is a slander . . . to lie without advantage or disadvantage to oneself or others is not to lie; it is not falsehood but fiction."[14]

If fiction is identified as a lie, it could hardly be adopted as an instrument in the study of history. What then must historical narrative become if it is to provide a resource in this regard? Nietzsche's genealogical analysis of factuality may be thought to provide a further deconstructive moment in the falling away of fact. But fundamental to Nietzsche's position is the continuity of our concepts of truth with our acts of valuing. Moral judgments in a tradition that wends its way from Greek philosophy to modern thought generally mandates varying degrees of subjugation of the instincts, repudiation of the trustworthiness of sense experience, or outright renunciation of the senses. But moral judgments require truth for their support, so much so that truth and goodness become indistinguishable. "The true world attainable for the sage, the pious, the virtuous man; he lives in it, he is it," says Nietzsche.[15] But even if the true world is merely a "moral-optical illusion," there are nonetheless truth and lies in Nietzsche's world: "By lie, I mean wishing not to see something one does see; wishing not to see something as one sees it."[16] In this view, to lie is not to refuse to see things as they are, but rather to refuse to see what one sees. If truth and morals are inseparable, they remain so even in their transvalued shape in a post-Nietzschean world.

The suggestiveness of Nietzsche's view for the study of history is evident in the work of Hayden White and Rancière, who themselves were influenced by Nietzsche's concerns. Truth that, for Nietzsche and pace White and Rancière, reflects the convictions of the historian involves a reflexive paradox that only reinforces the claim: the statement that truth is not disinterested is itself not a disinterested statement.[17]

Could it not be argued, however, that the difference between historical and fictional narratives goes all the way down once it is acknowledged that each is intended to belong to a different order of time? Thus Arthur C. Danto asserts: "The historian's statements are in history and belong to the same temporal order as the events that make them true. And this is not the case with fiction [even when the author is a contemporary of the characters she creates]."[18] But this claim holds for the lie that, unlike error, is an ambiguous form, belonging on the one hand to the historical time it purports to depict, on the other to the time stream of the illusion it hopes to create. Thus, one might ask, to which time stream does the narrative belong of the historian who, knowing his claim to be false and self-serving, writes that Stalin's labor camps reeducated counter-revolutionaries? And, one might add, do all putative "fictions" belong to a time stream other than that of their "factual" counterparts? To which order of time does a film about the life of Abraham Lincoln belong, that of historical time or filmic illusion?

In addition, what has been missed in identifying narrative with fiction is the sea change in the conception of fiction in writers such as Franz

Kafka and Jorge Luis Borges, so that not only are the usual conventions of narrative dissolved but the figures of narrative disclosure, what and how it reveals and conceals, are taken up into the narrative itself. The fact of unrepresentability itself is represented. Fictions have metamorphosed so that the alterity of the other can be made thematic without the other's actually appearing. By bringing forth the silences of the other rather than by coercing that silence into speech, by devising strategies of encounter that simultaneously attest and preserve that silence, silence itself becomes a speech-act. As Rancière remarks, "it is the world of silent witnesses that the historian brings into *signifiance* without lies."[19]

Both fact and fiction are transformed when shards of the metaphysical history through which they have passed, in a return of the suppressed, percolate at the surface of the narrative. Such fictions may bring to the fore not the old metaphors for truth and certainty but the very fact of their "wornoutness."[20]

Foucault's Remedy

It is perhaps no accident that Foucault begins *The Order of Things* by appealing to a Borges story to discuss the way in which cognitive regularities are constructed. Disdainful of the historian's analysis of the past as "thus it was," indeed of most ordinary ways of studying history, Foucault exhumes the discontinuities or breaks in the history of consciousness. These ruptures are neither the result of specific events nor of the initiatives of individuals, but rather the converse holds; events and behaviors are determined by the way the categories of representation force things to fall out at a given time and place. Thus Foucault brings to light multiple language practices, those of biology, geology, numismatics, and the like, each with its own protocols and rules that determine its objects.

Yet Foucault's historiographic lens retains a constant focus. In *The Archeology of Knowledge* he develops his notion of the episteme, "a discursive formation or ordered constellation of statements that point not to 'things,' 'facts,' 'realities,' or 'beings,' [but to] the law of possibility, rules of existence for the objects that are inscribed within it."[21] A statement's meaning is limited neither by its grammatical structure nor by what it refers to, but by the pattern of significations it inhabits. Just as the affirmation, "The world is made of atoms" does not mean the same thing for Democritus as it does for Niels Bohr, so too the assertion, "These are the facts," does not have an identical signification before and after the birth of modern science. There is no master narrative, no spirit of the age, no consciousness that knows and intends its objects as described by the conventions of phenomenology, strategies that constituted the philosophical lingua franca of Foucault's academic environment; there are only discursive practices. From the standpoint of preceding European historical writing, Foucault's discussion of such practices would appear to fasten upon details previously dismissed as marginal, so that the history of the West appears to be written from the perspective of its detritus. Historical epochs for Foucault, as Hayden White points out, are "an archipelago, a chain of epistemic islands, the deepest connections of which are unknown."[22] Like many writers of fiction, Foucault does not explain the shift from one episteme to another except to assert, "It happened." To seek a law that would explain the birth and death of a discursive paradigm would run counter to the notion of brute contingency that characterizes his description of epistemic shifts in history.[23]

In a move as much Lacanian as it is Nietzschean, Foucault believes that desire provides an escape hatch from the constraints of the discursive formations of modernity. Yet desire itself cannot break free of the push-and-pull of epistemic constraints, as Foucault makes abundantly clear in his extensive writings on sexuality. Even if desire is envisioned as a transgression of limits, as exuberant life, once it is encoded as the subject of a discourse, as has often been remarked, it becomes tedious. For Nietzsche, desire is both vision and orgy, dream and intoxication in which there is "sexuality and voluptuousness."[24] To follow Nietzsche one step further: "The sober, the weary, the exhausted, the dried up (e.g., scholars) can receive absolutely nothing"[25] from an art vivified by this orgiastic spirit. Desire described as commodified sexuality that awaits redistribution remains desire as commodity.

It is not difficult to fault Foucault both for inclusions and omissions in his selection of the voices he believes to have been suppressed by a given discursive practice. The outcome of Foucault's heady post-Nietzschean historicism can be perilous, as Foucault himself concedes:

> At the end of such an enterprise . . . one may be compelled to ignore influences and traditions, abandon definitively the question of origin, allow the commanding presence of authors to fade into the background; and thus everything that was thought to be proper to the study of history of ideas may disappear from view.[26]

Foucault's achievement is not that of altering the fortunes of any given constituency, but rather that of initiating discursive practices that make possible the genre of heterological history, history in which "the other is positioned between words and things."[27]

The Historian as an Artist of Time

I want to suggest by way of conclusion that the historian in fashioning narratives about the past is an artist of sorts, one who works in the medium of time. But as Walter Benjamin notes, history is not merely a sequence of events that transpire in the past, but rather a moment is drawn from the past into the present because of some urgent claim it has upon us.[28] Yet, to resurrect or remember the past "just as it was" the historian must somehow inhabit the past she wishes to recover. The historian's dream is to enter into the material and conceptual world she wishes to depict. Like the time traveller of H. G. Wells's famous novel, *The Time Machine,* she may inquire as an exercise in imagination why, if gravity can be resisted in flight, cannot human beings hope "to stop or accelerate their drift along the Time Dimension and travel the other way."[29]

Earlier I considered objections to the view that historical writing represents the past. I hope now to resolve some of the dilemmas bound up with these objections, but before doing so, the historian's relation to time must be clarified. The act of bringing back the past reflects two distinctive views of time. The first account sees time as passing, as moving from past to present to future, or as we experience it, as the future pressing in upon the present and the present, in turn, vanishing into the past. This view stresses time's mobility and is reflected in the time structure of narrative. To speak about time's passing enables one to slide back and forth along the time scale as well as to give emotional coloration to the experience of time's dimensions: "How sad I am that summer is over," or "I look forward to my trip." In short, the continuity of what Husserl calls lived time provides a useful framework for verbal or visual narration where the structure of the story replicates the structure of everyday experience.

As an example of stretched time, time as it moves along a chronological gradient, consider these sentences selected from the chapter on the Terror in June–December 1793 from Simon Schama's history of the French Revolution.

> The mass production of death through the marriage of technology and bureaucracy would have to wait another century and a half. But what happened in February and March was bad enough. With the military rebellion more or less extinguished, the republican armies embarked on a march of "pacification" [through the Vendée]. . . . General Turreau's twelve infernal columns were encouraged to massacre virtually every living person that stood in their path. . . . At Gonnard on January 23, Gen-

eral Crouzat's column forced two hundred old people along with mothers and children, to kneel in front of a large pit they had dug; they were then shot so as to tumble into their own grave. . . . By mid-April 1794 the military pacification of the Vendée was more or less complete.[30]

The narrative sustains its suspense as a temporal unfolding. By alluding to mass killings of the present, Schama's account reflects Walter Benjamin's claim that present concerns orchestrate narratives about the past.[31]

This view of time, however, is not without its difficulties. The status in existence of events changes with respect to their locations in time: events slip away, present events exist but future events do not yet exist, and past events no longer exist. A rephrasing of Schama's example should help to clarify the point: consider the sentence, "The pacification of the Vendée occurred 205 years ago." This sentence will no longer be true in the year 3000, for the number of years that pass between the time of the event and the year 3000 differs from the time span between the event and the year 1998. The conditions for ascribing truth and falsity to utterances about the past can now be seen as bound up with the movement of time that destabilizes truth values. Such time-tied sentences are not false in the usual sense, as is the sentence, "Hong Kong was a Spanish colony"; instead, a certain fluidity is intrinsic to statements about matters of fact. Changing truth values are the way in which narratives reflect time's passage.

The alternative view of time considers time as a sequence of separate now points that succeed one another and can be simply marked off as earlier and later, before and after: time as the pure succession of individual occasions. The "before-and-after" view of time put forth by philosopher Bertrand Russell was intended to solve a logical problem into which I need not enter here. Suffice it to say that statements that reflect the before-and-after view can be assigned permanent truth values: thus "It is true today and will remain so in the year 3000 that 'The French Revolution preceded the Russian Revolution.'"[32]

One might conclude that this arcane point might interest philosophers but has little relevance for the historian. Yet the before-and-after view is vital to the historian in that it supplies the framework for the ethical dimension of her work. To be sure, not every before and after is significant, but when there is a need to communicate that something momentous has occurred, before and after is the time dimension in which the historian is stationed. The before may be short or long, but in either case the after reflects a radical alteration in social, political, economic, and cultural circumstances. Consider an example. In the summer of 1794 "the architects of the Grande Terreur" identified as Saint-Just, Couthon, and Robespierre were guillotined. According to Schama, Robespierre, the "fastidious prophet of virtue," his jaw shattered in a possible suicide attempt, died in excruciating pain. The demise of Robespierre (by no means the only architect of the Terror) does not bring the event to closure but is premonitory of a change in historical consciousness: before and after the Terror. Before and after indicates the temporal positioning of the historian when she assumes a perspective, calls us to attention: "See. You must attend to the significance of what happened here." In so doing she addresses the claims of the dead others and those of her addressees.

In sum, each view of time, either as passing, i.e., as past present and future, or as before and after, opens a dimension of historical understanding depending upon whether the historian conveys what and how events happened or whether she speaks from the standpoint of ethics. Each of these views of time generates its own context. As narrative history, passing events are described in the indicative voice, whereas statements of the before-and-after form are uttered in the imperative voice. Thus, for example, before and after the Spanish conquest of the Aztecs may place a claim upon the historian to speak for a past event that would otherwise fall into oblivion.

Is There No True Story?

To see in what sense the historian may still speak of a true story, one has yet to ponder the significance of future time, time that has not arrived, in relation to the past. Does the "not yet" of the future in some way impinge upon the "no longer" of the past in a way that will enable the historian to prevent the unleashing of interpretations without constraints?

What appears to distinguish the future from the past is the future's seemingly unique relation to possibility. As the present moves ahead, the multiple possibilities of the future drop away; the future is lived as an annihilating of possibilities. It is a commonplace that with advancing age, people speak of the time they have left as a diminishing of their prospects. Yet does a past event, like an event that is present, not exhibit a relation to its future, the possibilities that were seen as before it then when it was present, possibilities now annihilated? The historian in her role can envisage her account of a past event as related to some past possible history, a history in the making, so that at any point an event before the fact could have come into being or not have come into being. To create a historical narrative, the historian must grasp occurrences in the manner of holding-in-front-of-her not only that which was but that which could have been, paths that could have been but were not taken.

A proposition about the past, "I stayed home last summer," is not merely a statement of fact but is accompanied by a penumbra of rejected possibles: my staying home may reflect a decision to avoid a camping trip I could have taken or to turn down an invitation for foreign travel that I might have accepted. Historical narration is a constructive act whose grammatical form is the indicative "it was thus and so," but a statement of this form is the limiting case, as it were, of what could have but did not occur: "It could have been but was not." In sum, the future is intrinsic to the past: what the historian narrates is that which occurred surrounded by a shadowy halo of negated possibilities, each of which is expressed in the form: "X was possible but X did not occur."

The historian in retrieving the past need not include these negated possibilities in her narrative. For example, before Hitler invaded the former Soviet Union, he could have honored his pact with Stalin and refrained from initiating this action; before the landing at Normandy in June 1944 the Allied command could have decided upon a later assault or a landing at some other point. If the past is to be retrieved, the not, the envisaging of that which could have but did not occur, is intrinsic to determining that which is to be recovered. The historian's reconstruction of the past is delimited by a further more restrictive negation, that which could not have been even on the broadest possible interpretation. Thus, for example, I may think of Charlemagne as son of Pepin the Short, as king of the Franks, or as emperor of the West, each of these identities producing a somewhat different story, but I cannot think of him as Leo XIII, pope of Rome. The historian is bound by the negative "grounding" of historical narrative: "It could never have been thus."

In/conclusions

It can be argued that radical epistemic skepticism can lead to a metaphysics of unamended difference and dissemination and that the latter could backfire. For the thinking of difference intended to support a justifiable anticolonialist discourse might be used in the interest of an intractable ethnocentricity and nationalism. But the historian can avoid this outcome without disregarding criticisms of representation. Although the historian cannot claim that she presents *absolute truth*, "It has to have been X, it could not have been otherwise," she can claim a *limited cer-*

tainty, grounded in a nonevent, "It might have been X or Y, but I am sure it could not have been Z." What is said about the past can be checked by a negative determination. Eliminative propositions—"it could not have been Z"—establish constraints on what can be said or shown to have happened in the past. Even if, as I have suggested, the historian is an artist who works in the medium of time, her freedom to interpret the past is checked by that which could not have been a past possibility.

What is more, the promise to tell the truth, which may at first suggest epistemological questions—what is to count as the truth criterion for the historian and how is it to be applied—can be seen to generate a different line of inquiry. The historian must ask, as did Foucault: "Whose truth is being told, to whom, by whom and to what end?" Is a given history the inalienable property of a people upon which an outsider has no purchase? Yet if an outsider is prohibited from inquiring into the history of the other, is this constraint not tantamount to an endorsement of historical solipsism? Although the historian as narrator may be, as I have suggested, an artist in the medium of time, these queries confirm metahistorian Hayden White's observation: "Every historical narrative has as its latent or manifest purpose the desire to moralize the events of which it treats."[33]

Notes

1. To avoid the awkwardness of using both masculine and feminine pronouns in each instance where such pronouns might be called for, I have chosen to use feminine pronouns throughout.

2. Gilles Deleuze and Felix Guattari, *What Is Philosophy?* trans. Hugh Tomlinson and Graham Burchell (New York: Columbia University Press, 1991), 64.

3. In my *An Ethics of Remembering: History, Heterology, and the Nameless Others* (Chicago: University of Chicago Press, 1998), a detailed portrayal of a figure I call the heterological historian is provided.

4. This view is cited by Richard Rorty in *Objectivity, Relativism, and Truth,* vol. 1 of *Philosophical Papers* (Cambridge: Cambridge University Press, 1991), 8.

5. See Arthur C. Danto, *Narration and Knowledge* (New York: Columbia University Press, 1985), xii.

6. Jacques Rancière, *The Names of History: On the Poetics of Knowledge,* trans. Hassan Melehy (Minneapolis: University of Minnesota Press, 1994), 97.

7. Emmanuel Levinas, "Language and Proximity," in *Selected Philosophical Papers,* trans. Alphonso Lingis (The Hague: Martinus Nijhoff, 1987), 109.

8. Davidson is cited and commented upon in Richard Rorty, *Philosophy and the Mirror of Nature* (Princeton: Princeton University Press, 1991), 158.

9. Donald Davidson, *Inquiries into Truth and Interpretation* (Oxford: Clarendon Press, 1984), 241.

10. Rorty, *Philosophy and the Mirror of Nature,* 158.

11. Jacques Derrida, *"Speech and Phenomenon" and Other Essays on Husserl's Theory of Signs,* trans. David Allison (Evanston: Northwestern University Press, 1973), 129–60, 64, and 152.

12. Derrida, *"Speech and Phenomenon,"* 7.

13. Jean-Jacques Rousseau, *Reveries of a Solitary Walker,* trans. Peter France (London: Penguin Books, 1979), 66.

14. Rousseau, *Reveries,* 69.

15. Friedrich Nietzsche, "The Twilight of the Idols," in *The Portable Nietzsche,* trans. Walter Kaufmann (New York: Viking Press, 1954), 485.

16. Friedrich Nietzsche, *The Anti-christ,* in *Portable Nietzsche,* 640.

17. Hermeneutical suspicion of this sort is linked to the claim that truth reflects interests in the shape of metaphors that come to seem canonical. In what is by now a vintage Nietzscheanism, he asks:

> What then is truth? A mobile army of metaphors, metonyms and anthropomorphisms—in short, a sum of human relations, which have been enhanced, transposed, and embellished poetically and rhetorically, and which after long use seem canonical and obligatory.

See "On Truth and the Lie," in *Portable Nietzsche,* 46–47.

18. Danto, *Narration and Knowledge,* 361.

19. Rancière, *Names of History,* 58 (emphasis added).

20. Ibid., 46–47. Derrida makes this passage a focus for his "White Mythology: Metaphor in the Text of Philosophy," in *Margins of Philosophy,* trans. Alan Bass (Chicago: University of Chicago Press, 1982), 207–29.

21. Michel Foucault, *The Archeology of Knowledge,* trans. A. M. Sheridan Smith (London: Tavistock, 1972), 91.

22. Hayden White, "Foucault Decoded: Notes from the Underground," in *Tropics of Discourse* (Baltimore: Johns Hopkins University Press, 1978), 235. White misses the anti-Hegelianism of Foucault.

23. Compare Rorty, *Philosophy and the Mirror of Nature,* 391n.

24. Friedrich Nietzsche, *The Will to Power,* trans. Walter Kaufmann (New York: Vintage Books, 1968), 798–800, 419–21.

25. Nietzsche, *Will to Power,* 801, 422.

26. Foucault, *Archeology of Knowledge,* 38.

27. Rancière, *Names of History,* 8. There is no reference here to Foucault.

28. Walter Benjamin, "Theses in the Philosophy of History," in *Illuminations: Essays and Reflections,* trans. Harry Zohn (New York: Harcourt Brace Jovanovich, 1968), 253–64.

29. H. G. Wells, *The Time Machine* (New York: Berkeley Publishing, 1977).

30. Simon Schama, *Citizens: A Chronicle of the French Revolution* (New York: Vintage Books, 1990), 790–91.

31. Schama, *Citizens,* 791. Schama dissociates his criticism of the military pacification of the Vendée from the stronger claim of Reynald Secher that they constituted genocide.

32. S. Sambursky and S. Pines, *The Concept of Time in Late Neoplatonism* (Jerusalem: Israel Academy of Sciences and Humanities, 1971), 20. They show

that the early sixth-century Neoplatonic philosopher Damascius had observed that the relation of earlier and later never changes. The statement that the Trojan War happened before the Peloponnesian War is true no matter when it is asserted.

33. Hayden White, "The Value of Narrativity in the Representation of Reality," in *The Content of the Form* (Baltimore: Johns Hopkins University Press, 1987), 14.

Some Aspects of the Ethics of History-Writing: Reflections on Edith Wyschogrod's *An Ethics of Remembering*

Allan Megill

What is the ethical problem that most compellingly confronts those who make it their business to understand the past? Clearly, it is not the task of historians qua historians to work out an ethics. Different enterprises make incompatible demands on their practitioners—first of all competing demands for time and attention, but also, and more compellingly, demands that are incompatible in the sense that to carry out one sort of enterprise one must do X and to carry out another sort of enterprise one must do not-X. Even in our post-Kantian age, in which "otherness" and "diversity" are all the rage, ethics unavoidably retains a connection to the universal. It is no accident, for example, that the United Nations Declaration of Human Rights is "The *Universal* Declaration of Human Rights."[1] On the other hand, history-writing (in the broadest sense of *writing*, which in the present essay I take to embrace *all* modes of representing the past) aims to tell the truth in particular cases, and one might ask in what ways such an enterprise can be ethical. My contention in the present essay is that an ethical history would be a history in which the rules for arriving at historical truth have been scrupulously followed. This is a partial requirement, for the ethical character of history-writing also hangs on other considerations—most importantly, on looking at the human world in such a way as to be able to see in it the possibility of ethical action in the first place. Here, however, my focus will be on the ethical aspect of historical epistemology. The epistemology of historical investigation is closely connected to the ethics of historical investigation, although, to the impairment of both, the connection is not usually attended to.

It is far from obvious that history-writing has an ethics. The core of this ethics resides in the historian's obligation to arrive at truth concerning the past (note that I did not say "*the* truth"), and to convey this truth to people in the present and future—which means to other historians, to scholars generally, and to whatever public exists. "The past is a place of fantasy," Hayden White has said.[2] This is exactly right. To say that the past is a place of fantasy is to say that it allows us to see modes of being that are different from the ones put before us by our present—different ways of living, different ways of meeting common human problems and opportunities. In presenting, as it should, such a past, history opens up a space of freedom and possibility, without which the present is impoverished. History adds to the present by *unpresencing* the present, so that the present comes to occupy less than the totality of our conceptual and experiential horizon. By presencing other ways of thinking and being than our own, history attenuates the hold of the present on us.

But this is not the end of the matter, for fantasy has opposing valencies and directions. What is the character of a place of fantasy? As White notes in *The Content of the Form,* the past has attributes "that we might ascribe to the psychological sphere of 'the imaginary,' the level of infantile fantasies and narcissistic projections."[3] The susceptibility of "the past" to narcissistic projection is visible in many realms of popular culture today. One sees the "imaginary" past in popular movies, in the pronouncements of politicians, in people's reaction to the "history" that they see in the form of battlefields, monuments, museums, and land- and streetscapes, as well as in the writings of popular and even (on occasion) of academic historians. The presence of "the imaginary" in the representation of the past gives us entry into the question as to how, primarily, the ethics of history-writing ought to be confronted.

1

What would be involved, then, in an ethics of history? In our time, when "memory" and "remembering" are greatly valued, a primary consideration is the need to distinguish between an ethics of history and an ethics of remembering (I evoke Edith Wyschogrod's stimulating and provocative book, *An Ethics of Remembering*).[4] It is important to distinguish between an ethics of history and an ethics of remembering because confusion between the two can lead to unfortunate, indeed to unethical, consequences. In the absence of a clear grasp of the differences between history and memory, the importing of mnemonic categories into the project of historical understanding is likely to be damaging to our knowing and even to our being. I do not reject mnemonically oriented categories but only insist on a clear awareness of their limits. Memory and history intersect, with elements of "memory" present in history and with history contributing in various ways to "memory," but the two are also in important respects opposed to each other.

My focus in the present chapter is on the ethics of history and not on the ethics of memory because in our time the distinctive characteristics of history need to be identified and defended. What is the historian's ethical orientation? Wyschogrod evokes the historian's "double passion," namely, "an eros for the past and an ardor for the others in whose name there is a felt urgency to speak" (xi). This double passion—I prefer to call it, rather, a *double orientation*—is certainly an ingredient in the historiographical enterprise.[5] I find Wyschogrod's portrayal of this doubleness both illuminating and affecting. It is a view that arises as a response to a set of phenomena that Wyschogrod, in an earlier book, called "man-made mass death."[6] One of the distinctive features of mass death is the fact that, by definition, its victims disappear and are thus radically unable to speak for themselves. There thus arises, as Wyschogrod points out, an urgency that their story be told somehow. The historian is certainly one who would tell their story, and in doing so he or she might well manifest "an ardor for the others in whose name there is a felt urgency to speak."

The relation to the past that is here envisaged is an ethical relation of the sort emphasized by Emmanuel Levinas, who sees the ethical as involving a face-to-face engagement with "the other." In this engagement, otherness is accepted in its alterity; it is seen as infinitely exceeding both the subject engaging with it and the world of objects.[7] I believe, with Wyschogrod, that in the attempt to understand the past there ought to be something very much like the ethical relation as Levinas sees it, for it is crucial that the historian not try to offer either a practically usable past, or a past, whether intended to be practically usable or not, that turns out when closely examined to be simply an instance in which we ourselves, as we are now, present *ourselves* in a slightly different, slightly exotic guise.[8] Yet, while agreeing that an ethical moment of this kind, involving a nonmanipulative relation to an "other," ought to be present in history-writing, I am uneasy about a conception of the historian's enterprise that highlights to such a large degree the "eros" and "ardor" of the enterprise of giving voice to the silenced others of the past.

Let me try to articulate the reasons for my unease. In brief, I find that Wyschogrod moves too quickly, too much on the basis of a presumed consensus about what was the case in the past. In her ethically oriented account she is *assuming* the patient work of historians, without fully taking account of the fact that she is doing so. Before we can begin to engage erotically with the past, attempting with ardor to attend to the past's silent voices, we need to ask two questions: What do we know about the past in question? and How do we know it? In other words, my claim is that an ethical relation to the past presupposes the results of historical research. I take "the past" as something that needs to be constructed or reconstructed on the basis of rules, tacit or explicit, of historical construction or reconstruction. I take the notion of an eros or ardor directed to the past, and to the past Other, as presupposing such a construction or reconstruction.

It is dangerous to confuse an ethics of remembering with an ethics of history because it is dangerous to confuse memory with history. R. G. Collingwood puts the matter well, if too briefly, in *The Idea of History,* when he suggests that memory needs to be confirmed by material traces before there can be history: "I remember writing a letter to So-and-so last week . . . and my memory is not deceiving me; because here is his reply." With the reply in hand, "I am basing a statement about the past on evidence; I am talking history."[9] As Collingwood implies, memory is often deceptive. Consequently, narratives about the past produced on the basis of memory need to be stringently corroborated if they are to count as probable.[10] Indeed, what is called "memory" often has more to do with the claims of present community than it does with the historical past. One such memory-related community is the community of those who remember, *on the basis of their own experience,* an event or set of events in the past: say, the community of those who managed to survive what later came to be called the Holocaust. Another type of memory-related community is memory-related in a looser sense: it is the type of community that exists on the basis of one or another kind of *virtual* or *invented* memory. An obvious instance of communities of this type is provided by such religions as Judaism and Christianity, which involve the commemoration, through ritual observance, of actual or alleged events in the past (as in Communion and Passover, to take only two examples). Ritual commemorations bind together, as a community, those who participate in them (although the old etymology that derived the word "religion" from the Latin *religare,* "to bind," is apparently false, it manifests an important existential truth). The commemorations that occur in religious and other rituals mark and promote a mutual recognition (an ethical relation) among those who believe in what is being commemorated.

For the most part, however, neither memory nor commemoration
has much to do with the historical past. To be sure, it is seductively easy
to think that memory is the raw material of history—that the historical
past is something that we *remember*. Slogans like "Never forget!" and *"je
me souviens"* attest to the presence of such a view. But it is a mistake to
think that we remember the past. Rather, we remember the present, in
the following sense. When we remember, what we remember has to be
something that continues to live *within our situations now*—something
that we believe comes to us from the past, and may well do so, but whose
primary connection is to our present. We encounter the past (in German, the *Vergangenheit*), which is something gone away (*vergangen*, as the
German has it), not by remembering it but by thinking it. We *think* the
past: that is, we construct or reconstruct it on the basis of *Quellen*
(sources, testimonies) and *Überreste* (remains, [material] traces), and on
the basis also of critical procedures applied to those sources and remains.[11] What do we *remember?* We remember what is in our minds now.
A helpful motto would be: Remember the present, think the past.[12]
When, on the contrary, historical understanding is described as "remembering," we can infer that an attempt is being made to promote one
or another presumably desirable identity in the present. Promoting and
sustaining particular identities is certainly part of what history does: as
Jörn Rüsen has pointed out, history has the social function of orienting
existence in the present, and there can be no such orientation without
an engagement with issues of identity.[13] But as Rüsen has also pointed
out, history involves methodological considerations, considerations that
do not arise within the sphere of memory.

What is the ethical demand that lies most heavily upon the historian? I do not believe that it is the demand to restore the actuality of the
past, or to make the voices of the past speak again, or to speak for the
dead or for others who cannot speak. All of these are tasks that historians, and others who have an interest in or commitment to the past,
might do or feign to do. But one should not lose sight of what is primary.
The historian clearly needs to have "an eros for the past"; but as
Wyschogrod also point out, he or she at the same time makes a "promise
of truth" (xi). I take the promise of truth to be ethically primary. Fundamentally, before anything else, the historian needs to be able to vouch
for the truth of the history that he or she writes, just as the accountant
needs to be able to vouch for the truth of the accounts that he or she
presents. If one is to claim to make the voices of the past speak, there
needs to be adequate reason for thinking that the voices have been
rightly constituted. Otherwise, they might be merely the product of the
historian's own compelling desire—whether the practical desire for

such and such a supposedly beneficial political or moral outcome in the present, or the aesthetic desire for representations that are dramatic or edifying, redemptive or horrible.

In short, it is a matter here of the above-noted double orientation. One orientation is toward the universal. This orientation amounts to a claim that the historian can speak beyond the particular interests, desires, and commitments pressing down upon her, articulating a truth that can be acknowledged by anyone willing to rethink the chain of evidence and argument that underlies this truth. The other orientation is toward particular communities, particular desires, and particular pasts, seen in all their contingency and partiality. What defines historical investigation and writing as an enterprise is the indissoluble, and at the same time unresolvable, intertwining of these two orientations. Thus history-writing properly carried out involves both a measure of transcendence and, at the same time, a deep embeddedness in particular mundane commitments. It is a delicate balance. I leave aside, here, the temptation to reject the history-writing enterprise altogether; instead I focus on another temptation, namely, the temptation to project our own wishes, and imagined wish fulfillments, onto the otherwise blank canvas of the past. At base we want people in the past to be just like us; we want drama and terror; we want edification and redemption. In short, we want a resolution of the tension between the opposing moments just noted. Such, at any rate, is what our time's popular history, and especially its historically related entertainments (see, e.g., *Schindler's List*), seem to be telling us.[14]

The ethics of history-writing resides above all in the moment of resistance to historiographical wish fulfillment. This moment of resistance is an epistemological moment. The epistemological moment is all the more needed the more an erotic investment is in play. Saul Friedlander rightly refers to "the unavoidable link between the ethical and the epistemological dimensions" in debates about history.[15] To be sure, in practical terms "epistemology" amounts here to procedural correctness in one's research and writing, and it may seem odd to think of the ethics of history in a procedural light. But any oddity is only apparent, for in crucial respects epistemology is like ethics. An epistemological commitment requires us to put aside what we wish would have happened in the past and instead to lay out what research and reflection compel us to think did happen. Similarly, an ethical commitment requires us to rise above the particularity of our own immediate desires and to attempt, however imperfectly, to follow a universal moral law.

Taking her cue from Levinas and from other heterodox philosophers, Wyschogrod posits what she calls the "heterological" historian, who is "bound by a responsibility toward the dead for whom she claims to speak" (3). Such a historian is ethical in her concerns. Ethics, in this context, involves an endeavor to encounter past historical agents and sufferers in a face-to-face manner, without imposing an external grid on them. The heterological historian must remain sensitive to "the nameless others" of the past, while at the same time conveying his or her own moral judgments concerning the past. I contend that historical investigation and writing, properly carried out, *ought* to be "heterological," and that if the heterology is left out the result is less than history. But what ought to define this heterology is not only a commitment to the nameless others. Rather, historical heterology is defined first by a certain alienation from the dominant logic, or logics, of the present. Indeed, precisely such an alienation seems to be a precondition for any proper historical work at all. Second, in addition to this, historical heterology is defined by a resistance to the seductive notion that the historian ought to articulate, against present orthodoxy, a counter-orthodoxy. But the articulation of orthodoxy of any kind involves the dissolving of the historian's double orientation. A history in which the tension between universal and particular is resolved into some sort of higher unity is no longer a history. It may be philosophy of history, or it may be theory, or it may be a political program, but it is no longer history.

The historian's alienation from the present deserves further discussion here, for it has some relation to Wyschogrod's insistence on the responsibility of the historian toward the dead. I suspect that many historians—although undoubtedly far from all—will acknowledge that it was some glimmer of discomfort with the present that first stimulated their interest in the past. But beyond issues of personal psychology, which is not really what is at issue here, there are theoretical reasons for finding in the historiographical enterprise a breach with the present. Historical investigation is prone to corruption when it is carried out under the dominance of the present. The historian's time stretches backwards, *away* from the immediate concerns of the present. Investigations of the past carried out with the intent of being practically useful—with the intent, say, of contributing to "policy studies" or to "policy science"—are bound to be systematically distortive, since such investigations are obliged to focus inordinately on those aspects of the past that fit the frame of the present. Similarly, history written in order to support some presumably good end in the present is all too prone to fall into various forms of special pleading.

However, I would not go so far as to say, as Wyschogrod does, that the historian's responsibility is "a responsibility toward the dead for whom she [the heterological historian] claims to speak" (3). Human beings do have responsibilities that one can plausibly interpret as responsibilities toward the dead. Consider, for example, debts that one owes to the dead—such as the debt arising from having benefited in some way from what a person or persons did when they were alive. A paradigmatic case is the debt one owes to parents and to other family members. Consider also legal and moral obligations, such as the obligation not to depart from the spirit of wills, bequests, foundations, and the like. Consider, finally, the act of "bearing witness"—by which I mean the making known of good or bad actions that were carried out in the past, so that one preserves the memory of heroism, on the one side, and of gratuitous cruelty and unmerited suffering, on the other. But while it is certainly proper to interpret these responsibilities as being, in some sense, responsibilities toward the dead, I wish to suggest that they are better interpreted as responsibilities toward the human community in general—or, if one will, toward the community of moral agents in general. The questions that one ought to ask, with regard to ethical matters, are questions of the following sort: Does one want to live in a society where just obligations are not carried out? Does one want to live in a society where a serious effort is not made to keep promises? Does one want to live in a society where the difference between lying and not lying is not taken seriously? From an ethical point of view, the questions are best seen, I contend, as having a more rather than a less universal form.

I do not deny that there is an ethical force that comes from thinking of a universal responsibility under the guise of specific imagined faces whom we might feel, despite their differentness from us, to be existentially closer to us than any abstract universal rule can be. I only wish to contend that it is best to see the historian's responsibility toward the dead (and perhaps all persons' responsibility toward the dead) in a way that highlights his or her responsibility to *all* human (moral) community. The epistemology of history-writing enters into the ethics of history-writing once one has come to see the historian's responsibility in this more universal light.

2

Beyond their common commitment to the universal, how, in more specific terms, is the epistemology of history-writing related to the ethics of history-writing? The first point that needs to be made is that history's "responsibility toward the dead" is *built on top of* the process of reconstructing the past. What is at issue in history are past particulars—

persons, places, situations, events. In every case responsibility toward the dead is based (in part) on an empirical assertion. It is based on the assertion that we actually do owe a debt to the people whom we honor, because they really did act in a way that puts us in their debt. It is based on the assertion that the legal document from which we infer an obligation on our part is an authentic document and that we have understood it rightly. It is based on the assertion that the atrocities, from mass murder to sexual abuse, to which we feel impelled to bear witness actually did occur, and occurred in the way that we suppose that they occurred. Justification for these specific assertions boils down in every instance to the mundane task of determining whether such and such things in the past were actually the case.

An ethical response to past events is certainly part of the historian's project. But the historian's ethical response to his or her object of study may well not be expressed in any explicit way. In fact, the preferred mode in the discipline is to be extremely reticent in the expression of ethical evaluations, to such a degree that historians who breach this implicit rule may well be sharply criticized for doing so. There are some sound reasons for this reticence. One reason was suggested at the beginning of this essay: the writing of a historical account makes different demands on its practitioners than does the enterprise of moral reflection. Historians have to focus on the former task. In consequence, any ethical evaluations that historians introduce into their historical accounts risk looking like mere statements of opinion and not like solidly worked-out judgments. If such statements appear to rely for their justification on an assumed moral consensus among the historian's contemporaries, they risk appearing unnecessary; if, on the contrary, they seem to diverge from the moral consensus of the historian's contemporaries, they risk appearing capricious and unjustified. In short, there are problems involved in historians' offering of ethical evaluations. In most circumstances, it may well be better for historians to hold themselves back from the offering of explicit moral statements in their historical work.[16]

But my point here is that the ethics of history-writing should not be identified with historians' offering of explicit moral evaluations in their historical writings. For the ethics of history-writing is ultimately located at a deeper level than this, at the level not just of the text but of the production of the text. We reasonably expect that the text the historian produces will have arisen from a commitment that is in part ethical, namely, the commitment to discover and lay out historical truth, insofar as historical evidence and historiographical procedures allow this to be done. Conceptual analysis of the project of history-writing shows that the historical text will contain four types of constructs: *descriptions,* in which the historian attempts to say what was the case in the past; *explanations*, in which the historian attempts to say why things were the way they were; *arguments* or *justifications*, in which the historian attempts to give the ground for holding that the descriptions and explanations in question are true; and *interpretations*, in which the historian attempts to say what the significance of the past events in question is for us, now.[17]

There are several places within this layout where questions of ethics enter into the picture. First, if one assumes that there is such a thing as ethical action (and not simply the pursuit of material interest), then to some degree the descriptions that the historian articulates will need to embrace the putatively ethical and unethical (morally wrong, even evil) dimensions of human reality. It is not at all rare at the present time that, either implicitly or explicitly, historians deny such an aspect to human reality, identifying in the past only those kinds of choices that conduce, or not, to one or another variety of material interest. (In a terminological irony that will be striking to anyone who has read Immanuel Kant, the choices in question are sometimes designated as "rational" choices.) The introducing of moral language into historical discourse raises complicated issues, as I have already suggested. Above all, there is always the danger of appearing to moralize—that is, of appearing to offer ethical evaluations that lack justification, that are simply imposed on the historical material.

Second, if one assumes that human life includes an ethical dimension, the historian's interpretive task also invites ethical reflection. For historical interpretation, as defined here, involves laying out the significance of past events and existence for us, now. Consequently, if there actually does exist an ethical dimension to human life, historians are obliged to reflect on the ethical significance of the past for us, now, and not only on its material, social, and political significance. Here, too, there is the danger of appearing to moralize. There is also a problem of definition, encapsulated in the question: Is it still history? For, to the extent that the interpretive function *takes over*, overwhelming the other historiographical tasks (description, explanation, argument and justification), the historian begins to turn into something else—into a critic, pundit, publicist, or moralist, to take the main possibilities. However, the boundaries between history and these other enterprises are not and cannot be precisely controlled: on the contrary, they have a certain porousness, like the boundaries between states within the European Union. The key point is that, within what are commonly taken to be the boundaries of history, there is at least *some* place for ethical judgment, albeit quietly and unobtrusively expressed. It seems reasonable to think that such judgment is often (almost always?) more effective when it is not shouted at the reader, but instead requires readers to do some thinking on their own.

It is striking how, in both the descriptive and the interpretive aspects of the historical account, the project of actually *stating* moral judgments appears somewhat problematic. As Agnes Heller has rightly put it, "the situation of the historian who chooses to pass moral judgments on actors of the past is awkward . . . we are unable to pass moral judgments over actors of the past consistently and methodically."[18] This conclusion, which Heller arrived at through philosophical analysis, is confirmed by historians' practice, which shies away from the making of explicit moral judgments. Admittedly, there have been exceptions. For example, as Perez Zagorin has noted, the prominent late-nineteenth-century British historian Lord Acton claimed that "moral judgment on past crimes and misdeeds is one of the supreme duties of the historian"; but as Zagorin also notes, Acton's claim "set him apart . . . from all the noted historians and thinkers about history of his own generation and thereafter."[19]

The awkwardness that accompanies the historian's making of moral claims at the levels of description and interpretation suggests that we need to direct our attention elsewhere if we are to get at the ethical dimension of historical research and writing. This "elsewhere" is none other than the level of argument or justification. Proper historians do not merely proclaim that such and such a historical description or explanation is true. On the contrary, they provide reasons for adhering to the historical claims that they make. This obligation is of course congruent with Wyschogrod's observation that historians are under an obligation to pursue and to tell the truth. The obligation to offer reasons for one's truth-claims is an ethical and not merely a technical obligation. It is ethical in at least two ways. First, the offering of reasons is a sign that one puts one's readers and interlocutors at the same level that one puts oneself, treating them, not as the merely passive recipients of a supposedly already established truth, but as fellow inquirers. The reciprocity here implied accords with the reciprocity that is generally seen as essential to ethics. Second, whatever the initial appearance might be, the offering of reasons is the historian's acknowledgment that he or she might be wrong. In carefully laying out the grounds for her assertions, the historian makes it possible for a community of inquiry to emerge around the questions animating the investigation. Community is likewise congruent with ethics as it is generally understood. Third, in searching for historical truth, and in demonstrating a commitment to that search by an attentiveness to the grounds for and against any specific historical claim, the historian stands apart from the notion that history is or ought to be immediately useful either to the present order, or to some part of that order, or to any particular alternative to that order. In short, the historian stands apart from the notion that history ought to be a form of propaganda for "the good cause"—whatever that cause may be—and instead engages in a pursuit that stands beyond such particular commitments. In thus adhering to a principle of universality, the epistemology of history again shows an affinity with ethics as it is generally understood.

Indeed, one of the things that history can and ought to do—and this is surely just as important as its putting forward of accounts of particular historical pasts—is to model truth-telling. I mean by this that it ought to model, not just truth-telling about the historical past, but truth-telling as such. In a social order where instances of deception proliferate, such modeling is of great importance. History-writing, so conceived, models attitudes and procedures conducive to arriving at truth, or at least to avoiding falsity, concerning human matters.[20] One can mention such practices and attitudes as a disinclination to jump to conclusions, however convenient these conclusions might be; a consciousness of the limits of our knowledge in any given case (limits that can be approached but that one ought not to overstep); a carefulness in weighing assertions against evidence (accommodating weight of assertion to weight of evidence); and an insistence on clearly identifying as speculative those aspects of a historical account that are indeed such (for speculation cannot be avoided in history-writing). Also relevant to the ethics of history-writing are the more technical rules of historical research and writing, such as preferring sources that are closer to the events to be described and explained over sources that are more distant, and the testing of testimonies and material traces against each other.

Proper history's truth-seeking involves, not the cultivated tendentiousness of attorneys, advertising agencies, travel brochure writers, spin doctors, and too-creative accountants, but the sifting of evidence and testing of assertions based on that evidence. Of course, what is here required is the breach, noted above, between the historiographical project and the present (which means a breach with the immediate desires of the present). To tell the truth—which is an ethical injunction—is almost always easier when there is some measure of distance from present desire. This is part of the reason why, at its best, history has a relatively large hope that it might model truth-telling, for its separation from the present is already part of what makes it history.

3

There is far more history than the history produced by historians: it is an evident fact that popular presentations of history are nearly ubiquitous in our culture. But I would argue that the historian's peculiar vocation for the sifting of the past's sources and traces ought to be at the center of the culture's orientation toward the past. The weakening of that vocation is a mistake, especially if the weakening occurs not through an illuminating interchange with other truth-seeking disciplines but through an attempt to emulate the vague territory of cultural "memory," with which history is sometimes confused. It is a mistake that can lead to ethical losses and wrongs.

As one writer has noted:

> history and memory are selective reconstructions, but they do not narrate the same history, for their criteria of selection are different. History (assuming that it claims to have something in common with scientific knowledge) has the obligation to orient itself on principle toward "truth." Memory orients itself toward "identity."[21]

To be sure, "truth" and "identity" are not absolutely divided one from the other: as noted already, history *also* orients itself, in part, to identity. But it ought to do so in a critical and methodologically disciplined way. The constituting of history as a discipline, in the nineteenth century, was closely connected with the then-prevalent notion that all particular histories will ultimately be embraced within a single "grand narrative" that is the narrative of human history as a whole. This assumed universal narrative presupposed, as its basis, a single identity that was male, political, and European. It seems clear that at the present moment we can no longer accede to the notion of a grand narrative: there are too many of them, and hence there is none. I have argued elsewhere that methodological criteria have come to take the place of the now-impossible grand narrative. In the absence of a grand narrative, it is these criteria that allow history to exist as something distinct from memory or fantasy.[22]

Wyschogrod poses a question that will always be asked by anyone aware of epistemological issues in history: "Whose truth is being told, to whom, by whom, and to what end?" (4). But although one needs to ask this question, one also needs to go beyond it. Unless one is able to deploy criteria for evaluating historical truth-claims, one will never be able to do so. Rather, as the question implies, it will be a matter of different truths for different identities, each truth constructed for its own particular end. A historical claim that serves a "good" function in the present will be "good," quite apart from whether it is factually correct (given the impossibility of comparing statements about the past to the past itself, "factually correct" equates to "not violating the rules, express and tacit, of historical method"). To abandon the notion that there are universal criteria of *some* kind, and to judge historical claims and narratives by how well they serve some allegedly good purpose in the present, is to destroy history as a discipline and as a field of concern. The break between present and past that is a precondition for historiography exists only because there are methodological criteria that make possible the establishing of a space that is precisely *not* that of the present.[23] These criteria establish a history that is different from memory. Memory in its various senses is tied too closely to an identity or identities in the present to get us anywhere near the other side of the breach between present and past.

It is extremely important to acknowledge that there *is* an other side. History's traumas—and, more generally, its obscurities—are not sufficiently acknowledged in the constructivist, Collingwoodian tradition of historical thinking.[24] One of the merits of Wyschogrod's *Ethics of Remembering* is that it acknowledges historical trauma. But the distance between past and present means that the historian cannot in fact speak the voice of the dead others, and historians who know what they are doing will not claim, or even appear to claim, to do so. Nor can the historian "represent" the past, if by *representation* we mean that the historian conveys to us the raw feel of the now-dead past. To be sure, a vast popular demand is placed on historians, and on others who in some way deal in the past, to do precisely this, to provide an *aesthesis,* a sensual or quasi-sensual representation, of the past. One sees this demand being catered to in large segments of popular and mass culture: in historical museums and historical sites of various kinds; in popular movies; in military and other historical reenactments; and in history documentaries and history channels. In the more serious of these enterprises much emphasis is put on making sure that the physical artifacts of the past—the weapons, uniforms, plates, silverware, and such like—look authentic, appearing now as they supposedly once were. Ideally, if possible, they ought to *be* authentic. The quest for authenticity of this sort is entirely understandable: there is a pleasure and pathos in viewing things that have a certain antiquity, or at least the appearance thereof. But such authenticity ought to be only a very small part of what the historian is engaged with, for the pursuit of authenticity of this sort brings with it a danger—the danger that a preoccupation with the *aesthesis* of history will lead us to think, wrongly, that we can resurrect the spirit, feeling, voices, and commitments of the past in the way that we can sometimes resurrect its furniture and tableware. In fact, it is almost always much harder to do the former than the latter.

Moreover, preoccupation with resurrecting the sight and feel of the past raises a problem with regard to the ethics of history-writing. No one has written better on historical representation, and by extension on the *aesthesis* of history, than has Hayden White. In a brilliant passage in *The Content of the Form,* White notes that since historical representation "purports to deal with 'the real' rather than the merely 'imaginary,'" the reading subject

> is treated to a spectacle that allows him to exercise his fantasies of free-
> dom under the aspect of a fixed order, or conflict under the aspect of
> resolution, or violence under the aspect of an achieved peace, and so
> on . . . historical representation permits the reader to give free reign to
> "the imaginary" while remaining bound to the constraints of a "symbolic
> system" . . . historical representation can produce in the subject a sense
> of "the real" that can be used as a criterion for determining what shall
> count as "realistic" in his own present.[25]

In this passage White rightly characterizes an important part of the psy-chology of historical representation. The difficulty from an ethical point of view when the reader (or, increasingly, the viewer or Web surfer) treats—and is encouraged to treat—historical representation as "a spec-tacle" is that the ethical dimension of history arrives on the scene only belatedly, in the form of an ethical response to that representation. For example, one might well come to the ethical conclusion that it would be obscene to write about the Holocaust in the comic mode.[26] Here, ethical judgment appears as an arbitrary, "after the fact" addendum. It appears, further, not as an actual part of the historian's work, but as a kind of be-lated response to it, articulated in a form that looks suspiciously like an arbitrary expression of taste.

It is a mistake to think of the ethics of history-writing in this be-lated way. What needs to be understood is the extent to which ethics is—or, more accurately, ought to be—embedded in the process of historical research itself. At least if one has any concern with ethics, it is much bet-ter to conceive of history as a public inquiry than as an attempt to offer an *aesthesis*. History is inquiry because it is a process of investigation into truth. It is public inquiry because it is enmeshed in a process of argu-ment, and because the argument is about matters that are far from purely technical, so that the substance of the argument is in principle open to a "public," understood as people without arcane technical train-ing but with the capacity to apply themselves seriously to evidence and argument. The process of argument in question is intersubjective, even though it is not always "face-to-face" (to evoke again Levinas's notion of ethics). From the beginning, the historian knows or ought to know that she has to make a case for the claims that she advances, for in history apodictic certainty is not possible. The case is not one that is made in some sort of abstract Platonic space. Rather, it is made before living interlocutors—interlocutors who, one hopes, will be capable of entering into the gist of the matter, as one hopes the jurors in a criminal trial will.

Historians are undoubtedly engaged in the enterprise of "declar[ing] something as something," as Wyschogrod puts it (7). The phrase evokes Heidegger's point that to interpret something is to see it "as" something.[27] In fact, much of the historian's discourse is interpretive in this sense: it is the making visible to an audience of realities that the audience was previously unaware of, because it had no interest or curiosity directed toward those realities. Certainly, the historian's discourse is representational and aesthetic—representational in the sense that, at its best, it *presents* a historical reality to its audience, and aesthetic in the sense that, at its best, it renders that reality vivid. Yet at the same time the historian's discourse is, or ought to be, argumentative. The historian's "declaring" something does not arise out of superior aesthetic or prophetic insight. When a historian "declares something *as* something," the claim has an argumentative rather than an intuitive or prophetic basis. He or she is under an obligation to give reasons. These might be reasons for our concurring that such and such phenomena occurred in the past (e.g., certain instances of violence in the years 1939–45), and also reasons for our seeing these phenomena "as" such and such a thing (e.g., for seeing these instances of violence as "the Holocaust"). In practice, of course, the two moments—the moment of the thing and the moment of the interpretation of the thing—blur together. But both should be present in the historical account; neither should be reduced to the other.

The presentation of the reasons is as important as the presentation of the claims themselves. The model ought not to be that of the utterly confident eyewitness declaring what she has seen: in fact, eyewitnesses are unreliable for a variety of reasons, including inattentiveness, limitations imposed by the particular perspective of the witness, the unreliability of memory, self-deception, vanity, and, perhaps least important, outright lying.[28] The model ought rather to be that of the modest searcher after truth presenting both what she has discovered and her reasons for thinking that this is what she has discovered. The historian ought to avoid a language that would suggest declaration in a very strong sense of the term; he or she ought to propose, more than declare or reveal. To give or to appear to give a prophetic or revelatory dimension to historiography is, I am persuaded, a mistake, the mark of a defect, perhaps the mark of a moral defect. It is the Nietzschean temptation, or at any rate it is *one* of the Nietzschean temptations: Thus it is so; therefore believe.

Memory, as already noted, orients itself to identity; and the identity speaks from the present. What is needed for history to exist in contradistinction to memory is the breach between present and past. As de Certeau puts it, "modern Western history essentially begins with differentiation between the *present* and the *past*. In this way it is unlike tradition . . . "[29] (One might add that tradition is very much like memory, and is connected to memory in various ways.) But note that there are actually *two* breaches in the historiographical project. First, there is the breach between the historian, as one who seeks out the past, and the present in which he or she lives. Second, there is the breach between the historian, who lives in the present, and the past, which in its otherness from the present turns out not to be fully recoverable. The fact of this double breach limits the extent to which history can "speak for" the silent dead. To put the matter another way: to divide the present from the past is to "draw a line between what is dead and what is not dead."[30] Accordingly, the object of historiography is quintessentially other—"the other is the phantasm of historiography," to follow de Certeau again. But more than this, and perhaps more disturbingly, the "other" is "the object that [historiography] seeks, honors, and buries."[31]

This is why I find that the ethics of history-writing does not lie primarily in a relation to the other—to this "real" that, as de Certeau writes, is both the "result" of historical analysis and its "postulate."[32] Rather, the ethical relation of history-writing is primarily to one mode of the present—namely, the *continuing* present. Historiography is a set of continuing practices, not just a set of texts. The historian claims to tell true stories about the past. The test of that claim is not whether the stories correspond to the past that actually existed (since we have no independent access to the past that actually existed, but only to the testimonies and material traces out of which the historian's past is constructed or reconstructed). Analogously, the test of the ethical rightness of a historical account is not primarily a matter of its relation to people who lived and suffered, spoke or remained silent, in the past. The test of a history's truth has to do primarily with whether the historical claims being made stand up when scrutinized according to the rules of historical research. The test of a history's ethical rightness has to do primarily (although I think not entirely) with the skill, openness, honesty, and imagination with which those rules are deployed. It is a matter here of process, and of the openness of the process to continuing investigation by others (a historical account can come to be judged passé, outdated by subsequent research, while still retaining a rightness in this sense, which I think is not only epistemological but also ethical).

There are similarities and differences that are worth considering between ethics in history and ethics in the legal system.[33] Like the historian, a court applies rules of evidence to the body of evidence that is brought before it, deliberates on the evidence that survives this application, and thence arrives at a decision in each particular case. An ethical court is one in which the evidence is gathered diligently, presented clearly, and assessed with scrupulous attention to the rules of evidence and to the law. In essence, historians do the same thing that law courts do. Just as an ethical court does not bow to the immediate desires of the community but instead follows its own distinctive rules and practices, so also does the ethical historian. The ethical practice of history derives from a combination of training, intelligence, thoroughness, care, and honesty, and from an unmixed intention to follow, not an agenda, but the argument where it leads.

Still, in a number of significant respects legal judgment and historical judgment are different. Courts focus on a limited range of issues—normally, in criminal cases, on the guilt or innocence of an accused person. Legal cases are also constrained in time: a case is not supposed to be inordinately delayed, and once a decision is reached there are limits on the right of appeal. Neither constraint applies to historical judgment. But the crucial difference between the legal system—in its Anglo-American variant—and historical research and writing has to do with the peculiarly adversarial character of truth-seeking within the former. Opposing counsel shade the truth, telling it only partially and putting one or another "spin" on it. Indeed, as law is practiced in America today, there is reason to suspect that many attorneys countenance perjury by their clients, and that some sail perilously close to telling untruths themselves. The rationale for tolerating such behavior is to be found in the thought that the conflict between two opposing sides, each telling a distorted truth, will in fact conduce to the actual truth eventually winning out. This may or may not occur: there is in fact a permanent danger that the adversarial system will fail to function adequately in particular cases.

What history offers, or ought to offer, is an ethical model that is superior to the model just described. What it ought to offer is an ethics of truth-seeking argument, applied to the sphere of humanity (a difficult field, given the unpredictabilities of the human organism and the implication of historians in the very passions and interests that they seek to study). The ethics of history-writing has to do less with an attempt to encounter the dead than with the argumentative speech situation of seekers for truth within the continuing present. Certain rules and commitments attach to this situation. They include the following: a commitment to direct and explicit argument, as distinguished from insinuation. A commitment to the open canvassing and display of evidence. A commitment to modulating the strength of one's claims to accord with the strength of the evidence for those claims. A rejection of the lawyerly tactic of employing arguments that one knows, or ought to know, are distortions of the facts of the matter. A rejection of the lawyerly tactic of *suppressio veri*—in which the attorney does not actively lie, but nonetheless conceals from his or her opponents and from the judge facts of a materially relevant nature. An engagement toward ultimate clarity (although obscurity may be encountered along the way). An openness to the possibility that one's own stance may in some way be defective. An awareness of modes of seeing and arguing that go beyond the narrowly historical. And so on. It is primarily in this, the sphere of argument and justification, that the ethics of history resides.

Consider again de Certeau's claim that a breach between present and past is crucial to the structure of modern historiography. Thucydides, whom Hegel once identified as writing a type of history in which the spirit of the historian is the same as the spirit of the events that he describes, would not have been able to make sense of such a claim.[34] The same is probably true for all historians until, at the earliest, the seventeenth century. But the breach that de Certeau identifies amounts to a brilliant conceptual innovation. It is a conceptual innovation with epistemological consequences and—what is more relevant in the present essay—with ethical ones as well. For it asks the historian to stand aside from the immediate demands of the present community within which he or she lives. History that is not detached from the present falls too easily into the temptations of lawyerliness and self-deception, where a tendentiously justified account of the past serves to support the desires of one or another collectivity within the present. In history, as in any enterprise of truth-seeking, we are dealing with a work, an *ergon,* that is not reducible to an interest-serving machine. A work of the sort envisaged here is a matter of desire restrained. Such restraint is more easily achieved where there is a breach with the present than in those situations where there is a passionate and immediate engagement with the present's unresolved issues. The historian functions in a more ethically engaged manner when he or she resolves to assess matters dispassionately and to let the chips fall where they may. Such a stance is morally superior to the stances both of the advocate and of the teller of edifying stories.

Does it need to be said that ours is a social and political order from which the disinterested and committed pursuit of truth is often lacking?

Tocqueville, especially the Tocqueville of *Democracy in America,* is popular in America not only because he was in many ways an acute observer of the American scene and a brilliant theorist of democracy, but also because *Democracy in America* flatters the sensibilities of Americans. To Montesquieu, who saw civic virtue as the essential motivating force of republics and who had a strong sense of the fragility of such virtue, ours would appear as a corrupt republic. What is most relevant to the subject of the present paper is the absence or corruption of argument in large sectors of public life. In the face of such absence or corruption, there is some advantage to a discipline that attempts to stand apart from present desire (while at the same time taking desire as one of its central objects of study). Consider, again, the double breach that marks out the historian's work. One breach separates the historian, or anyone else, from ever knowing the past in its essence. The other breach, a condition of possibility of historical investigation, detaches the historian from the practical concerns of the present, and enables the disinterested pursuit of the admittedly defective (but not negligible) knowledge to which the historian can lay claim.

4

People disagree about the ethics of history-writing. Consider a comment that Wyschogrod makes in *An Ethics of Remembering* on a position that Hayden White articulated in *Metahistory:*

> for White, the ethical moment of a historical work is derived from a synthesis of plot, "an aesthetic perception" and argument, "a cognitive operation," so that the prescriptive emanates from the descriptive without further explanation.[35]

Wyschogrod remarks critically that White has here

> not noticed that the ethical referent goes all the way down, that the alterity of the other grips the historian prior to her narration and not as an inference from it. (22)

Wyschogrod calls attention to the victims of twentieth-century genocides. She also evokes the legal system, observing that the assumption has recently come to the fore that "the ethical dimension of historical writing can be construed in terms of jurisprudence." She draws attention to the plaintiff-victims of the genocides, who have been deprived of the opportunity to establish their own victimhood. "Who is authorized to speak for the victims? How is victimization to be ascribed?" (23).

Obviously, I would conceptualize the ethical problem in a different way, as having to do primarily with the truth-telling aspect of the historical discipline. The ethical dimension of history, then, would not primarily have to do with speaking for victims. Until we have established these matters by systematic inquiry, we should not say that we know the nature of the victimhood. In other words, victimhood cannot first be *ascribed.* Rather, it must first be established, by evidential procedures that are akin to juridical procedures (although not identical with them). Establishing claims about the past is not an easy thing to do. It requires immense care. Further, as suggested above, it is a task that extends over time, involving arguments among historians about matters that cannot offer apodictic certainty. Accordingly, the historian can speak for the silenced dead only with the greatest circumspection. Perhaps the historian can speak for the silenced dead not at all, only pointing to the place of a victimhood, describing the victimization and attempting to discern what led to it.

In the passage cited above Wyschogrod takes exception to the view, which she attributes to White, that in history-writing "the prescriptive emanates from the descriptive without further explanation." Precisely so: this is how history in the modern era is most often written. Consider Peter Gay's well-known discussion of the end of book 7 and beginning of book 8 of Ranke's *Französische Geschichte*. Henri IV had dominated Ranke's text for scores of pages. Now he is assassinated, and book 7 closes. Book 8 then begins with a stunning sentence: "*Ein Mann weniger war in der Welt*": In the world there was one man less.[36] As Gay points out, Ranke's "tight-lipped, ostentatiously understated reference to the actor who has just left the world stage forever" imparts to the dead king "the most monumental stature."[37] But the effect is not only dramatic; it is also ethical. For Ranke's understatement offers an implicit moral observation: *sic transit gloria mundi* (so the mighty are fallen). Life is contingent, and we must understand that tomorrow or the next day we also will die. Here is an example of an ethical judgment arising more or less seamlessly from a descriptive text. Clearly, Ranke thought that there was no need for him to make an explicit ethical statement—indeed, an explicit statement about the contingencies of the world would have ruined the drama, undermining the ethical frisson that the text seeks to impart.[38] What Ranke says is not cast as a prescription applicable to our own situation now, but rather as a judgment arising from events that have already taken place. An implicit ethical observation arises seamlessly and unobtrusively from a description of events.

This seems to me to be entirely right. The temptation to turn history into a moral or policy science is ever present and should ever be resisted. The fundamental tasks of history are to describe events and existents in the past; to explain these wherever it is possible and interesting to do so; to offer arguments and justifications for the truth of the claims made; and to comment on the significance for us, now, of what has been claimed. None of these tasks is primarily ethical, although they have ethical connections and implications. For the most part the ethics of history-writing ought to remain unstated, as in the passage just cited. The offering of explicit ethical judgments, let alone the making of ethical prescriptions for the present and future, is for the most part not essential to the historian's enterprise, and should usually be avoided. The true is not the the same as the useful or the uplifting. But this does not mean that history-writing is an un- or nonethical enterprise. The fundamental obligation of historians is to the maximal telling of truth, maximally keyed to the weight of the available evidence. Here is where the only ethics of history worthy of the name is to be found. As for the silenced others, the crucial point is that it is unfaithful to the enterprise of maximal truth-telling *in the present* to fail to take account of them. If, for example, a historian were to write an account of "the frontier" in South African history, while treating the frontier as exclusively that of the Europeans and failing to deal adequately with the fact that non-Europeans were also to be found on the scene and presumably had frontiers of their own, this would fail the test of maximal truth-telling.[39]

There are two important clarifications that must be made concerning the rule of maximal truth-telling and its relation to the silenced others. First, the historian's obligation is not to speak *for* the silenced others—or for anyone else in the past. The historian ought not to be an attorney for one side or the other in the past: the historian is judge, not advocate. That is, the obligation of the historian, and of historians collectively, is to provide accounts of the past that are maximally true and maximally illuminating; and the wishes of particular groups need to be subordinated to this obligation. Advocacy leads to subtle corruptions of the search for truth that are dangerous if uncorrected.

Second, the rule of maximal truth-telling requires that one take account of the ultimate impossibility of speaking for the silenced others. What defines the silenced others *as* silent is that they were silenced: they did not and do not speak. How can historians reproduce voices that left no record? The simple answer is: they cannot. Moreover, the rule of maximal truth-telling, and the internal conventions of the historical discipline, require that historians not pretend to do what they cannot do. Historians are required to make *justified* claims about the past, but in the absence of evidence no justification is possible. If historians do not respect the limits of their evidence, they open the way to lies about the past. They make it appear that the making of claims that cannot be adequately supported by evidence is acceptable in academic life, and presumably a fortiori elsewhere. This is not a conclusion that one should wish to accept. In history-writing, the unevidenced voice remains silent.

5

It is an austere prescription, that the historian acknowledge scrupulously the limits of his or her evidence. Does the severity of the prescription mean that there are no resources left—no possibilities for addressing the silences of the past? On the contrary: it is indeed possible to address these silences, while at the same time not violating the ethical demands of the discipline. There are in fact two modes of approach: from within the discipline, and from outside it. I shall here address them only briefly and suggestively.

From within the discipline. Famously, Collingwood held that a justified historical conclusion is knock-down drag-out true. In his view, the claims that the historian makes ought to follow "inevitably" from the evidence; it is thus the case that a historical argument proves its point "as conclusively as a demonstration in mathematics."[40] *The Idea of History* is one of a small number of works in the philosophy of history that *must* be attended to by anyone seriously interested in the subject.[41] But Collingwood's claim that conclusions in history ought to be demonstrably certain is glaringly wrong. The fact is, the discipline does not sustain the level of certainty that Collingwood attributed to it. Rather, it sustains different, and lesser, levels of certainty in different contexts.

One way of responsibly coming to grips with the suppressed voices of the past is by attending to the different degrees of certainty that are possible in history. The historian ought to make it clear, at any given moment within the text, what degree of certainty is to be attributed to the claims that he or she is making. Roughly, one must distinguish between what one can know to be true with something approaching certainty; what one can know to be very probably true; what one can know to be possibly true; and what one has to put beyond the bounds of historical knowledge altogether. Note that this is a set of *rough* distinctions: on a conceptual level it is not possible to divide sharply the different degrees of historical knowing or nonknowing, which occupy a continuum. Nonetheless, it is not only useful, but essential, to keep these different degrees of certainty in mind in the researching and writing, and also in the reading, of history.

Collingwood, and perhaps no one else, held that historical knowledge is certain knowledge. Admittedly, there are propositions about the past—e.g., World War I began in 1914—that few would want to question. But by far the greater part of historical knowledge occupies the overlapping territories of the probable and the possible (overlapping territories, because there is no systematic way of distinguishing what is probably true from what is possibly true). Much historical knowledge is empirical and *inductive*—in other words, it is a matter of collecting data and then of producing descriptive generalizations on the basis of these data. But I wish to suggest that many historical conclusions are only *possibly* true. The model of collecting data and then of inducing descriptive generalizations from those data is adequate only in partial degree to what historians actually do. Rather than seeing historical knowledge as empirical and inductive, one needs to see it as being, under many circumstances, empirical and *speculative* or *abductive*. On this model, the historian collects a body of data, which then suggests to him the *possibility*—the hypothesis—that X is true. Far more historical research than is usually recognized proceeds in an abductive manner.

Abductive reasoning most often comes into play when it is a matter of attempting to reason back from a fact that the historian knows to the antecedents of that fact. For example, a "result," C, is well known: World War I began in 1914. In search of an explanation for this result, the historian begins to postulate "rules," such as: If imperialistic rivalries between great powers, then major wars. Finally, the historian articulates a statement about the particular "case": [Perhaps] imperialistic rivalries caused World War I. Here, without further evidence being supplied (and it is quite possible that further evidence *cannot* be supplied), the claim generated by the historian is only *possibly* true—it is the statement of a "perhaps" rather than of a "probably." I have here chosen a case from political history, one that evokes the possibility that large sociopolitical forces are at work. But abductive reasoning equally well comes into play when one seeks to go from observable personal actions to hypothesized personal motivations. And it likewise comes into play when one attempts to grasp the significance, for us, now, of past historical events and situations.[42]

Finally, historians need to acknowledge that there exists a domain of things that they cannot know. Collingwood to the contrary, there is an unknowability in the past, a zone of incomprehensibility that some have called sublime.[43] We can conceive of this aspect of the past as a domain inhabited by that which is either too traumatic to be put into language;

too foreign to be understood in the present; or cannot be constructed or reconstructed because of a lack of evidence.

Prompted by Wyschogrod, let us consider again the historian's approach to the voiceless others of history. The first point that needs to be made is that one cannot ethically approach the voiceless others in the mode of certainty. To claim certainty is to lie—or, worse, to be blithely and dangerously self-deceived. Any historian who wants to claim that the knowledge of the past that he or she produces is certain knowledge will have to steer clear of the voiceless others. For of all historical questions, the question, "What does the voice of the voiceless other say?" least allows the historian to speak with an air of certainty. Nor can such difficult-to-grasp matters be adequately dealt with in the mode of probability. For it is a matter here of presumed historical facts that the historian cannot know. The historian cannot know the speaking of a past person or collectivity in situations where there remains no record of that speaking, indeed where we do not even know for sure that speaking took place at all. Consequently, when it is a matter of unheard voices in the past, the historian cannot follow the path of induction, collecting data and then articulating generalizations from those data, because the only immediately telling data are inaudible. Thus the historian cannot arrive at probable generalizations, let alone at certainty, concerning the voiceless others.

The unheard music of which we are speaking here can only be played by historians willing to operate in the abductive mode, the mode of speculation. And I believe that historians *should,* at times, operate in such a mode (as well as in the modes of induction and of definition or tautology). That is, I believe that historians ought to speak (speculatively) about matters of which they cannot have probable knowledge. To be sure, some would argue that agnosticism is the better course to take in historical thinking. As the American legal historian Annette Gordon-Reed noted in an online discussion of her book, *Thomas Jefferson and Sally Hemings: An American Controversy,* "agnosticism serves as a check on active error making." Thomas Jefferson himself declared, in his *Notes on the State of Virginia,* that "he is less remote from the truth who believes nothing, than he who believes what is wrong." If the historian follows Jefferson's dictum, it would follow that, lacking evidence that P, he or she ought to steer completely away from saying P. But notice what this does to the voiceless others: it leaves them hors de combat. Gordon-Reed, interested in Jefferson's relations with his slaves, is disinclined to follow the Master on this particular point. And I think that she is right. As she puts it, "the value (ethics) of agnosticism on a question depends heavily upon what is at stake." The defect of agnosticism is that, while lessening active error, it "can also promote passive (largely hidden) error."[44] In other words, it can promote error by leading us to not consider what might *possibly* have happened, on the grounds that the evidence is lacking to allow us to come to *probable* conclusions concerning the matter. Yet, as I have noted, much historical reasoning is in fact concerned with historical possibilities, not probabilities. To reject reasoning about possibilities is to reject much of what constitutes the discourse of history.

Abductive (hypothetical) reasoning is required in situations where the past is obscure. The explicit deployment of abductive reasoning allows the ventriloquizing of hypothetical departed voices, and the describing of possible but not definitively known past situations, while still making clear the hypothetical character of such voicings and descriptions. In the abductive mode—assuming that it is clearly identified *as* abductive—the demand for truth-telling and the demand that voiceless others be recognized are both satisfied. In short, a responsible epistemology of history (responsible to our contemporaries and to those who come after us) demands the recognition and explicit deployment of different degrees of probability or possibility in the historian's attempts to confront the past. To speak in a speculative mode is acceptable, as long as the speculation is identified as such and is both clearly marked off from, and clearly connected with, what is not a matter of speculation.[45]

From outside the discipline. But history is not the only discipline, and it is not even the only way of confronting the past. History's merit is in its prosaic pursuit of truth, but the prosaic pursuit of truth is not the only thing that makes up the world, and it is not even the only road of inquiry or meditation. Here I can only evoke, and not adequately canvass, those modes of inquiry that lie outside the discipline. In particular, the advantage of literature and of philosophical or theological speculation is that in these domains possibilities can be entertained and turned over in our minds in ways that stand much further away than even an abductively argued history does from the claim to be factually plausible. It is on such grounds that a book like Wyschogrod's *An Ethics of Remembering* finds its justification. It is likewise on such grounds that the much-disputed genre of historical fiction can also find justification—or such a work as Primo Levi's *The Periodic Table*, which, in its combination of memoir and Montaignean essay, is certainly not historical discourse but instead occupies a completely different register.

As a historian I am glad that history, with its project of historical construction or reconstruction, exists, for confrontation with something that one has to believe was and is *there*, solidly and unequivocally, is a rational limitation of desire—a limitation of desire that seems to be needed for living in the world without being devoured by it. Yet, while the ethics of literary fiction and of theological and philosophical speculation lie beyond the borders of the ethics of history-writing, I do want to emphasize that the contrast between history on the one hand and literature and speculation on the other does not amount to a contrast between the factual and the fictive. On the contrary, what is speculative and fictive also has its place inside historiography, just as literature contains true facts about the world. But there are limits as to precisely how much the fictive and the speculative can operate within history, for their indiscriminate pursuit could well lead to the impairment of historical epistemology, and hence to the impairment of history as an intellectual practice. From this point of view, literature and speculation can be seen, not as irresponsible rivals to history, but as indispensable stimuli to its more conscious and imaginative pursuit.

Notes

1. The Declaration's claim to universality was a bone of contention from the very beginning, even as it was being drafted in the late 1940s, but one could hardly have a declaration of human rights *without* the universalistic claim, and indeed many of its articles include the words *everyone, all,* and *no one.* Johannes Morsink, *The Universal Declaration of Human Rights: Origins, Drafting, and Intent* (Philadelphia: University of Pennsylvania Press, 1999), offers an exhaustive analysis of the Declaration. On the claim to universality, see especially ix–xiii; for the text of the Declaration, briefly annotated, see 329–36.

2. Hayden White, *Encounters: Philosophy of History after Postmodernism,* ed. Ewa Domańska (Charlottesville: University Press of Virginia, 1998), 16.

3. Hayden White, "Droysen's *Historik:* Historical Writing as a Bourgeois Science," in *The Content of the Form: Narrative Discourse and Historical Representation* (Baltimore: Johns Hopkins University Press, 1987), 83–103, at 89.

4. Edith Wyschogrod, *An Ethics of Remembering: History, Heterology, and the Nameless Others* (Chicago: University of Chicago Press, 1998). Further citations to this work appear parenthetically in the text.

5. The unresolvable doubleness of history-writing, variously named, has been a minor and usually unnoticed theme in the philosophy of history literature. See, e.g., Agnes Heller, *A Theory of History* (London: Routledge and Kegan Paul, 1982), 117, who refers to historiography's "double task" of understanding the past and of communicating universally; and Leonard Krieger, *Ideas and Events: Professing History* (Chicago: University of Chicago Press, 1992), who juxtaposes events particularized in the past, and ideas by which historians and others in the present give a measure of coherence to those events.

6. Edith Wyschogrod, *Spirit in Ashes: Hegel, Heidegger, and Man-Made Mass Death* (New Haven: Yale University Press, 1985).

7. Emmanuel Levinas, *Totality and Infinity,* trans. Alphonso Lingis (The Hague: Mouton, 1969), 291 and passim. I have been helped in attempting to

understand Levinas's work by a number of the essays in *Ethics as First Philosophy: The Significance of Emmanuel Levinas for Philosophy, Literature and Religion*, ed. Adriaan T. Peperzak (New York: Routledge, 1995).

8. For one argument against the notion of a practically usable history, see Michael Oakeshott, "Historical Experience," chapter 3 of *Experience and Its Modes* (Cambridge: Cambridge University Press, 1933), 86–168, especially 157–58.

9. R. G. Collingwood, *The Idea of History*, rev. ed., with *Lectures 1926–1928*, ed. J. Van der Dussen (Oxford: Oxford University Press, 1994 [original edition, 1946]), 252–53. See also Collingwood's interesting remarks on history, memory, and authority at 234–35, as well as at 366–67 in his "Lectures on the Philosophy of History" (1926), which are included, at 359–425, in this revised and expanded edition of *The Idea of History*.

10. Note that if Collingwood here intended to *require* the existence of material traces if what happened in the past is to be known, his view was too restrictive, for it is possible, *even in the absence of material traces of any kind*, to reconstruct the past with a fair degree of confidence, provided that a number of informants have independent, overlapping, and similar recollections of the same set, or type, of events. For example, even in the absence of any other evidence, weight has to be accorded to multiple, independent assertions that such and such a priest carried out acts of sexual abuse. In fairness, one must say that Collingwood dealt with memory issues only very marginally, an unsurprising fact in view of the marginality, even nonexistence, of such phenomena in history-writing in Collingwood's time.

11. For one account of the distinction between "sources" and "remains," see Johann Gustav Droysen, *Outline of the Principles of History*, trans. E. B. Andrews (Boston: Ginn, 1893), 18ff.

12. Compare Johannes Fabian, *Remembering the Present: Painting and Popular History in Zaire*, with narrative and paintings by T. K. Matulu (Berkeley and Los Angeles: University of California Press, 1996).

13. See Jörn Rüsen, *Grundzüge einer Historik*, 3 vols. (Göttingen: Vandenhoeck und Ruprecht, 1983–89), especially *Lebendige Geschichte: Grundzüge einer Historik III, Formen und Funktionen des historischen Wissens* (1989).

14. *Schindler's List*, directed by Steven Spielberg, produced by Steven Spielberg, Gerald R. Molen, and Branko Lustig, based on the novel by Thomas Keneally (Amblin Entertainment, 1993; MCA Universal Home Video, 1994).

15. Saul Friedlander, "Introduction," in *Probing the Limits of Representation: Nazism and the "Final Solution,"* ed. Saul Friedlander (Cambridge: Harvard University Press, 1992), 9.

16. This is the conclusion to which Agnes Heller comes, by a different route, in her chapter on "Moral Judgments in History," in *Theory of History;* see especially 123–25.

17. On these constructs, which correspond to four distinct but interrelated tasks of historiography, see, more fully, Allan Megill, "Recounting the Past: 'Description,' Explanation, and Narrative in Historiography," *American Historical Review* 94, no. 3 (1989): 627–53. This is, of course, not the only way of slicing the historiographical cake; but I believe it to be one of the most illuminating ways of doing so.

18. Heller, *Theory of History,* 123, 124.

19. Perez Zagorin, "Lord Acton's Ordeal: The Historian and Moral Judgment," *Virginia Quarterly Review* 74, no. 1 (1998): 1–17, at 4–5.

20. The attitudes and procedures of historical research are described in many handbooks; for one of the most literate, broadly gauged, and interesting, see Jacques Barzun and Henry F. Graff, *The Modern Researcher,* 4th ed. (San Diego: Harcourt, Brace, Jovanovich, 1985).

21. Alessandro Cavalli, "Gedächtnis und Identität: Wie das Gedächtnis nach katastrophalen Ereignissen rekonstruiert wird," in *Historische Sinnbildung: Problemstellungen, Zeitkonzepte, Wahrnehmungshorizonte, Darstellungsstrategien,* ed. Klaus E. Müller and Jörn Rüsen (Reinbek bei Hamburg: Rowohlt, 1997), 455–70, at 470.

22. Allan Megill, "'Grand Narrative' and the Discipline of History," in *A New Philosophy of History,* ed. Frank Ankersmit and Hans Kellner (Chicago: University of Chicago Press, 1995), 151–73, 263–71. For the notion of "grand narrative" generally, see Jean-François Lyotard, *The Postmodern Condition: A Report on Knowledge,* trans. Geoff Bennington and Brian Massumi, foreword by Fredric Jameson, Theory and History of Literature, vol. 10 (Minneapolis: University of Minnesota Press, 1984), xxiii.

23. See Michel de Certeau, "The Historiographical Operation," chapter 2 of *The Writing of History,* trans. T. Conley (New York: Columbia University Press, 1988), 56–113, especially 57, and 103n5.

24. I argue out this point in Megill, "History, Memory, Identity," *History of the Human Sciences* 11, no. 3 (1998): 37–62, at 51–53. On the constructivist and reconstructivist traditions, see Megill, "Philosophy of Historical Writing/Historiology," in *Encyclopedia of Historians and Historical Writing,* ed. Kelly Boyd, 2 vols. (London: Fitzroy Dearborn, 1999), 539–43. I do not mean to *reject* the view that the historiographical object is constructed in the course of historical investigation; on the contrary, constructivism identifies and usefully characterizes *one moment* in historical research and writing.

25. White, "Historical Writing as a Bourgeois Science," 89. Note how this passage evokes a series of unresolvable tensions in historiography—products, I would argue, of history's double orientation.

26. See White's subtle discussion of the question as to which literary forms are acceptable for representing the Holocaust in "Historical Emplotment and the Problem of Truth," in Friedlander, ed., *Probing the Limits of Representation,* 37–53, at 39–42.

27. Martin Heidegger, *Being and Time,* trans. Joan Stambaugh (Albany: State University of New York Press, 1996), §32, pp. 139–40.

28. See the deflating account of eyewitnessing in Allen Johnson, "The Basis of Historical Doubt," chapter 2 of *The Historian and Historical Evidence* (New York: Scribner's, 1926), 24–49.

29. De Certeau, *Writing of History,* 2. The breach was of course not always there, but was invented toward the beginning of the modern age, as part of the invention of the modern age itself. Because classical historiography (the paradigmatic instance is Thucydides) emphasized writing about things one had witnessed oneself, it was in some ways close to memory.

30. Ibid., viii.

31. Ibid., 2.

32. Ibid., 35.

33. I am not aware of any study that systematically compares legal and historical modes of evidence and argument. Consequently, the following account is somewhat speculative. See, however, two interesting background works by Barbara Shapiro: *"Beyond Reasonable Doubt" and "Probable Cause": Historical Perspectives on the Anglo-American Law of Evidence* (Berkeley and Los Angeles: University of California Press, 1991), and Shapiro, *A Culture of Fact: England, 1550–1720* (Ithaca: Cornell University Press, 2000).

34. G. W. F. Hegel, *Lectures on the Philosophy of World History: Introduction: Reason in History,* trans. H. B. Nisbet from the German edition of Johannes Hoffmeister, introduction by Duncan Forbes (Cambridge: Cambridge University Press, 1975), 12–14.

35. Wyschogrod here cites Hayden White, *Metahistory: The Historical Imagination in Nineteenth-Century Europe* (Baltimore: Johns Hopkins University Press, 1973), 27.

36. Leopold von Ranke, *Französische Geschichte,* vol. 2, in Ranke, *Sämmtliche Werke,* 54 vols. (Leipzig: Duncker und Humblot, 1867–90), 9:108–10, quoted in Peter Gay, *Style in History* (New York: Basic Books, 1974), 60.

37. Gay, *Style in History,* 61.

38. A question arises: would the ethical effect of the text be visible to a reader who did not already understand at some level the moral lesson that is being taught? That is, does the text teach something new, or does it merely reinforce what the reader "always already" knows? I suspect that for the most part it is the latter that is true—of history and literature, of sermons and life.

39. Note, however, that the test of maximal truth-telling does not mean that every history must attempt to be a "total history" of the time and place with which it is concerned; in fact, the notion of total history is a chimera. The point is rather that, within the frame of historical investigation that has been chosen, there should be no arbitrary omissions.

40. Collingwood, *Idea of History,* 262, 268.

41. I say this in spite of the fact that recent scholarship has established that the book, which was published posthumously, is textually rather questionable, having been cobbled together in a quite arbitrary way by its first editor, T. M. Knox, out of Collingwood's manuscripts. See Jan Van der Dussen, "Collingwood's 'Lost' Manuscript of *The Principles of History,"* *History and Theory* 36, no. 1 (1997): 32–62.

42. My account in this paragraph is suggested by C. S. Peirce. See Peirce, "Deduction, Induction, and Hypothesis" (1878), in his *Chance, Love and Logic: Philosophical Essays,* ed. Morris R. Cohen (New York: Harcourt, Brace, 1923), 131–49. In other, later writings, Peirce tended to favor the term "abduction" over "hypothesis" in this context; he also characterized abduction as a form of "presumption." See Peirce, *Collected Papers,* vol. 2: *Elements of Logic,* ed. Charles Hartshorne and Paul Weiss (Cambridge: Harvard University Press, 1932), 496–97. See also Peirce, *Collected Papers,* vol. 7: *Science and Philosophy,* ed. Arthur W. Burks (Cambridge: Harvard

University Press, 1958), especially chapter 3: "The Logic of Drawing History from Ancient Documents," §6: "Abduction, Induction, and Deduction," 121–25. To be sure, Peirce wanted to get beyond abduction; it was, for him, "merely preparatory" (§8: "Abduction," 136). But in historical understanding, abduction can never be entirely gotten beyond. This is because history depends not only on fixed ("objective") data points, but also, in its unavoidable interpretive aspect, on the stance of the observer, which is subject to change. On the essential role of the historian's point of view, see Arthur C. Danto, "Narrative Sentences," chapter 8 of *Narration and Knowledge* (including the integral text of *Analytical Philosophy of History*) (New York: Columbia University Press, 1985 [1965]), 143–81.

43. Observe the logical interdependence pertaining among (1) Collingwood's conviction that conclusions in history are certain, (2) his rejection of a domain of incomprehensibility in the historical past, and (3) his notion that the historical past is constructed by the historian. These three views are of a piece. Each reinforces the other. One could not say that historical conclusions have the quality of being certain while at the same time acknowledging a domain of incomprehensibility. Similarly, if one holds that the historical past is constructed by the mind of the historian, there can be no domain of incomprehensibility in the historical past. Finally, if history (like a geometrical figure) is constructed by the knower, then certainty becomes conceivable within it.

44. Response by Annette Gordon-Reed to an online review by Harry Hellenbrand of Gordon-Reed, *Thomas Jefferson and Sally Hemings: An American Controversy* (Charlottesville: University Press of Virginia, 1997), posted on H-SHEAR (http://www2.h-net.msu.edu/~shear/), the discussion list of the Society for the History of the Early American Republic, on February 11, 1998. For the Jefferson quotation, see Thomas Jefferson, *Notes on the State of Virginia*, ed. Merrill D. Peterson (New York: Literary Classics of the United States, 1984 [Library of America 17]), 156.

45. I note briefly two instances where the speculative mode has surfaced in a prominent way in disciplinary historiography—both instances where the "voiceless others" come into play. First, Natalie Zemon Davis's *The Return of Martin Guerre* (Cambridge: Harvard University Press, 1983) explicitly and consciously employs the speculative mode in her attempt to puzzle out the attitude and behavior of the peasant woman Bertrande de Rols. (Her doing so became a matter of debate in Robert Finlay, "The Refashioning of Martin Guerre," *American Historical Review* 93, no. 3 [1988]: 553–71, to which Davis responded in her "'On the Lame,'" *American Historical Review* 93, no. 3 [1988]: 572–603.) Second, there is the discussion concerning Jefferson's relations with African-Americans, and particularly with Sally Hemings, at Monticello, which was much stimulated by the publication in 1997 of Annette Gordon-Reed's *Thomas Jefferson and Sally Hemings* and became headline news in November 1998, when DNA evidence strongly suggested that Jefferson was the father of Sally Hemings's son Eston. This discussion has prompted a good deal of recourse to the speculative mode, as is evident in *Sally Hemings and Thomas Jefferson: History, Memory, and Civic Culture*, ed. Jan Ellen Lewis and Peter S. Onuf (Charlottesville: University Press of Virginia, 1999); see especially, among pieces in this collection, Rhys Isaac, "Monticello Stories Old and New," 114–26.

Prudence, History, Time, and Truth

Arthur C. Danto

In the very first paragraph of his history, Herodotus of Halicarnassus declares the twofold goal of his researches: "To preserve the memory of the past by putting on record the astonishing achievements both of our own and other peoples; and more particularly, to show how they came into conflict."[1] The analytical philosophy of history has mainly connected itself to Herodotus's second sort of goal, which concerns historical explanation, an inquiry prompted by the question of whether there is anything distinctive in the logic of historical explanation, or whether it exemplifies a general pattern to be found throughout the scientific representation of the world. A prior commitment to some principle of the unity of science explained the positivist analyses which very largely defined the field, and under which obstacles to that unity were bit by bit removed, demonstrating that history is a science in the same sense in which physics is, albeit in a concededly sketchier state. I have already insinuated an explanation in my account by citing a belief in the Unity of Science as explaining the kind of analysis presented half a century ago by the late C. G. Hempel—"an astonishing achievement," to invoke Herodotus's criterion in justification of my recording it.

Reference to beliefs as explanatory must have been believed inconsistent with Hempel's account, for otherwise it is difficult to explain the conflict engendered between Hempel's views and the views of those who felt that some kind of internal understanding of the minds of agents would always distinguish historical from general scientific explanations. But Hempel's own examples characteristically do refer to the mental states of historical agents, e.g., that Louis XV died unpopular because of his fiscal policies—for what is unpopularity save a negative attitude, and why are fiscal policies unpopular other than through the fact that we would prefer to use our money in ways other than paying taxes? It is doubtless true of Hempel, as a positivist, that he would have regarded such explanations as half-measures, in some way accounting for the sketchiness of historical explanations, and would have defended some eliminative program through which references to mental states could be dispensed with. But once it was conceded that a belief which explains an action is a reason, and that reasons are causes of actions, it was easy enough to treat rational explanations as conforming to Hempel's model. One had merely to count the reasons of historical agents among the initial conditions, and to bring explananda under laws (or lawlike descriptions) of a form grown familiar in the philosophy of mind: If an individual wants p and believes that q is a means to p, then he or she does q, all things being equal. As such analyses became commonplace in the philosophy of action, there seemed no further point in the philosophical conflicts over the problem of historical explanation, and so history receded as the kind of problem with which at least analytical philosophers felt there was something to worry about.

Once we begin explaining actions in terms of the beliefs and attitudes of agents, there is no obstacle to explaining them through their *moral* beliefs and attitudes. Even if one is a non-cognitivist in ethical theory, as so many at the time were, one should have no metaphysical qualms in allowing that moral beliefs and attitudes can be explanatory if beliefs and attitudes ever are. The belief that Louis XV's monetary policies were unfair, for example, is a moral belief because unfairness is a moral concept; and that makes resistance to them by not reporting income morally justified as well. Indeed, when we read such histories as those of Herodotus, we are instantly caught up in moral explanations and moral conflicts. The conflict between Greeks and Asiatics was a conflict, as Herodotus saw it, in moral attitudes, and especially over what he terms "woman stealing." According to the Asiatics,

> Abducting young women is not, indeed, a lawful act; but it is stupid, after the event, to make a fuss about it. The only sensible thing is to take no notice; for it is obvious that no young woman allows herself to be abducted if she does not wish to be. The Asiatics, according to the Persians, took the seizure of the women lightly enough, but not so the Greeks: the Greeks, merely on account of a girl from Sparta, raised a big army, invaded Asia, and destroyed the empire of Priam. From that root sprang their belief in the perpetual enmity of the Grecian world toward them.[2]

"Such then is the Persian story," Herodotus says, planting a doubt, but adding that he "has no intention of passing judgment on its truth or falsity." For Herodotus already recognizes that beliefs can be explanatory, even when they are false, and that it is an objective truth that Persians believed, whatever the belief's truth, that "it was the capture of Troy that first made them enemies of the Greeks." He meanwhile intends to "point out who it was in actual fact that first injured the Greeks," beginning his story with Croesus, who was "the first foreigner so far as we know to come into direct contact with the Greeks." But we may at this point take leave of Herodotus's explanatory project, for whatever explanation he comes up with, it will not differ in any *philosophically* scrutable way from the one subscribed to by the Persians. It might, to be sure, greatly reduce hostilities to demonstrate that their explanation was false. But it is difficult to suppose the explanation at which Herodotus finally arrives will not take into consideration the ways in which Greeks and Persians alike interpret events, and whether these interpretations have any basis in historical truth. So far as scientific representation is concerned, we cannot go greatly further in dealing with human history. If a tribe whose source of food diminishes interprets this to mean that their gods wish them to relocate, then nothing we might invoke in explanation of the diminution of food explains their action: their action is explained by the interpretation given by their wise men and prophets, which then accounts for the migration we hoped to understand. In a relatively recent and certainly momentous decision, it was the Soviet interpretation of the Star Wars initiative which disposed them to abandon a conflict they no longer believed they could win—even if their belief was false that there was in fact a Star Wars initiative in place. They felt they could not afford to go any further. And everyone can find similar examples wherever there are events noteworthy enough to make the pages of our daily newspapers. Herodotus was the father of history not so much because he was the first historian, but because the structures of explanation with which he dealt have defined the practice since him, and doubtless before him as well. Think of the *Iliad*.

Connecting morality to history through opening human actions up to explanation through reasons and then recognizing that reasons themselves are often moral—that agents do *this* because it is right, *that* because it is in their view just—seems to me too weak a basis to justify devoting a philosophical conference to the relationship between morality and history. Neither, it seems to me, is a philosophically interesting topos to be identified through recognizing that beliefs themselves have a history, and that a fortiori so do moral beliefs have a history. The Persian's belief that no woman is abducted against her will, so that forcible rape does not exist, remains a widely subscribed attitude even today, against which the belief that women are in fact victims of such acts and not lusting participants, has made very slow progress. The belief that rape is of moral consequence only because women are men's property still justifies, in many cultures, seeking revenge against the perpetrator while holding the woman disgraced. Only with a change in beliefs regarding female sexuality has the "stealing of women" come to be regarded contrary to the women's will and hence a felony, and these beliefs continue to be resisted in traditional societies. Replacing beliefs, especially moral beliefs, is rare in any event, and it is a tribute to feminism that it has been able in a relatively few short years to achieve transformations in attitude nearly parallel to those wrought by Christianity two millennia ago, when it had to sound nearly insane to urge people to turn the other cheek and not retaliate, and that the poorest of the poor had a better shot at salvation than the richest of the rich, so that there are some things money cannot buy. Examples of changes in moral belief can be registered in histories, and explained in ways that would have been immediately understandable by Herodotus, who after all knew whatever there was to know about being human (which is why it is appropriate to class his text as a classic in the *Humanities,* as much about us, today, as about the Greeks and the Trojans in the ancient world). So moral beliefs may have a historical explanation without it following that there is, since Herodotus, a history of that form of explanation. And in any case the history of changes in moral beliefs are, as in the case of female attitudes toward the female body, based in large measure on factual claims, the history of which is fairly straightforward. In brief, moral beliefs are merely a further topic for history and for historical explanation, without implying any more intimate a relationship with history itself than any other topic—the history of artistic beliefs, or of superstitions, or science. So where are we then to find a connection of the intimate sort one would suppose a conference on history and morality must seek?

One way, of course, would be to invert the relationship, making history a topic of morality, a pageant of progress toward some moral end state, which, for whatever reason, could not have been attained to other than through the actual agony of wars and genocides and dislocations. Usually the progress is considered the enactment of a divine plan, in the existence of which men stop believing when events occur which seem to have no such justification—the Lisbon Earthquake in the eighteenth century, or the Holocaust in our own. But thinkers who were not in any further sense committed to a belief in god retained the form of such a theory, moving them to justify terrible suffering in the name of history, and as necessary to the terminal utopia as the cracking of eggs to the making of omelettes, to use the cynical cliché. The belief in history having the shape it does was justified by the belief that the terminal state could come about in no way other than through this suffering, making the suffering morally justified because the end was. And in any case, the belief was that there is no room for human intervention in the dialectical evolution in which the screams of men and women were the chorus of moral progress: once it was begun, the sequence of stages was irresistible. The inversion means a shift from the question of explanations in history, such as those Herodotus provides in abundance, to the stammering question of explaining history as a whole, as a necessary evil because it is the only way to attain a certain state which makes it an instrumental good. Sir Herbert Butterfield begins his Rede Lecture of 1971 by quoting from the Fourth Book of Ezra, in which the author wonders why humanity had to be created in a series of successive generations, rather than all being made at once, "a thing which at the least would have shortened the long tale of human misery."[3] The famous answer is that men and women were in fact set in a paradise, which it is their (our) fault to have lost, and a history of sacrifice was needed in order that this responsibility should be dissolved and humanity redeemed. In any case, the inversion treats history as a moral problem, and the philosophy of history as a way of identifying its solution. This indeed gives us the intimate relationship between history and morality, in that there is now a moral reason for history as a whole. Since providential explanations have scant philosophical credibility, in light especially of the history of communism in our time, I cannot see this as a direction to pursue. So where shall we find something stronger than morality as a topic for history but weaker than history as a topic for morality on which to base a discussion of the two?

My proposal is to have a look at the first of Herodotus's reasons for publishing his great book: "to preserve the memory of the past by putting on record the astonishing achievements both of our own and other people." This has not in any respect had the philosophical appeal that the topic of historical explanation has had for philosophers, dominated as we are by the vision that science is the great source of human knowledge and that history is cognitively significant only if it can be assimilated somehow to science. Herodotus's first reason connects historical recording with "astonishing achievements," and I would like to begin a discussion on where this connection has itself a significance which gives a moral reason for writing history. Certainly there is a connection between morality and truth, in the sense in which it is a duty to tell the truth—one of the best examples of a duty which can be universalized under Kantian considerations, since a world in which people did not tell the truth would parallel the world in which people made promises with no intention of keeping them. It would be a world in which social bonds would wither, since we could not count on one another for information. But this is a world in which everyone always told lies, and hence an epistemologically disordered world in which at the very least people would quickly learn not to ask questions. Still, there is a difference between truth in the sense in which it contrasts with lying—between *Wahrheit und Lüge*, in Nietzsche's early distinction—and truth in the sense in which it contrasts with ignorance. After all, *istoria* means, etymologically speaking, knowledge which is the result of inquiry or learning, hence knowledge we would not possess without some special cognitive effort. But since the knowledge here is specified as knowledge of the past, the question is what basis in morality we can identify which makes this truth a duty? With Herodotus, finding out the truth of the "present conflict," of why it exists, might go some distance toward mitigating it. If the truth is worse than we imagined, the conflict might instead be exacerbated. But in any case the hostilities between Greeks and Asians has no particular meaning for us today—we can be as disinterested in the inquiry as we are alleged to be in responding to works of art. And so the question becomes what moral basis there is for learning the truth of something which has no bearing on our lives, and towards which disinterestedness is the only attitude practically available to us?

To be sure, we would have a hard time understanding a great deal of our literature without reference to just the issues pursued by Herodotus—without reference, say, to Achilles and Priam, "the girl from Sparta" and Agamemnon, Hecuba and Hector—let alone Croesus and Gyges and Cyrus. But how important is it that these should be historical truths? In the Confucian tradition, appeal is made, over and over, to the so-called Sage Kings, possessed with what we might call perfect moral pitch. So we can consult the annals to find out how the Sage Kings would respond to this or that contingency—and then seek to adapt the insights we gain to our own situations. Would it make any difference if it turned out that there were no Sage Kings? So that the Sage Kings might occupy the kind of fictive status occupied by the Ideal Observer in ethical theory, or the makers of original choices in Rawls's account of justice? A practice which used the Sage Kings as paradigms and authorities could continue to use them, since that practice had proven itself long since in making difficult political decisions: it might still be of great value to ask what someone with perfect moral insight might say, even if there were none. Euthyphro appealed to the stories of the gods to clarify moral questions, but would it have made any significant difference if the gods were mere postulates, adopted for the precise purposes of making moral decisions? Once the foundations of Troy were discovered, in the nineteenth century, it became clear that Homer was historical. But the stories of Troy had by that time so penetrated Western consciousness that it hardly mattered. So where is the imperative to find out the truth grounded? What makes the practice of history a moral practice as such, even if the truth would make no practical difference in the conduct of human life?

A possible direction for finding an answer might be to shift ground entirely from the present to the past itself: have we some kind of duty to the past itself to find out its truth? Not because it does us any good beyond the fact of doing that good as such, like keeping a promise when the person to whom it was made is dead and no one would know the difference if we broke it? Are we in some sense fulfilling a moral duty to those personages who did the astonishing things Herodotus speaks of by preserving the knowledge that they did them? Not because it is valuable to us to have this knowledge but in some sense valuable to them? Does history, on this view, exist for the sake of the past which somehow has a right correlative with our duty not to allow it to vanish from consciousness—a right not to be forgotten and a duty not to forget?

I do not know the answer to this question. But I would like to explore it in the remainder of this text.

At the beginning of his essay on *The Use and Abuse of History,* Nietzsche gives us an amusing portrait of animal consciousness: "They know not the meaning of yesterday or today; they graze and ruminate, move or rest, from morning to night, from day to day, taken up with their little loves and hates and the mercy of the moment, feeling neither melancholy nor satiety."[4] Humankind cannot, he goes on to say, regard animal being without a twinge of regret—"for even in the pride of [our] humanity [we] look enviously on the beast's happiness."[5] There are two correlative questions to which the difference between the beast and us gives rise—why can the beast not remember and why can we not forget? What we envy the beast for is that it "forgets at once and sees every moment really die, sink into night and mist, extinguished forever."[6] The beast, in brief, "lives *unhistorically.*" It follows from this that to be human is to live *historically*—that history is the mode of our being, a dimension of our ontology. The reason we cannot forget is intertwined with our essence. But so, if indeed we are historical beings, is the reason we want to be remembered. Kant undertook to ground his ethic in an anthropology, based on the dignity an autonomous being merits. Nietzsche, like Hegel, grounds it in the fact that we are, lamentably perhaps, historical beings whose happiness is in thrall to our memories. We see this everywhere confirmed. A sixteenth-century mosque in Ayodhya was destroyed in 1992 by a group of Hindu fanatics, believing that it had been built by Babur, the first Mughal emperor, on the site of a Hindu temple marking the birth site of the god-hero Rama, and which they vowed to restore. The Serbs justified the barbarity of their behavior on memories of the medieval Battle of Kosovo. Even if these memories were false, the mere fact that they are believed and appealed to implies an essential historicality, a way of existence we cannot help, however little good it does us to be built that way. "One who cannot leave himself behind on the threshold of the moment and forget the past, who cannot stand on a single point like a goddess of victory, without fear or giddiness, will never know what happiness is."[7] The real problem for humanity, as Nietzsche states it, is learning how to forget. "There is a degree of . . . 'historical sense,' that injures and finally destroys the living thing, be it a man or a people or a system of culture."[8] As George Eliot observed, the happiest women, like the happiest nations, have no history.

It is clear that Nietzsche admired human beings in whom animality was dominant—who have enough of the concept of making promises that they give their word, but manage to forget that they have done it, as if the past which precisely sinks into "the night and mist" gives way to a present on which it leaves not the slightest mark. He sees in humans of whom this is true a certain health and a certain danger. There is a frightening discussion in the second essay of *The Genealogy of Morals* in which he uses the history of torture in dramatizing the problem of creating what he terms a "moral memory" in human beasts. "Ah reason, seriousness, mastery over the affects, the whole thing called reflection, all those prerogatives and showpieces of man: how dearly they have been bought! how much blood and cruelty lie at the bottom of all 'good things.'"[9] Nietzsche speaks of the "forcible sundering from [our] animal past, as if it were a leap and plunge into new surroundings and conditions of existence, a declaration of war against the old instincts upon which [our] strength, joy, and terribleness had rested hitherto."[10] On the other hand, the existence of an "animal soul turned against itself was something so new, profound, unheard of, enigmatic, contradictory, and *pregnant with a future* that the aspect of the earth was essentially altered."[11] This condition Nietzsche famously called *schlechtes Gewissen*—Bad Conscience—to which we owe our humanity. To which, if he is right, we owe our historiality, which means that morality and historical consciousness arise together, at least so far as our paradigm of morality is, as witness Kant, the keeping of promises. So entertaining this as a hypothesis, under what obligation does the past put us to inquire into its truth? Is there something analogous in society to the melding together of past and future in the individual under which history is like memory? Do we have the kind of commitment to the past which the individual has to his uttered oaths, no longer forgotten the moment they are made? So that history is the morality of society? And not forgetting is pivotal to our moral well-being?

These are questions which take us very far indeed from the analytical philosophy of history, as I, at least, understood and sought to contribute to it; and I have nothing much by way of precedent to guide me to an answer. It would be wonderful if we could connect the past and present in such a way that only by honoring the past through knowing could we acquire knowledge of what we are now—so that in enjoining us not to forget it, the past promises that compliance will bring self-knowledge, a knowledge of who we are, construed as being historical. But this kind of knowledge constitutes what Nietzsche called monumental history, which is what Herodotus provides. "What is the use to the modern man of this monumental contemplation of the past, this preoccupation with the rare and the classic? It is the knowledge that the great thing existed and was therefore possible, and so may be possible again."[12] I think this violates the general intuition of historical possibility and impossibility. The art historian Heinrich Wölfflin says, profoundly, that not everything is possible at every time. We cannot today paint Virgins and Holy Infants the way Botticelli did, not because the knowledge of how to do so has been lost but because there is no room in the objective structure of the art world for paintings in the spirit of the Tuscan master. In a way, the monuments demonstrate the structure of history through their unreproducibility. "Putting on record," "preserving the names [and the] astonishing achievements" of the past is worth doing because it shows what is no longer possible and hence what is possible. The looming presence of the past in the present teaches lessons in what we cannot do because of the way history is shaped. We can only admire or deplore them. Herodotus provides a museum of great actors and great deeds. But the museum is not filled with truths we can use in life. There will not—this is Nietzsche's example—be another Renaissance just because there has been a Renaissance.

On the other hand, preservation keeps the monuments present to our consciousness, and indeed, in a good many cases, our moral consciousness. And in some way it would have been of great importance to know that they would be known even in the far distant future. Even Nietzsche's human beasts would not have been indifferent to glory, and hence coloring the consciousness of others with an aura of awe and admiration. Had they the vocabulary of Sartre, it would be in their dimension of *pour autrui* that they did what made them famous. That their *pour autrui* should exist in the consciousness of the future, well past the time in which it could have done them, in their other dimensions of being, any practical good would be a motive for doing what they did. Riches, power, beauty, are true gifts, but fame, especially fame which perdures after death, is a vastly less tangible good, and a good, moreover, made possible only because we live in history. We want our stories not simply told, but sung and painted and taught. And, because we participate in that same mode of being, with the *pour autrui* of past figures and events in our own consciousness, we comply. But when we comply as historians, it is critically, and against the truth as we can know it. Do the figures in the past deserve our admiration? Were they good or bad or indifferent? Truth is in the service of morality when these issues are raised.

There is a drawing by Tiepolo, executed in the 1750s, titled *Prudence and History*. Prudence—one of the cardinal virtues—can be identified through her attributes—a mirror and a serpent. History is a winged creature with an open book. There is an unidentified third allegorical figure in the drawing, but as the connection that concerns me is between Prudence and History, we can erase the third figure, who does not turn up in the fresco for which this is a preparatory study. Prudence, as a virtue, is defined in my dictionary as "the capacity for judging in advance the probable results of one's actions." The mirror, of course, is a natural symbol for self-consciousness, of seeing oneself as others do, and modifying one's actions on the basis of their likely effects. "How will it look?" is the question the mirror of prudence is able to answer, and while there is a certain philosophical reluctance, deriving from Plato, to give appearance much weight, how we appear has a great deal to do with our effectiveness in practical life. Plato imagines a perfectly just man who appears perfectly unjust, and his opposite, who appears perfectly just though in fact a swine, and asks why it is better to be than to appear just. I suppose Dorian Gray would be the most familiar example of the apparently virtuous conjoined with an evil reality, but in the unfolding of time, Dorian's appearances coincide with his moral being, and he stands forth as a monster revealed. Wilde's story means to argue that one cannot hide one's true character forever—that moral truth will sooner or later out. That I think is why we have History recording Prudence's actions. Prudence acts in such a way that her mirror image is congruent with her historical representation. How she is to appear controls how she acts. And what gives depth to the connection is that the historical representation will outlive the mirror-image, and how she appears to futurity has to be distinguished from how she appears to those who can do her some practical good, based upon how she appears to her contemporaries. And one question is why Prudence should be that concerned with futurity, since she will not be there to benefit? Why should she *care*?

That human beings do care is certified by the conduct of the worst offenders against history, those who try to assure their future historical representations through controlling their appearances so as to present a fair moral face. The various Ministries of Truth that define so much of twentieth-century political reality, with their apparatus of doctored photographs, deletions from the record, the insertion of fraudulent claims as if historical truths, would hardly have come about if those who ordered them did not care about history. Indeed, they pay it the highest tribute by seeking to preempt how they are to be regarded from the vantage point of the future—determined that no one will know the truth. As the opened archives of the KGB and the Stasi have demonstrated, it takes a lot more than dirty tricks to suppress the truth, and while I have no argument to show that the truth must inevitably prevail, we now see through so many of the appearances they sought to erect that we can at least see the practical difficulty of Plato's paradigm swine with the angelic features, and appreciate, in consequence, how intricately appearances are woven together. The doctored photographs are incredibly crude, and though we now have digitization as a way of smooth alteration, I am reasonably certain there will be features the method will inevitably overlook, say in the placement and tonality of shadows. Experimental pigeons discriminate between two slides taken seconds apart of the same motif, which human vision regards as identical. The experimenter discovered, but only after the most careful and protracted examination, the minute differences in the shadows which to the pigeons were stridently evident. Goodman has famously argued that however alike a forgery is to an authentic work, sooner or later protracted scrutiny will disclose differences sufficiently marked that we will wonder how we could ever imagine they were indiscernible. In this he articulates the very principle of connoisseurship, as practiced by Morelli, who was able to establish authenticity not in terms of manifest features, but through details—the way an artist did earlobes or fingernails. The slogan of the Warburg Institute was *Le bon dieu est dans les details*. So Prudence would be prudent not to feign attributes she counts on history to bestow: if she is interesting enough to history to consider at all, the truth will be revealed in time. Prudence is not an especially attractive virtue—it is too calculating. No one wants to be remembered for their prudence. Still, as we can see from the terrible archives of past horrors, even moral monsters were prudent in the sense of putting what we today call spin on their actions, concealing from the eyes of present and future the true nature of their enterprise, and replacing it with a false image. They do not want to be morally condemned.

I would like to conclude with the help of another work of art. This is Peter Paul Rubens's *Time Uplifting Truth,* which is the final panel in his tremendous cycle of paintings glorifying Marie de Medici for the Palais de Luxembourg in Paris, now installed in the Louvre. Truth is a woman—*Vorausgesetzt daß die Wahrheit ein Weib ist?* Nietzsche asked—and she is naked as only a woman by Rubens can be. Time is an elderly powerful male figure, who lifts Truth out of the shadows of ignorance toward the light in which Marie de Medici and her son, King Louis XIII, are shown joined in what their contemporaries would have read as a gesture of concord. It is a little sad to reflect that this pictorial tribute to truth is false. There was no such concord. Marie de Medici was a scheming difficult lady, and her son loathed her and ordered the murder of her councilors. And he put her under a state of house arrest. In this respect the final panel belongs to the tone of the great cycle, in which Marie de Medici commissioned the services of the greatest living artist to fix her *pour autrui* forever. It belongs with the great image of the magnificent woman disembarking in France, stepping out of an ornamental boat, accompanied by Neptune and his watery consorts. It is a kind of pictorial overkill. We are immeasurably grateful to possess this magnificent exercise in spin management. But somehow the truth really has been uplifted in the face of all this baroque misrepresentation, and despite it. The cycle belongs to the project of concealment and distortion which defined Marie de Medici's practice in the conduct of her political aims. It defines her as a person. And when we see this, we realize, once more, that truth will be uplifted in time. I have tried to suggest, in passing, a philosophical argument for this faith.

Rubens's painting made a certain impression on me when I saw it in Paris, in the early 1960s, when I was writing the *Analytical Philosophy of History.* Because that book was about time—or at least about tensed statements—and truth, I thought it would be amusing to use it as my frontispiece. It would have served as a kind of cartoon of the connections I was concerned to explain. At that time, like most of us brought up in the ascendancy of logical positivism, I had no serious philosophical interest in moral discourse, thinking it lay outside the domain of science, which one naturally took for the domain of philosophy in those years. But now I see Rubens's painting differently, and in connection specifically with Herodotus two intentions. History and morality, mediated by the ontological reality of other consciousnesses, form, it now seems to me, a metaphysical knot. We live historically as moral beings and moral judges. Just because something is past does not remove it from moral scrutiny. I would not at this point use the painting as a frontispiece in the spirit of frolic. There is an historico-moral judgment, if you care for an example.

Notes

1. Herodotus, *The Histories,* trans. Aubrey de Selencourt (Hammondsworth, Eng.: Penguin Books, 1973), 41.

2. Herodotus, *Histories,* 42.

3. Sir Herbert Butterfield, "The Discontinuities between the Generations in History: Their Effect on the Transmission of Political Experience," Rede Lecture (Cambridge: Cambridge University Press, 1971), 1.

4. Friedrich Nietzsche, *The Use and Abuse of History,* trans. Adrian Collins (Indianapolis: Bobbs-Merrill, 1957), 5.

5. Nietzsche, *Use and Abuse,* 5.

6. Ibid.

7. Ibid., 6.

8. Ibid., 7.

9. Friedrich Nietzsche, *On the Genealogy of Morals,* trans. Walter Kaufmann (New York: Random House, 1969), 62.

10. Nietzsche, *Genealogy,* 85.

11. Ibid.

12. Nietzsche, *Use and Abuse,* 14.

Part 2

Postmodernist Challenges

No Tear Shall Be Lost: The History of Prayers and Tears

John D. Caputo

It is not enough that tears be wiped away or death avenged; no tear
is to be lost, no death to be without a resurrection.

—Emmanuel Levinas

History is written with prayers and tears. History, a certain history,
critical and driven by ethical desire, is written in the memory of
prayers and tears now long gone and extinguished, even as it itself
constitutes a prayer, a certain praying and weeping, for a time to come, a
time of salvation and rebirth. History, a certain history, the history of a
historian who would, as Walter Benjamin says, "brush history against the
grain," recalls and meditates upon tears long since shed and prayers
long since sighed in vain, in an act of remembering that is to be compared to the way the saints remember the dead in their prayers; in such
a history no tear is to be lost, no death without resurrection. History is
no less a prayer for the future, heaving and sighing its *viens, oui, oui,* its
deep *amen* to the coming of the Messiah, heaving and sighing, yes, yes,
for a messianic time, for a time in which it will have been the case that
no tear is lost, no death without resurrection.

1. Irrecuperable Loss

I begin with what I will call irrecuperable loss, irredeemable suffering,
suffering lodged irremissibly in the past and beyond repair. The irremissible past is a time of ruin, *mal-heure,* ruined time, a time that seared and
scorched the souls of the dead, and then slipped away, forever, without

repeal or compensation, without redemption or any possible remuneration. The time of irrecuperable loss is essentially an-economic; it cannot in principle be worked into an economy, cannot in principle be entered into a balance of payments. The sufferings of the irrecuperable past were not undertaken voluntarily, in exchange for the reward that follows, like a long period of punishing, grueling physical training in preparation for an athletic event, or of study for an examination. It is not the pain of sacrifice, willingly undertaken in exchange for a higher good. It is not even the suffering, involuntarily suffered, that finally issues in an unforeseen and unintended reward. Of this ruined and irrecuperable time we will never be able to say "it was all worth it." This is not the pain that crowns and accompanies gain, but the misery of ruined time, of pure loss, of disaster. A child born with AIDS, whose life is short and painful, which no one can justify or compensate, which one can only try to comfort or ameliorate. Or the years of confinement, abuse and humiliation suffered by a man or woman unjustly imprisoned, which cannot be returned or restored, for which there cannot be any compensation, whatever monetary considerations the state may later offer. The strongest argument against capital punishment is the irrecuperability when the accused is innocent. The lost time, the ruined life, is gone forever, without return. Misery and grief have imposed themselves upon us with impunity, escaped like thieves in the night. The damage having been done, the forces of destruction make their escape, and we are left without recourse, defenseless against the destruction, abandoned to the wanton violence.

There is no good face to put on the face of irrecuperable loss, no theodicy to explain it which is not an obscenity. As Lyotard has said, the Holocaust is not a "sacrifice" of the Jews . . . and the very attempt to offer some sort of rationale or explanation for the Holocaust is an obscenity which defiles its very name.

Irredeemable loss escapes the order of economy in a way that is precisely contrary to the gift: unlike the gift, it is not an expenditure without return, not the unlimited giving, the unconditional affirmation of the other, but a destruction without return, sheer destruction, without compensation, repair, redress.

History, I want to say, a certain history, is the record, the archive and the treasury, of irreparable loss. History is haunted by the voices of the dead, whose unrequited misery and persecution cry out for justice. But history and justice come too late for the dead. Justice, however swift, is not swift enough to return to the moment of their misery and redress it. History, however sweeping and complete, cannot erase the misery of their lives. In the Middle Ages, certain Scholastic masters wanted to know whether God could change past time, could extend his almighty reach back into the past and make it to be that the sinner did not sin, which would constitute the most marvelous and perfect forgiveness. History would be like that, would be like God, although it cannot. All that history has is fragile memory, which is a poor substitute for justice, but the only one available.

How are we to console the dead who are long since dead? How are we to repair their irreparable loss? That is the hopeless and impossible demand—the demand that, as Levinas says in our epigraph, "no tear is to be lost, no death to be without a resurrection"[1]—that is placed upon history. And in keeping with the dynamics of what Derrida calls the aporia—that it is only when we see that things are impossible, when we find ourselves up against *the* impossible, that we are truly on the move—we will maintain that historical writing begins in earnest, the tensions of historical writing are fully engaged, only when it experiences this impossible exigency.

2. Levinas

To pursue this impossible question, of how to repair an irreparable loss, which is the hopeless task it imposes upon historiography, it will be necessary to reconstitute the context of this beautiful citation from Levinas. So I ask for your patience and indulgence with a bit of exegesis of Levinas, on the basis of which I shall return, in the conclusion, to consider the question of history more directly. The text is taken from the very difficult and enigmatic analyses of *De l'existence à l'existant,* a book written in part during the Holocaust, during his imprisonment in a labor camp, which must be read in connection with *Le temps et l'autre,* also published in 1947. *Existence and Existents* bears the marks of the Holocaust, although it does not want to invoke the Holocaust for validation, and this above all in its discourse on suffering and the instant. One cannot avoid the impression that Levinas's reflections on the instant, on the "irremissibility" of the subject's "captivity" by the instant, written as they are "shortly after the liberation (*au lendemain de la Libération*),"[2] are very closely linked to his experience of the instants of captivity, the steady drip of inescapable presence that marked his time in the camp. At the end of *Existence and Existents,* an unusual and compelling book, Levinas makes a series of remarkable observations about the irredeemability of *douleur,* of pain, grief, and suffering, and about the absolute impossibility of including pain in "economic time" or the "time of compensation." We cannot exchange suffering for something which pays it off, which means that suffering is priceless, that you can not put a price on it which would take its measure and enter it into a marketable exchange. Not priceless as *beyond* exchange, more precious than anything for which it could be exchanged, like the gift, but *beneath* exchange, so that one would never be able to rise to the level of exchange, and there is a certain indecency, even obscenity, in proposing something that one could exchange for it. The moment passed in suffering is an irreparable loss.

How then are we to repair this irreparable loss? How can there be any "salvation"? What hope is there if all is hopeless? For that impossible hope, Levinas says, for that hope against hope, we require the coming of the Messiah. But we are moving too quickly.

We first need to follow what Levinas says about the constriction, the contract and contraction, the confinement of the self to the present, the now or the instant, something which, as he will say, reaches its "purity" in the case of suffering.

The process in which the existent, the concrete subject of existence, rises up from the anonymity of *il y a*, from the indeterminate sea of being (*il y a de l'être*), is conceived by Levinas as a process of seizing upon existence, of taking hold of and mastering unmasterable being, while in the very same process finding oneself fixed in being or existence in such a way that the existent itself cannot extricate itself from existence. The triumph of the existent, the mastery exercised by the I or hypostasis over the indeterminate primal mix of existence, turns into an equiprimordial defeat. The victor, the existent, is taken captive by the vanquished in a kind of odd play of the master/slave dialectic. The triumphant existent is brought to bend all its efforts to escape being held captive by that in which it has first established itself by its virile efforts, seeking to find a way out of the contract into which it has entered with existence. The existent contracts existence to itself, constricts and confines existence to its individual subjectivity, in which is concentrated all the stability and substantivity of its individual subsistence. But in the process the subject is subjected to what it has subjected. In the process of entering into this contract, the existent subject finds that it has "contracted" existence like a disease that it cannot cure, at least not by its solitary efforts. The individuality of the existent, its subsistent subjectivity, its identity and privatization, its contraction to itself amidst the disseminating, dissipating sprawl of *il y a*, its "definition" amidst the infinite play of forces called *il y a,* constitutes the very victory and virility of subjectivity. But the solitude and isolation of the existence thus achieved or "accomplished" becomes a kind of original sin that comes along with the birth of the existent, a sin originating in its very origin or beginning.

Existence and Existents describes the "birth" of the existent, its beginning (*commencement*), in a kind of phenomenology of creation, not *ex parte creatoris* but *ex parte creaturae,* not from God's point of view but from ours, from the point of view of the "time of a creature."[3] It describes what Levinas calls the *accomplissement* of the existent, the process by which the existent achieves and effects existence, by which it carries out the act of existing, brings it to a successful completion or outcome. But this outcome leaves no way out, no exit or issue (*sans issue*), no way for the existent to be carried away from the achievement in which it is completely steeped. Because the existent is steeped in existence, filled to completion—*accomplissement*—by existence, the existent is imprisoned in its own wealth, held captive within its own walls, walled in by the existence thus achieved. While it achieves definition, it is simultaneously confined within the definition it has carved out for itself amidst the anonymous rumbling, weighed down by the existence with which it is replete. The birth of the existent is accompanied by a birth defect, a congenital illness—Levinas curiously speaks of being or presence as "evil" in these pages, where it is not matter that is evil, as in Gnosticism or Manicheanism, but presence—of which it cannot cure itself. The virile victory of the existent is its very undoing, springing the trap of solitude and solitary existence that encloses the subject without escape (unless it encounters something otherwise than virile). The way that leads from existence to the existent leaves no way out. The horror of the *il y a* is its faceless infinity, the bad infinity of its indeterminate no-thingness, which is neither this nor that nor nothing at all. But the resolution of this horror, which is the upsurge (*surgissement*) of the finite subject, in turn provokes, not horror at the *il y a*, but a kind of claustrophobia before existing, not the madness of the abyss, but a kind of boredom with the sameness of the same, not a terrifying insomnia but the confinement and constriction which imprisons me in the solitude of the I and me and mine. To be something existent, to be a subject, is to be fashioned from the abyss of *il y a* but then, starting out from there, to be held captive there (*y*), in being, where it has (*il a*) us, from which we need salvation (*salut*).

To exist is to exist in the now, in the present, in the instant. Solitude is the prison of the present where the now is all in all. What interests me in this remarkable essay is the temporal coefficient of this process, the provocative way that this strange quasi-phenomenology of being created and of beginning is cast by the young Levinas in terms of time. This *commencement,* this *accomplissement,* is a work of time, a temporal genesis, a work not of being beyond time and becoming (Platonism), nor of time as the horizon of being (Heidegger), but of a time *beyond* being. But that also means a time beyond the present. The beginning transpires in the time of the instant, of the instant whose temporality is so impoverished as not yet to merit the name of time. The present is time only in the sense that is *not yet* time, in the sense that it awakens the need, the desire, for time, that is, for the time of the other, which is time indeed. The prison of solitude is the prison of the present, of what he calls somewhere the monotony and the tick-tock of solitary instants. In the solitary confinement of the solitary instant, the monotony is, we might say, a "mono-chrony," a solitary time, a solitude of the "instant."

The existent exists in the *instant*, comes to stand in existence, stabilizing the flow of *il y a*. As *instans*, the existent takes a stand, acquires the standing or status of an existent, a hypostasis, in the instant of existence. The existent is insistent, *in-sistere, in-stans*, and its existence is carried out in the instant in which it seizes upon existence and, in seizing, is itself seized. To be, to be an existent, to exist as an individual existent, is to be in the present, but to achieve the definition that the existent accomplishes in the anonymous *milieu* of the indeterminacy of existence is likewise to be defined and confined by the present.

The existent is weighed down, fatigued, by the exertion the act of existing requires, and indolent, too weary to lift a finger to do anything more. Fatigued by the exercise, it abstains or holds back from the future itself. Its tragedy is to lack a future, to be too weary for the future. "The beginning (*commencement*) does not solicit it as an occasion of rebirth, like a fresh and joyful instant, like a new moment. . . . It perhaps indicates that the future, a virginal instant, is impossible in a solitary subject."[4] The existent is weighed down by its existence, trapped in and condemned to the presence of the instant, with no way out (*sans issue*), no way forward, to a new instant that would be something more than a repetition of the same—not by itself, at any rate. It cannot find the way to joy and rebirth, cannot save itself (only a God can save it). Unlike the magician—or the creator God of Genesis—who can achieve everything with an effortless word, without meeting resistance, without being drawn into the instant of creation, the creature is condemned to labor by the sweat of its brow, and all the effort of existing is drawn through the drain and duress of the instant's duration. The existent endures (*duratus*, "hard") the duration (*duritio*, "lasting") of the instant, with blood and sweat and tears, and unlike the magician is deeply "engaged in the instant" in which its work is carried out.[5] It does not move lightly like a melody, in which instant melts indiscernibly into instant, but, like a child (a beginner) laboriously picking out notes on a piano, its fatiguing movement is made up of stops (*arrêts*) lurching discontinuously from instant to instant, punctuating the "anonymous flow of existence,"[6] tearing or ripping out little commencements or beginnings from the flow without beginning. [7]

Levinas embraces the very instant that is denounced by Bergson, the fractured, fragmented, and discontinuous moment that lacks flow and the ability to join up with the next instant. Each instant starts out from (*à partir de soi,* "all over again"), begins anew, begins a new instant. Each instant is in relation, not with an adjoining instant with which it would seal a pact of harmony, but with existence over which it represents a momentary triumph in constant need of renewal, as in the Cartesian and Malebranchian conceptions of time.[8] The cup of existence is drained in each instant, nothing is left for tomorrow[9] or borrowed from yesterday. Each instant is a stop (*arret*). But not in such a way as to threaten annihilation, but with an "irremissible," inescapable bonding to being or existence, so that one cannot escape the steady but staccato beat of existence in which the existent is established. The present is the first appearance of a subject which has taken on existence and wrestled with its nocturnal, anonymous *bruissement,* with the muffled and indiscernible sounds of some strange nocturnal visitor, some force more strange than the mysterious angel with which Jacob wrestled through the night (which some say was Him).

Nothing better illustrates the oppressive presence of the present, let us say the pain of the present, than the presence of pain. We are condemned to the pain of the present, to the effort of labor, caught up in an "event of irremissible engagement, without the possibility of being redeemed" (*sans pouvoir de rachat*) from it[10] in a "state of purity" in pain:

> In pain (*peine*), sorrow (*douleur*), and suffering (*souffrance*), we once again find, in a state of purity, the definitiveness (*définitif*) that constitutes the tragedy of solitude.[11]

Pain, not moral pain, or—as in Heidegger's tasteless reading of Trakl— pain transmuted into a figure for the ontological difference, but real, physical pain, what philosophers "lightly" (*à la légère*) call physical pain, represents "in a state of purity" the bond of the subject to itself, the tragedy of solitude, and this because:

> [P]hysical suffering in all its degrees entails the impossibility of detaching oneself from the instant of existence. It is the very irremissibility of being. The content of suffering merges with the impossibility of detaching onself from suffering. . . . In suffering there is an absence of all refuge. It is the fact of being directly exposed to being. It is made of the impossibility of fleeing or retreating. . . . In this sense suffering is the impossibility of nothingness.[12]

In physical suffering, I live through phenomenologically—on the level of "experiences" that can be described—the ontological structure of being riveted to being—which Levinas calls an "event" (*événement*), which transpires below the level of conscious experience, of being locked into the presence of the present, of being imprisoned inescapably in the instant. What is painful about pain is not only the pain, not only the "content" of pain, as Levinas says, but its temporal coefficient, its irremissibility, its inescapability, the absence of refuge. The painfulness of pain lies in a sense of unremitting assault, of being pinned to existence, "backed against being"[13] of existence. It is one thing to be beaten, but quite another to be held down while one is beaten, to be rendered defenseless against the assault, "exposed" to the beating without protection, reduced to the vulnerability of utter passivity before the pain, utterly disabled and unprotected. It is one thing to stand tall and take a beating, like a virile Heideggerian, but quite another to be beaten senseless, reduced to "crying and sobbing" (*le pleur et le sanglot*), turned inside out from a subject to subjection, my activity thrown in reverse into passivity, which is what happens when suffering "attains its purity":

> Where suffering attains its purity, where there is no longer anything between us and it, the supreme responsibility of this extreme assumption turns into supreme irresponsibility, into infancy. Sobbing is this, and precisely through this it announces death. To die is to return to this state of irresponsibility, to be the infantile shaking of sobbing.[14]

(Levinas's phenomenological analysis of suffering is strikingly confirmed for us in Elaine's Scarry's well-known book *The Body in Pain* . . .)

The disabling effect or essence of suffering portends or "announces death,"[15] not just in the sense that suffering can lead to death, but in the sense that death is the figure of something "even more rending (*déchirant*) than suffering,"[16] something still more disabling than suffering. This still more disturbing thing about death is not nothingness, about which we know nothing and which in any case would seem to promise a release, but, in virtue of the impossibility of nothingness, of our being riveted to being and presence, it is the experience of a still deeper vulnerability, of an exposure to something that absolutely eludes our grasp, something that for the first time broaches alterity, for it does not come from me, is none of my doing.[17] The more disturbing thing about death is the exposure to a "mystery" absolutely unknown in fact and unknowable in principle, which even more profoundly divests the ego of itself—it does not come from me—and dis-ables the subject—it is nothing I am doing—reducing its activity to passivity. Against the supremely enabling experience of *Sein-zum-Tod* in *Being and Time,* in which authentic *Dasein* gains possession of itself, of its "solitude"—by assuming possession of its own (*eigen*) uttermost possibility of being (*Seinkönnen*), being before death in Levinas means exposure to the first breach of solitude, to an abyss of disablement where the subject loses control utterly, "seems to reach the limit of the possible . . . finds itself enchained, overwhelmed, and in some way passive," which "renders every assumption of possibility impossible,"[18] making every possible impossible. Contrary to Heidegger, mortality does not strip us down to our naked *solus ipse,* but is the first encounter we have with something *not* coming from ourselves. Far from giving us ownership of our *können* or *pouvoir,* it leaves us alienated and divided from our power, utterly disabled. The subject, he says, is no longer able to be able (*nous ne pouvons plus pouvoir*), it is able only to undergo.

The subject is imprisoned in the solitude of the present, and the approach of death is the first breach of that solitude and hence the first break with the present, the first approach of a future that does not come from me. But the futurity of death is a hollow or false futurity which does not belong to true time. The futurity of death is never to be present, which means never to be a possibility of mine in the present on which I can act; it always eludes my grasp because it is never present, and when it is present, I am no longer on the scene and able to engage it. It is one thing to have a fair fight, face-to-face, out in the light of presence, and then to fall before the other's sword in a good, manly battle; that at least would have a ring of Heideggerian virility about it. "At least we'll die with harness on our back," Macbeth says.[19] But it is quite another to do battle with a faceless force, a mysterious alien power, with an unknown and unknowable mystery that is never present to engage me in battle, with some invisible specter that undoes my ability to do battle without ever giving me a target at which I could take aim, that only shows up when I am no longer able to be able. How is Macbeth to "take on" (assume) one not born of woman, the portent of which cowed Macbeth's better part and put an end to his virility? Death is never present yet always coming and there is no hope of stopping it, no way to "take it on." How would it be possible to "take on" or "assume" what is never present and structurally withdrawn? It is hopeless and I am defenseless against such impossible odds. But I am not dead yet, for my very being is to be bonded to being and presence, so while the ego is present and death is not, while I breathe, *spiro,* there is hope, *spero,* hope in a hopeless situation, hope against hope. So rather than a projective *Vorlaufen* upon death I do not go gladly into that dark night, instead I fight, fight against the fading of the light. I act in the present, while the present lingers, for the present is the sphere of activity, even as I am reduced to passivity against death, left as powerless against elusive death as Macbeth is to do battle with one not born of woman. I am condemned, not precisely to death, but to a present which is haunted by the mysterious power of death, and to a moment saturated by suffering.

Death is what happens to us, an *événement*, beyond anything that we can assume, for death does not arraign itself before the compass of our a priori projects, but simply disables every projective *Vorlaufen*, every project. Death "gives" a future[20] and absolute alterity, but not of a true alterity and an authentically futural time, because in the end death simply annihilates the subject and returns it to faceless anonymity, wiping out one of the terms of the relation with the other. My solitude is not, as in Heidegger, "confirmed" by death, that is, it does not constitute me in my authentic selfhood and strip me down to the *solus ipse,* but rather my solitude is "broken" by the approach of something that does not come from me.[21] But this break is not a true release from solitude but rather a simple destruction of the solitary subject. It breaks the bonds of solitude by exposing it to an alien power, but it ends only in shattering the subject.[22] It opens a way out of solitude only by crushing this solitude.[23] Death cannot be a true future because it is a faceless future, *nobody's* future.[24] No one is there, and the subject, far from transcending or trans-ascending, has been returned to *il y a,* leaving its momentary triumph over *il y a* in ruins. It exposes the subject to an "other" (*autre*)—death does not come from me—but not to the other one (*l'autrui*). The subject is indeed exposed to an alien power, but a faceless one. But what is that power except the lapping of the waves of *il y a* against its shores, threatening to draw the subject back into the abyss from whence it came, to pry apart the bonding of the existent to its existence? We seek a way to open up the subject to another existent, a relationship of existent to existent that would relieve the tragic solitude of the existent and "nonetheless preserve its conquest over the anonymous '*il y a.'*"[25] Enter *l'autrui*.

Death cannot and does not relieve the tragedy or "curse" of solitude because it cannot "give" (*donne*) the future; death cannot give time.[26] Neither can I give time or the other to myself. There is nothing that death or I can do to transcend my solitude. I cannot give transcendence to myself. I must instead be *for-given* my solitude by the other. The radical breakup of my solitude—that means to be pardoned ("*c'est être pardonné*").[27] The givenness of my being in which I am steeped can only be forgiven by the other. The other comes and forgives me, forgiving not my trespasses, not my doing, but my being, as an event which breaks down the prison of my present. The coming of the other is time and forgiveness. In classical metaphysics, time is a mark of our insufficiency and limitation, a changing image of the plenitude of eternal being. But for Levinas, our being is all too sufficient and self-sufficient, all too saturated and replete with itself, and time is "a remedy for the excess of the definitive contact [with being] which the instant effects." That, says Levinas, is "the fundamental theme of the conception of time which directs these investigations."[28] Duration as otherwise than being, "on another plane than that of being," exceeding the present and the being of the subject, but "without destroying being," resolves the tragedy of being. Time is salvation (*salut*) from the present.

The ego (*le moi*) carries itself (*le soi*) around with itself, the way the body is always accompanied by its shadow. I never leave home or return without it. *Moi* and *soi* are an inseparable pair and there seems to be no saving me from myself. The duality and distance of the distinction between the ego and itself awakens a "nostalgia for escape," a dream of another shore, which the inescapability of the ego from its shadow blocks, seeing to it that the ego lacks the means to achieve it. Thus is constituted what is no more than a glimmering hope for escape to another order, but one altogether lacking the means to "unleash the future."[29] So the ego hopes against hope, hoping for what one cannot do or reasonably expect. But for Levinas—and this is a motif with which the works of the later Derrida are punctuated under the name of "*the* impossible"—that is just when hope is really hope. Hope is truly itself when hope is more or less impossible, when nothing permits it. Otherwise hope is nothing more than a reasonable expectation of how things are likely to go in the foreseeable future. The more gravely I am weighed down by the present, the sharper and livelier the hope. Hope flourishes most when the situation is most hopeless:

> The irreparable is its natural atmosphere. Hope is hope only when it is not permitted. Now what is irreparable in the instant of hope, is that this instant is itself a present (*c'est son présent même*).[30]

When we are lodged inescapably in the present, when suffering cannot escape from the prison of the self, when escape is impossible, then hope is hope. What is more "irreparable" than the instant, the bond of the present to itself? And when is this irreparability suffered more acutely than in suffering, when the subject is riveted to itself in pain? Even if the future, the subsequent course of moments, brings relief, consolation, or even "compensation," still "the suffering of the present remains like a cry whose echo will resound forever in the eternity of spaces."[31] The moment of suffering, imprisoned within itself, the suffering of the moment, remains what it is or was, irreparable in virtue of its very atomicity and discontinuity with the present.

The moment of suffering cannot be entered into a system of exchange or, if it can, that occurs only in what Levinas calls the time of the "world," the "time of economy,"[32] which is marked by the breezy lightness of an "I" which presides over our conscious acts and barters with them. In the time of the world, time is already "given," taken as constituted, synthesized in the synchronized contemporaneity that represents no great feat. In economic time, the ego moves more or less lightly and freely from moment to moment, "accompanying every representation," as Kant would say, so that it can be on hand at a *later* moment to receive "compensation" for the misery of an earlier moment. The ego oversees the exchanges of moments, weighs one against the other, and decides on what will amount to a fair trade, what it will take "for its trouble." This is a commercial operation in which the ego evaluates what sort of market value "effort" has, what sort of objects it might bring in return. These objects then "indemnify" (*indemnisent*) our pain and suffering, and see to it that they produce no loss, no damning loss (*in + damnatus*), instead of "releasing (*détendent*) the torsion of the instant upon itself," thereby letting the intensity of pain be what it is, insisting on or in, standing in the pain of the *instans*. The "profound exigencies" of the pain are in that way nullified instead of being lived through, taken for themselves, in all their irreparability. Then the ego loses its traction, is contracted to the instant, stopped and arrested, mired in the misery, the *malheure* of the moment, experiences the hopelessness. "The world is the possibility of wages," Levinas says. The world is the life of the naive ego, sincere in its love of nourishments and *jouissance,* and willing to strike a bargain about pain and suffering, constantly maintaining the ability to detach itself from its definitive attachment to itself, to settle into and exploit the distance between *moi* and *soi*. The time of the world dries all our tears, and it enables us to forget "the unforgiven instant and the pain for which nothing can compensate."[33] It is just this unforgiven, uncompensated quality of suffering, of the moment of suffering, that strips away the mask of the ego with which it masquerades in the world and exposes the fraudulent lightness of its mundane adventures. It is just this suffering for which nothing can compensate that constitutes the "torsion" and "exigency" of the moment—what pain and sorrow and suffering of the moment truly demand—which gives it the force or energy to "unleash the future." Life in the world is a balance of payments, of work weeks and Sunday, lightly moving between effort and leisure. It is "monotonous," Levinas says, by which he also means monochronous, for all instants are equivalent, interchangeable, part of a larger economy. In the time of the world, Levinas says, the "engagement in existence which is effort is repressed, compensated and amortised"—like a "mortgage"—"instead of being repaired in its very present."[34]

The economic world includes not only the unavoidable wage earning of daily life, but more broadly, more deeply, "all the forms of our existence where the exigency of salvation has been haggled over (*marchandée*)," put on the market, put up for sale.[35] In the economic world, we seek compensation. In what will eventually be called the ethical sphere, we demand or require salvation (*exigence du salut*). The "world" is through and through "secular" (*laïque*), that is, the world is the place where everything is for sale and everything has a price, everything is done for a salary. That is a corruption from which religion itself is not immune. One thinks of Derrida's critique of the "celestial economy" that is invoked in the Gospel of Matthew against the pharisees, which makes the children of the light simply more enlightened investors, buying stocks in goods that will not perish.[36]

But the time of the world, economic time, will not suffice and does not measure up to hope, cannot take the measure of hope, which is without or beyond measure. Hope transpires in—unleashes—another time, otherwise than economic time, a time of "salvation" (*salut*) in which one instant cannot be compensated for by another, where it does not suffice to wipe away a tear or avenge a death, to makes things "even." Instead, Levinas says, "no tear should be lost"[37]: we do not want to wipe away these tears but save them, for they have a saving power, and they are precious beyond any price. Likewise, he says, "no death should take place without resurrection": it is not a question of avenging death, of putting a price on a priceless life and counting ourselves even by exchanging death for death, but of following death with resurrection. In short, the exigency of suffering is not for compensation but salvation. It does not suffice to receive some compensating exchange or account-balancing substitute, some salary that pays off the debt, for that is to pass over the instant too lightly and to cheapen the moment of suffering. What is required and demanded (*exigence*) is a double gesture in which the subject first undergoes irreparable loss and then *without losing the loss*, in a precisely *nonindemnifying* movement, *demands repair,* not as a worker demands a wage, but as death demands resurrection. In short, the exigency of suffering is not for a salary but for salvation, *salut non salaire,* while economic life occurs precisely when the exigency for salvation is put on the open market where it can attract the best market price.

But how are we to repair the irreparable? How to resurrect the dead? How are we to hope if it is hopeless? Still, is that not what hope is? Small comfort that, to know that hope is *the* impossible, for how are we to do that? Hope, for Levinas, is not satisfied with this easygoing, market-wise ego, who moves lightly across the flow of instants trading in his most marketable moments precisely for the highest price. "The true object of hope is the Messiah, or salvation."[38] But what does that mean? It means I need the Messiah, a paraclete, a consoler, to console me. I need the Messiah, a healer to lay hands on me and release me from myself. Like Lazarus in the grave, I need the Messiah to lift me up, to call me out. I need the miracle of the caress:

> The caress of a consoler, the lightness of his strokes in our pain, do not promise the end of suffering, do not announce any compensation, and in their very contact, are not concerned with what is to come *afterwards* in economic time. They concern the very instant of physical pain, which is then no longer condemned to itself, is transported "elsewhere" (*ailleurs*), by the movement of the caress, and is freed from the vise grip of "oneself" (*soi-meme*), finds "fresh air," a dimension and a future.[39]

To be sure, this is not an erotic caress, and perhaps it is "non-erotic par excellence," as he will say later on. Still, it can hardly be denied that the erotic and nonerotic caress would belong to a more general sphere of corporeality, of touch and contact, face to face, flesh to flesh, or even that they communicate with each other, which happens whenever the lover caresses the ill or wounded body of the beloved. In *Totality and Infinity*, Levinas will say that "the doctor," the healer, "is an a priori principle of human mortality."[40] The alterity of death, the alien force, that menaces the sufferer, far from stripping me down to my authentic *Selbstsein*, pries open my solitude, opening up an "appeal to the Other, to his friendship and medication."[41] The threat of death elicits hope in the Other, in the messianic coming of the Other.

In any case, there is no question of "salvation" for the market-wise ego, which is always concerned with a movement of *return* to oneself (*soimeme*). The "street smart" ego makes its way along a road that leads inevitably from *moi* to *soi*, from me to myself, from I to me and mine. Economic time moves along the circle of the same and so cannot effect a genuine release from the present, from the vise grip of "oneself" (*soimeme*), from the presence of the subject in the present, from the insistence of the subject in the instant, its miredness in the moment, in itself. Only the Messiah can save us from that. That can be effected only from without, from a movement that is initiated *elsewhere*, by a laying on of hands by the other, by the coming of the Messiah who has come to save us, who is defined by and is interchangeable with salvation: "that is the Messiah or salvation," that is, the Other. It is the other who opens up the *moi* to what is otherwise and from elsewhere, who releases the subject from the insistence of the instant, and who thereby opens the ego to the future, to time and the future, which it cannot give itself. The voice that consoles, the hand that gently touches, the vow to be with you through this long night, to stay by your side, the promise, absolute and unconditional, to be there when you awake: *c'est le Messie ou salut.* That is the messianic time and the salvation, the coming of the Messiah for which we pray and weep, *viens, oui, oui,* as Derrida says (prays, weeps). The time of salvation and of the Messiah is irreducible to economic time, to the time of the world, to "secular" time.

The future that thereby opens up is more than a "simple future," more than the foreseeable future that we can reasonably expect on the basis of present investments. This is instead a "future where the present will have the benefit of a recall (*rappel*),"[42] a future that, if it can be said to be the effect of compassion, is the effect of an infinitely mysterious compassion, one that infinitely transcends the balanced payments that transpire in the time of the world, in secular time. For pain does not belong to secular time; it cannot be bought off or paid for (*ne rachète pas*). Pace the utilitarians, you cannot justify the misery (*malheure*) of an individual by saying that it purchased the happiness (*bonheure*) of many. *Malheure* and *bonheure* do not constitute an economy. The rewards of the future do not wipe out the misfortune of the present. There is no justice—here Levinas means a "retributive" justice—wise enough or swift enough to "repair" the present, which has been irreparably damaged. Such "repair" of the irreparable is the effect, not of justice, but of salvation; that is the exigency of salvation. Salvation requires the reparation of the irreparable, beyond anything that can be imagined in compensatory or redistributive justice. Reparation requires the impossible: one should have to return to that instant, or be able to resurrect it.[43] Reparation requires time travel, a miraculous return to the present to repair it, to resuscitate it, the way that Lazarus was resuscitated, rather like the debate conducted in the Middle Ages about whether God could change past time, whether God could forgive sin so completely as to "return to that instant" and change it! Beyond the wise but calculative justice of Solomon, who knew how to split the difference and was willing to roll the dice, reparation requires the caress of the Messiah himself, for whose appearance we can only hope against hope. Reparation requires hope, messianic *hope.*

> To hope then is to hope for the reparation of the irreparable. It is to hope for the present.[44]

The hope is for now, for the subject caught in the grips of a present misery and misfortune. Hope is not a hope in an afterlife, for gaining

entrance to the "world behind the scenes," the *arriere-monde*, which
would be no less worldly or secular for Levinas, for the very reasons
pointed out by Derrida in *The Gift of Death*. World-time is any economic
time, including the celestial economy of that after-world time called
eternity, "which does not seem to us indispensable," Levinas says.[45]
Heavenly rewards bear witness to the sphere of salaries, not of salvation.
Salvation is situated not in a heavenly kingdom to come, but in pain of
the present, "the very instant of pain." It is effected when pain is not
compensated but comforted, healed, released, caressed, in the balm of
flesh softly stroking flesh, and it transpires not in eternity, but now, in a
night of anguish and suffering. Is that not the essence of time? "Does
not the essence of time consist in responding to this exigency for salvation? Is not the future above all the resurrection of the present?"[46] To
hope, is that not to hope in the coming of the Messiah, of the Other,
autrui, in what Derrida calls *l'invention de l'autre*, which we translate: the
incoming of the other? Time then is not the stream of moments across
which the subject freely moves, trading off one for another to its
economic advantage. Neither is it Bergsonian duration, in which the
present impinges or "encroaches"[47] upon the future by the sheer precip-
itancy, the headlong rush of the *élan vital*. Nor is it the headlong rush,
the *Vorlaufen*, of ecstatic *Dasein*'s anticipatory projection upon its own
most possibility to be. Both Bergson and Heidegger are too precipitous
for Levinas, building the future too quickly into the present, so that the
present is never given its moment in the sun, its time and duration, but
is too quickly swept off into the future, which in turn never allows the future to be truly accomplished as a release from the present. The Levinasian notion of resurrection—we live time and the future more deeply
as the resurrection of the present—requires the "indispensable interval
of nothingness"[48] which separates the instant and allows it to be constituted. The present must first surge up in its discontinuous density, for it
is only then that the *exigency* of the present can be nourished and engendered. The enchainment to the present needs to be constituted before
the need for release is felt. But it is not enough, and there is no salvation, simply to lurch from instant to instant, simply to pass discontinuously but unchanged from moment to moment. It is not enough to
enter the next instant "identical and unforgiven (*impardonné*)," which
would be no more than the repetition of the same. The knot by which
the subject is tied to itself, the definitiveness of its confinement to itself,
is not cut by the mere evanescent flow of instants, but only by a new beginning, by beginning again, by a *rebirth*. This exigency is not a demand
for the perseverance of the same but for *dénouement*—for something that
unties the knot by which it is tied to itself—and *recommencement*, for a new

beginning, a commencing anew this time free from the definitiveness that confines it to itself. The exigency is a demand for a "miraculous" beginning, a "beginning again as other,"[49] not a beginning from itself (*à partir de soi*), but beginning from the other, from the caress of the other.

This exigency is the subject's "very need (*besoin*) of time," what would later be called the "desire" (as opposed to need) of the time of the other. But it cannot "give itself" this alterity; it cannot give itself time. That is to say, the subject cannot save itself, even as it cannot effect the movement of time by itself. Neither time nor salvation are possible in the solitary ego. Because the tragedy of the human situation is its very solitude, because it is the definitiveness by which the subject is confined to the present, salvation "can only come from elsewhere, while the subject is always here." Levinas means thus to overturn the Augustinian motif (which made its way into Kierkegaard and Heidegger), when Augustine said do not go elsewhere, *nolite foras ire*, for God is here, within us. For Levinas, on the contrary, what is here, *ici*, is a prison from which we hope to be saved by the coming of the Messiah, who comes from elsewhere (*ailleurs*).

Truly to shatter the instant, to move into a next instant that is no mere repetition of the same, that does not carry the shadow of the same along with it, truly to break outside into the "absolute alterity of another instant," is not possible for the solitary subject. "This alterity comes to me only from the other."[50] The time that flows in the solitary subject, the very idea of "internal time consciousness," is fraudulent for Levinas. Such false time amounts only to a repetition of the same in which the instant is "negated" only in order to resurface in the next instant as the same, and that is nothing more than a successful strategy of self-perpetuation, self-preservation, self-regeneration, and not a new birth. Such internal negation is not true alterity but a self-assertion that deploys the mediation of self-negation. Such negation as remains within the interiority of the subject—whether that be the process of retention and retention in Husserl, the projection upon death in Heidegger, the dialectical power of the negative in Hegel, or the freedom derived from *le néant* in Sartre's *pour soi*—is nothing—it is monotony and monochrony—in comparison with genuine alterity.

Every such internal self-negation, every such attempt to give oneself time, is a false freedom and a false time, and altogether different from pardoning, *pardoner*, from being pardoned by the other (*autrui*):

> Classical philosophy left aside the freedom which consists not in negating oneself, but in having one's being *pardoned* by the very alterity of the other.

It underestimated the alterity of the other in dialogue where the other frees us, because it believed there existed a silent dialogue of the soul with itself.[51]

The pardoning pardons the ego not for its trespasses but for its being, not for what the subject does but for what it is, viz., a subject imprisoned in itself, given wholly to itself, saturated with itself. The *pardoner* relieves the subject of the futile and solitary work of trying to give itself time, of trying to save itself. The pardoning extends the saving hand of the healer who heals the subject trapped in the tension and intensity of suffering, of the consoler who gives the subject consolation. The *pardoner* gives us freedom and frees us from the futile attempt to free ourselves, to effect escape from the confines of the self.

The text of *Existence and Existents* concludes with a confusing shift of focus, a reversal of the terms of the self (*moi*) and the other (*altrui*). Before now, the subject is who suffers and is released by the coming of the other, where the other is "the Messiah or salvation." But in the conclusion of the work it is the other who suffers—the other is "the weak one whereas I am the strong," or "the poor one, 'the widow and the orphan,'" or the other is the enemy and stronger.[52] In either case, the other is no longer one who alleviates the suffering of the subject. By the same token, the "caress" shifts from the caress *by* the other, by the healer or consoler who alleviates the suffering of the subject, to become the erotic caress, the caress *of* the other by the subject who reaches out into the infinite mystery and exteriority of the feminine other, groping in a distance that cannot be crossed. The caress is not the one by which the subject is lifted out of its misery and misfortune, but the caress whose loving futility would cross the distance of the other which is maintained in the very proximity of the embrace. In these final pages alterity, salvation, and pardon are quickly sketched in terms of eros and the ethics of the other, terms which will require the lengthy analyses in *Totality and Infinity* to make sense. But what interests me in these pages is the first appearance in them of the healing gesture of the other who comes, like the Messiah, to save the subject from itself.

3. Historical Desire (Dangerous Memories)

History, I am claiming, is written with prayers and tears. The historian who writes against the grain of history recalls tears long since shed in the irremissible past, even while heaving and sighing a messianic prayer for a time in which no tear shall be lost. Let us now address that claim directly.

History always runs the risk of nostalgia, of a voyeuristic desire to go where it is impossible to go, to what is no longer there, to revisit ancient sites, to witness ancient events, to observe, invisible and unnoticed, as bygone worlds unfold. That desire feeds the historical novel or film, seducing us into suspending our disbelief so that we may walk again the streets of medieval Europe, pray again in Gothic cathedrals, dine with the landed gentry of Austenian England, and slip unnoticed into vanished worlds. That knowing relation to the past, as Levinas would say, is too possessive, too violent, too voyeuristic, too obsessed with truth as representation, too much aimed at reappropriating or reconstituting the alterity of the past. A history written with prayers and tears lets justice precede truth, and ethics precede episteme, and finds itself in the impossible situation of desiring to repair the irreparable. That does not mean to wipe away every tear but to see to it that no tear is lost, like Benjamin's chronicler who records every event, however minor, who, like the biblical God, counts every tear and every hair on our head. The needs of nostalgia are filled by witnessing ancient worlds, reconstituting their costumes and ambience precisely, without interfering with them, disinterestedly, without understanding that memories are dangerous, without hearing the prayers and tears.

The medieval debate about whether God can change the past seems to me a most profound reflection upon history. I am interested not in the technical conundrum it poses for modal logic, which is from this point of view merely an intellectual amusement, but in the desire, the aspiration, that lies beneath it, which lies in hearing the sighs of prayers and tears now long gone. Can God restore lost virginity, the Scholastic masters wanted to know? Can God see to it that a man or woman who wants *now* to live a life of religious celibacy *after* having had carnal experience should now get a second chance? Can God give one who has been "reborn" in the love of God a new lease on life, so that the person would be quite literally reborn? Can God make it to be that the sinner did not sin? Can God so completely forgive sin as to wipe the sin out, so that there is—there would be, there was—no sin to be forgiven? A sensible realist and Aristotelian like Thomas Aquinas, much as he loved God, demurred. Thomas was not saying that God, try as He might, was just unable to do this particular thing, that this was a test that even God's omnipotence failed, that it was too much to ask even of God. Thomas simply said that the suggestion made no sense, so that no "thing" coherent or possible was being sought. God was neither able nor unable to do "it," because there was no "it," nothing really going on behind those words, which were merely a *flatus vocis* (we would say "hot air"). In terms of the modal logic, Thomas is right enough, even too right, a little too logical and sensible, for he misses the soaring aspiration for a miracle, the dream and desire for the impossible, the heart and the love, the prayers and tears that lie behind the suggestion.

What Thomas said is true enough, too true, too preoccupied with truth: the time of forgiving past wrongs, or of healing past injustice, is an impossible time and an impossible desire. Taken strictly in terms of modal logic, it is an immoderate request, quite excessive. But that is why we love it so much. We are carried by the wings of historical desire above the constraints that time and being place upon us, to brush against the grain of history, across the—alas irreversible—flow of moments, to a moment that is no longer there so as to undo the damage and destruction, to stay the hand of the oppressor, to change the heart, *metanoia,* of the offender.

But Levinas, who is not lacking in heart, is no less realistic about the past. He too would insist that the past is irrevocably what it is, that the injury done in the past cannot be undone, that it is not to be undone but "saved." I would say that is because, in this context, Levinas has in mind not the time of the sinner or trespasser, who needs forgiving, but the time of the sinned against, the trespassed. He is thinking about releasing the sufferer from solitude, not about forgiving the trespasser. In these early works of 1947, the past is past, over and done with, the time is irrevocably ruined, irreparable. That raises the stakes, provokes an impossible desire to repair the irreparable, to revisit the irreparable moment, transpose ourselves to that impossible site, and offer a hand of comfort, caress, and consolation, and even of resurrection. In Levinas's phenomenological ontology, as we have seen, the moment is marked by its self-enclosure, by the captivity of the instant within itself, so that the tear that is shed is shed forever and irreparably, and the life of the victim is forever taken and death is forever. But Levinas does not speak of altering or undoing the past, but offering it what he calls "salvation." The logic, the ethics, the pathics of the tear do not call for wiping away every tear but of seeing that "no tear is to be lost, no death without resurrection."

In the 1947 texts, salvation requires the time of the other, of the consoler who lifts the subject out of himself by way of the caress, whose soft and gentle stroke, whose light embrace, *effleurer,* opens up the self-enclosed subject to the other, allowing an even momentary escape. Blessed are those who give comfort. Levinas would save the tear, not wipe it away, and save the death by following it with resurrection. The time of the consoler is to divide the self-enclosed instant in half and share it. If I may be forgiven a tasteless gesture of self-citation, I would put it thus:

> Therapists and clinical psychologists and counselors of every stripe belong, on this view, to an ancient but very unscientific jewgreek paradigm, the paradigm of the "healer," people who "drive out devils," usually by "laying on hands." I imagine that what is behind such old jewgreek stories is the power of a man or woman of compassion to calm a troubled heart, to take the hand of the troubled one in their hands, literally to lend them a hand, to be on hand. They did not have anything special to say to them or the miraculous power to suspend the laws of nature. They did not know anything special. Who does? But they talked with their troubled friends through long nights or lonely days, hand in hand, flesh in flesh. It is not what they said (*le dit*) that matters but the saying (*le dire*)—and the flesh of their hand. That was the miracle of what they did. . . . The hand heals of itself, because it is a hand, because it is flesh. We all have the hands of healers and we all heal by laying on hands. . . . It is not a question of finding an answer to the night of truth but of sitting up with one another through the night, of dividing the abyss in half in a companionship that is its own meaning.[53]

To divide the abyss in half, to break open the tragic solitude, to divide the instant by sharing it between us, that is the time of the consoler.

The time of the consoler, I contend, enters—by an impossible gesture—into the structure of writing history with prayers and tears. For the historian who would brush history against its grain is driven by the impossible desire to console the dead and grant them resurrection, which is to be distinguished from the desire to change the past, to heal the dead and make them whole and well, to feed the victims of famines past, to resurrect them from their graves. Note well that Levinas speaks of "resurrection," not of "resuscitation." This impossible desire is not to break down the walls of the prison camps and liberate the inmates, like the famous pictures of Allied soldiers entering the death camps, but by an historical act to visit them in prison and offer them an—impossible— consolation.

The historical act is to record their tears, to keep them in our heart (*re-cordari*), to keep the prayers and tears of broken hearts in our heart. The historian re-cords with the feeble tools of memory, not a passive, reproductive memory, but an active, heartfelt, searching and researching memory, that understands that history is the archive of countless tears and untold deaths. In the New Testament it is said that God will wipe away every tear and that God has counted every hair on our head,[54] an operation that I would say very beautifully describes the biblical God, as opposed to the impassive, apathetic, tearless *nous noetikos* of the Athenians, who thought of God in terms of thinking instead of prayers and tears. Now I would assign that divine operation, recording or counting the countless tears of time, to historical desire that would write with prayers and tears. I would say that the desire of historians is to save those tears and see that they are not lost, to reach across the uncrossable space of time and comfort those who weep and are persecuted, to record their prayers and tears, to tell the death of the untold dead and to offer them resurrection.

In "Diachrony and Representation," Levinas says that I am commanded by the "mortality" of the other, by his very weakness and vulnerability. I am commanded, he says, "not to remain indifferent to his death, to not let the Other die alone, that is, to answer for the life of the other person"—lest I become an "accomplice" in that death.[55] The authority of the Other is his precariousness, his strength is his weakness. I am not overpowered by his overpowering upsurge of Being, as in some Heideggerian extravaganza of *physis,* but thrown deeply into question, made acutely conscious of the murderousness of my power, by the Other's mortality and vulnerability. But if I am commanded by the "mortality" of the other, then I am no less commanded by their actual death, commanded *post mortem,* after their death. The command that comes to me from the living Other, "thou shalt not kill," comes no less from the dead, comes no less from those that have already been killed. The command of the dead comes back to me from the grave and fixes me in its gaze, accusing me. The blood of the dead cries to us from their graves, like the blood of Abel, making us all responsible, making us all the children of Cain.

Walter Benjamin speaks of the "chronicler who recounts (*hererzählt*) events without distinguishing between major and minor ones," who believes that "nothing that has ever happened should be regarded as lost for history." For a "redeemed humanity," Benjamin says, every moment in the past deserves memory and citation.[56] Every moment of the past is to be remembered, the way someone is remembered in prayers. We must become like saints who remember everyone in their prayers, even the least of God's creatures.

That is why the memories of the historians are dangerous, what Johann Baptist Metz calls, in a magnificent expression, "the dangerous memories of suffering," the memories of countless tears and untold deaths.

The historian does revisit these ancient sites like a tourist, looking on helplessly at the frozen faces of the dead petrified at the foot of

Mount Vesuvius, having arrived too late on the scene to lend a helping hand. Instead the historian is to supply the voice of these mute dead, to sigh their sighs, to weep their tears, and to offer them resurrection. If the dead constitute those whom Levinas calls the "subjectivity poorly heard in history,"[57] then the historian must make them better heard. The historian of prayers and tears must in a certain sense rise to the revisionist historian's challenge that Lyotard denounces in *Heidegger and "the jews,"* to let those who were gassed to death step forward and register their complaints, to let the untold dead of nineteenth-century Ireland register their complaints from the grave, to transform them from the *differend* to which the revisionist historian would confine them, into historical litigants, with new voices and new life, restoring their prayers and tears.

That would issue in rather a different history than the one that Levinas denounced in the "Preface" to *Totality and Infinity,* not a "teleological" history, which was a very economic affair, in which the untold dead and countless tears were cost accounted as a good investment in the progress of the world spirit, the high but affordable price the Spirit must pay for advancing from one *Gestaltung* to the next. The sufferings of the past would eventually bring a good return, an absolute return, an excellent "result," and Auschwitz would be an "example" of a deeper and more sweeping law. Teleological history is one in which many an innocent flower is tread on the way to *savoir absolue,* very brilliantly explicated in "Result," the central chapter of *The Differend.* Teleological history always gets a return for its tears and is well compensated for the deaths it has contributed to the course of progress. Thus instead of opposing eschatology to historiology, one would speak instead of an "eschatological history," a history of prayers and tears, a history that goes beyond history, to that end beyond or beneath the sweep of world history in order to settle upon the innocent flowers, the tender shoots that are trampled under the boots of teleology. Eschatological history would tend to the secrets of the heart which are unknown to the judgments of history, that are revealed only in the judgment of God, the *kardiognostes,* the God who knows the human heart.[58] Eschatological history would be intent on counting these tears, on saving them from loss, and it would respect the secret in every heart that history does not know, the moments long past of irrecuperable loss. Rather than entering these losses into a long-term gain, eschatological history would let the loss be a loss and seek, by an impossible gesture, to comfort it. The historiographer, Levinas says in *Totality and Infinity,* is a survivor who calculates the contributions of the dead to the living, a historical cost accountant who computes and recapitulates the investments of the past in terms of the return they make in the present. In the time of the historiographers, "particular existences are lost (*se perdent*),"[59] taking a position that perfectly reproduces the one struck by Johannes Climacus against Hegelian world history. But as long as I am alive, as long as I have breath enough to protest, I take a "leave of absence" (*congé*) from world history, I postpone the reckoning against which I will be defenseless in death, when I will not be on hand to explain myself. To be alive is to withdraw into the citadel of my interiority which is kept secret from the calculations of the historiographer, where no tear is lost, no grief allowed to dissipate in the economy of historiographical reckoning.

Eschatological history is not economic; it does not concern itself with how the past can be entered into the ledgers of world history, how the books of history can be balanced. It does not seek to wipe away the tears of the past, but rather to return to the moment of irreparable loss and death and release what Levinas calls its "tension," its torsion, to reconstitute the intensity of the past so that its "exigency" may be released. This work of the historian is to offer the dead not compensation but salvation, an impossible salvation, for its caress is not made of flesh but of memory and re-cord, its gentle hand is stretched out to those who no longer receive its touch. The tension or torsion of the past is its cry not for retributive justice, which is not enough and never truly possible; for that would require either returning to that past instant and undoing it, "resuscitating" the dead, or putting a price on the sufferings of the past which the present would then have to meet. The exigency, Levinas says, is for salvation, which means both to release them from the solitude of the present and to offer hope for the future.

The historian cannot, of course, caress and give hope *to* the dead, save them or release them from the present of their suffering, now long gone; the historian can only offer hope and a future *for* the dead, on their behalf, pleading on their behalf for the future, for a new birth, new life. That means that historical desire is directed at an opening on the future that would not be the "afterwards (*après*) of economic time," like returning the art stolen from the victims of the Holocaust, but the future of hope. That would come about *as if* we had assisted at the sufferings of the past, as if we had been on hand to lend a hand to their grief, like the consoler "*qui effleure dans la douleur*," and offer them a word of consolation. That is impossible now; we are too late to help. It is impossible now to answer their prayers or wipe away their tears. What remains now is to *hope*, and to hope, Levinas says, requires first to be driven into a state where, calculatively speaking, it is hopeless, where the odds are hopelessly against us, to hope against hope. Hope, says Paul, is not hope if you can see what you are hoping for on the horizon. We need hope when we cannot see the way out. Hope requires blindness. Hence the work of the historian is the impossible one of giving comfort to the dead by way of memory and hope, to answer their prayers and tears with prayers and tears for the coming of the messianic time.

By memory we mean not a Hegelian memory that interiorizes, that sucks up the interiority of the dead into the present and makes it our own, but a memory like mourning, which preserves the distance of the dead, their fallen tears, the irreducible loss, then offers hope for the future they will never know, seeing to it that their lives are a gift without return, because they cannot return, to the future, so that their memory makes its impossible that the future would ever close, that we would ever give up or give in to the odds against us. The irreparability of the past goes hand in hand with the open-endedness of the future, with the radicality of the *to come,* so that the more intensely we experience the tension and intensity of the past, the prayers and tears of the past, the more radically we pray and weep on their behalf for a future to come, the more radically we pray and weep *"viens, oui, oui, viens!"*

For as Walter Benjamin says, not even the dead are safe from the assaults of the anti-Christ, whom the Messiah must subdue.

The correlate of the irreparable past is the irrepressible future, the future of the "come," the *"viens"* of the *"à-venir,"* the unforeseeable, unprogrammable future, whose unforeseeability is directly proportionate to the irreparability of the past. That is the future of hope, the time of hope, the time of the gift, beyond calculation, reparation, and redemption, the future that converts the past into a gift without return. Only the dead can give a gift without return. A genuine gift must be given beyond my death, for an absolute future that will never become present. That is possible for the dead alone. For the dead alone cannot be compensated, cannot draw some secret, unconscious payment for their expenditures, and so they alone stand able, by the strange dynamics of the gift, to give a gift without return. The gift alone outstrips all economy. The future of the gift alone provides for a "resurrection" which, beyond resuscitation, alone grants new life. The comfort that the historian extends to an irrecuperable past is to offer it the caress of the gift, the gentle stroke of the gift. Levinas all along thought the time of the other in terms of the *child,* the gift of fecundity. It is the child for whom he prays and weeps in these early analyses. The child is the future, the other that is the same and not the same, the one to whom past and present generations are asked to give without return. The child is no less a paradigm for the historian, for the children are the ones to come in history no less than in the family. History is being written *for* the children, *to* children, and it is to the children that we call "come," for whom we pray and weep, *viens, oui, oui.* The historian writes in the time between the dead and the children, between irreparable suffering and hope for the unforeseeable to-come. By recording their prayers and tears and by recounting the countless dead, by awakening the dangerous memories of their prayers and tears, the historian says "come," says and prays, *viens* to the messianic time. History is written *in* prayers and tears, *with* prayers and tears, *about* prayers and tears, now long gone, praying and weeping over the coming of the messiah, the time of salvation, of the messianic time which has counted countless tears, recounted unaccountable death.

Notes

1. Emmanuel Levinas, *Existence and Existents,* trans. Alphonso Lingis (The Hague: Martinus Nijhoff, 1978), 91; French edition: *De l'existence à l'existant* (Paris: J. Vrin, 1947), 155.

2. Emmanuel Levinas, *Time and the Other and Additional Essays,* trans. Richard A. Cohen (Pittsburg: Duquesne University Press, 1982), 33; French edition: *Le temps et l'autre* (Paris: PUF, 1983), 11.

3. Levinas, *Existence and Existents,* 76; *De l'existence à l'existant,* 131.

4. Levinas, *Existence and Existents,* 39–40; *De l'existence à l'existant,* 29.

5. Levinas, *Existence and Existents,* 32; *De l'existence à l'existant,* 46.

6. Levinas, *Existence and Existents,* 34; *De l'existence à l'existant,* 48.

7. Levinas, *Time and the Other,* 52; *Le temps et l'autre,* 32.

8. Levinas, *Existence and Existents,* 73–75; *De l'existence à l'existant,* 125–29.

9. Levinas, *Existence and Existents,* 77; *De l'existence à l'existant,* 132.

10. Levinas, *Existence and Existents,* 34; *De l'existence à l'existant,* 49.

11. Levinas, *Time and the Other,* 68–69; *Le temps et l'autre,* 55.

12. Levinas, *Time and the Other,* 69; *Le temps et l'autre,* 55–56.

13. Levinas, *Time and the Other,* 72; *Le temps et l'autre,* 59–60.

14. Ibid., 60.

15. Compare Levinas, *Time and the Other,* 71; *Le temps et l'autre,* 57.

16. Levinas, *Time and the Other,* 69; *Le temps et l'autre,* 56.

17. Levinas, *Time and the Other,* 57; *Le temps et l'autre,* 70.

18. Levinas, *Time and the Other,* 71; *Le temps et l'autre,* 58.

19. *Macbeth,* act 5, scene 5, cited by Levinas in *Time and the Other,* 72; *Le temps et l'autre,* 60.

20. Levinas, *Time and the Other,* 79; *Le temps et l'autre,* 68.

21. Levinas, *Time and the Other,* 74; *Le temps et l'autre,* 63.

22. Ibid., 63.

23. Levinas, *Time and the Other,* 77; *Le temps et l'autre,* 65.

24. Levinas, *Time and the Other,* 79; *Le temps et l'autre,* 68.

25. Levinas, *Time and the Other,* 77; *Le temps et l'autre,* 65.

26. Levinas, *Time and the Other,* 79; *Le temps et l'autre,* 68.

27. Levinas, *Existence and Existents,* 85; *De l'existence à l'existant,* 144.

28. Levinas, *Existence and Existents,* 85–86; *De l'existence à l'existant,* 147.

29. Levinas, *Existence and Existents,* 89; *De l'existence à l'existant,* 153.

30. Ibid.

31. Levinas, *Existence and Existents,* 89–90; *De l'existence à l'existant,* 153–54.

32. Levinas, *Existence and Existents,* 90; *De l'existence à l'existant,* 154.

33. Ibid.

34. Ibid.

35. Ibid., 155.

36. Jacques Derrida, *The Gift of Death,* trans. David Wills (Chicago: University of Chicago Press, 1995), 97–98.

37. Levinas, *Existence and Existents,* 91; *De l'existence à l'existant,* 155.

38. Ibid.

39. Ibid.

40. Emmanuel Levinas, *Totality and Infinity: An Essay on Exteriority,* trans. Alphonso Lingis (Pittsburg: Duquesne University Press, 1992), 234; French edition: *Totalité et infiniti* (The Hague: Martinus Nijhoff, 1961), 210.

41. Levinas, *Totality and Infinity,* 234; *Totalité et infiniti,* 210.

42. Levinas, *Existence and Existents,* 91; *De l'existence à l'existant,* 156.

43. Ibid.

44. Ibid.

45. Ibid.

46. Levinas, *Existence and Existents,* 91–92; *De l'existence à l'existant,* 157.

47. Ibid.

48. Levinas, *Existence and Existents,* 93; *De l'existence à l'existant,* 158.

49. Ibid., 159.

50. Ibid., 160.

51. Levinas, *Existence and Existents,* 94; *De l'existence à l'existant,* 161.

52. Levinas, *Existence and Existents,* 95; *De l'existence à l'existant,* 162–63.

53. John D. Caputo, *Against Ethics: Contributions to a Poetics of Obligation with Constant Reference to Deconstruction* (Bloomington: Indiana University Press, 1983), 243–44.

54. Mt. 10:30.

55. Emmanuel Levinas, *Entre Nous: On Thinking-of-the-Other,* trans. Michael B. Smith and Barbara Harshav (New York: Columbia University Press, 1998), 109.

56. Walter Benjamin, *Illuminations,* ed. Hannah Arendt, trans. Harry Zohn (New York: Schocken Books, 1969), 254.

57. Levinas, *Totality and Infinity,* 182; *Totalité et infiniti,* 158.

58. Luke 16:15.

59. Levinas, *Totality and Infinity,* 55; *Totalité et infiniti,* 26.

The Tomb of Perseverance: On *Antigone*

Joan Copjec

The term "Greek tragedy" is what we commonly use to refer to it, but it would be more accurate to say "Attic" or "Athenian tragedy"; since it was *only* in the city-state of Athens that this aesthetic form was nourished and thrived. Yet not even this correction sufficiently discloses the intimate relation that bound this particular city to this particular form, for tragedy was not simply founded in Athens (between 534 and 530 BC) and there declared dead (by Aristotle, in 414 BC), it also reached out a hand to help invent the very city that invented it.[1] As Jean-Pierre Vernant has argued:

> [Athenian] tragedy is contemporary with the City [Athens] and with its legal system. . . . [W]hat tragedy is talking about is itself and the problems of law it is encountering. What is talking and what is talked about is the audience on the benches, but first of all it is the City . . . which puts itself on the stage and plays itself. . . . Not only does the tragedy enact itself on stage . . . it enacts its own problematics. It puts in question its own internal contradictions, revealing . . . that the true subject matter of tragedy is social thought . . . in the very process of elaboration.[2]

That is, not only did the Athenians insert themselves into their tragic dramas—as chorus members, who judged the actions of the protagonists in the same way as the tribunal of citizens in the audience was judging the unfolding tragedy against others performed for the same contest—they also posed, through their tragedies, the juridical and ethical questions they were currently confronting in actuality.

But if the form of Athenian tragedy is so local, tied not only to a specific place, a particular and precisely datable time, and a unique set of social problems, it would seem, then, according to the historicist-relativist thinking of our day, to offer nothing that might help us think through the juridical and ethical issues raised by the modern city. In fact, to begin a consideration of contemporary urban issues with a reference to Athenian tragedy is automatically to brand oneself with the sin of anachronism. I propose, however, that the question should not always be, "How can we rid ourselves of anachronism?" for it is sometimes more relevant to ask, "What is the significance of anachronism?" How can we account for the temporal nomadism of figures from the past? And, in this context, how is it possible that the drama of Antigone still concerns us?[3]

The simplest initial response would be to point out that German idealism *resurrected* Antigone at the beginning of our own era and refashioned her as the paradigmatic figure of *modern* ethics. Hegel, Schelling, Hölderlin all wrote with deep fascination about this young Athenian woman and it is their fascination that commands contemporary interest in her.[4] Voicing, undoubtedly, the sentiments of his colleagues in addition to his own, Hegel proclaimed *Antigone* "one of the most sublime, and in every respect most consummate works of human effort ever brought forth."[5] Despite this trans-historical judgment, however, before the intervention of German idealism, the play had not received any special attention and had, in fact, been relatively neglected. It was only after paeans such as Hegel's began to revive the play that it became a major reference point of ethical speculation, including that of Kierkegaard, Brecht, Anouilh, Irigaray, Derrida, and, of course, Lacan. In 1978 *Germany in Autumn,* a compilation film produced by nine New German Cinema directors, was released. Focusing on questions of a family's right to bury its dead and the right of citizens to rebel against their government, the film loosely associated actions taken by the Red Army Faction and the Baader-Meinhof terrorists against the German state with Antigone and Polynices' rebellion against Creon and the city-state of Thebes. More recently, Jean-Marie Straub and Daniele Huillet's release, in 1992, of their film version of Brecht's adaptation of Hölderlin's translation of Sophocles' *Antigone,* has demonstrated that the legacy of German idealism's retrieval of Antigone lives on. If our interest in her is an archaism, then it is a peculiarly modern one. What will concern me in the following analysis is less the historical conditions that reawakened interest in *Antigone* (the Hellenistic bent of German idealism has been amply explored) than the play's own susceptibility to a rereading in the modern context (how is it possible to resurrect such an old drama?); for this issue is closely linked to the ethical issues raised in the play.

My approach to these issues begins with a single rereading of *Antigone,* or, more accurately, a rereading of a prior rereading: Lacan, in

Seminar VII: The Ethics of Psychoanalysis, reinterprets Sophocles' play by challenging Hegel's interpretation in *The Phenomenology of Spirit.* Though later, in the *Philosophy of Right,* Hegel would read the play straightforwardly as a modern drama of ethical action, in the *Phenomenology* he reads it as a tragedy belonging to an earlier moment which he describes (perhaps metaphorically) as that of the Greek city-state; at this moment the opposition between the universal and the particular, the state and the family, human and divine law, man and woman could not be practically overcome. Hegel argues that classical Greek society held the two poles of these oppositions together, in a precarious equilibrium, through *custom,* which provided the community with a concrete unity. But when any decisive action was taken, this equilibrium collapsed into real and irresolvable conflict. Through the ethical *act,* the ethical *community* was dissolved, for the act "initiates the division of itself into itself as the active principle and into the reality over against it, a reality which, for it, is negative. By the deed, therefore, it becomes guilt. . . . And the guilt also acquires the meaning of *crime,* for as simple, ethical consciousness, it has turned towards one law, but turned its back on the other and violates the latter by its deed."[6] Only *inaction,* then, can remain innocent in the Greek polis; every *act,* insofar as it decisively chooses one pole of the opposition, one law, over the other, renders the actor guilty. This inevitable and tragic result is, according to Hegel, the very point of these dramas in general and of *Antigone* in particular, for there each protagonist, each ethical consciousness, "sees right only on one side and wrong on the other, that consciousness which belongs to the divine law sees in the other side only the violence of human caprice, while that which holds to human law sees in the other only the self-will and disobedience of the individual who insists on being his own authority" (par. 466).

Hegel here effectively argues that Antigone ("that consciousness which belongs to the divine law") and Creon ("that which holds to human law") are, in their very decisiveness and intransigence, *both* guilty, both in the wrong, insofar as they both abandon or alienate one principle through the very act of embracing its opposite. Acting on behalf of a particular individual, her brother, Antigone betrays the community and terrorizes the state, while Creon acts on behalf of the city-state and thus sacrifices Polynices and the values of the family.

Lacan attacks the deep undecidability of this reading in order decisively to side with Antigone, praising hers as the only real, ethical act in the play and condemning the actions of Creon as crimes. In this reading it is *only* Creon who, through his actions, renders himself guilty. This is not to say that Antigone's implacability goes unnoticed by Lacan; he is as strict as Hegel is in observing the raw, untamed, and uncompromising nature of Oedipus's daughter's rebellion. "The nature of the girl is savage, like her father's, and she does not know how to bend before her troubles," is what the chorus says of her, and Lacan is quick to agree.[7] But as a psychoanalyst—and here we catch a glimpse of the difference between psychoanalysis and philosophy or psychology—he does not read the *behavior* of each of the protagonists, he defines the *structure* through which their acts must be read. Thus, while Antigone and Creon may be equally stubborn in the performance of their duties, this stubbornness, according to which fantasy structure it enters, admits of a fundamental distinction that Lacan will use to ruin the symmetry Hegel so carefully constructs.

In *Three Essays on the Theory of Sexuality*, Freud warns us not to conflate *Fixeirarbeit*, which is an inexplicable fixation that persists despite every external attempt to dislodge it, with *Haftbarkeit*, "which is perhaps best translated by 'perseverance' but has a curious resonance in German, since it means also 'responsibility,' 'commitment.'"[8] It is this distinction introduced by Freud which lies behind and undergirds Lacan's insistence that Antigone, and she alone, is the heroine of Sophocles' play; her *perseverance* in carrying out the burial of her brother is ethically different from Creon's *fixation* on enforcing the statist prohibition against his burial.

How Freud is able to distinguish between these two kinds of acts is what we will have to determine, but Lacan gives us a clue when he refers to them as separate effects of "the individual libidinal adventure" (*SVII* 88). Whatever else needs to be said about the distinction, it is clear from this that it cannot be drawn without taking into account the *sexual* being of the subject who acts. The reason Hegel's reading has received so much feminist attention is precisely because it seems to be attentive to this issue insofar as it foregrounds the sexual difference that separates the play's main protagonists. But this difference turns out to be, in his reading, only a gender or biological difference, not a sexual one; that is, Antigone and Creon enact a division of labor which is defined sociologically, according to the spaces they are allowed to inhabit and the roles they are encouraged to assume, given their biology. In fact, Hegel consciously aims to *avoid* sex as far as possible, which is why he chooses to focus not on the husband/wife but on the brother/sister relation. This relation, he says, provides a truer or "unmixed" picture of the difference between the sexes insofar as it excludes sexual desire. This positing of a family relation free of libido is problematic to begin with—Freud and Foucault have both, in different and definitive ways, exposed the family as a hotbed of desiring relations—but it is absolutely stupefying in light of the fact that the family in question here is Oedipus's and no stranger, then, to the taint of incest. The Greek text, which loads Antigone's references to her brother with libidinal overtones, never lets us forget the fact that the tragedy which plays itself out before our eyes is in some sense a consequence of the incestuous union between Oedipus and his mother. It is necessary to conclude then, I would venture to argue, that there is in this section of Hegel's *Phenomenology* no sex and no sexual difference, properly speaking. This has the effect of leaving the notions of work and act undisturbed or unproblematized by sexual enjoyment.

According to Freud, however, between sex or libidinal satisfaction and work there is a permanent antagonism that threatens work (or the act) with extinction. As he notes in *Civilization and Its Discontents,* "No other technique for the conduct of work attaches the individual so firmly to reality as laying emphasis on work . . . [which is] indispensable to the preservation and justification of existence in society. . . . And yet . . . work is not prized by men. They do not strive after it as they do after other possibilities of satisfaction."[9] By rethinking the notion of work through that of pleasure, Freud opens Aristotle's distinction between the *act,* in all its rarity, and mere *action* to a redefinition in which what matters is the kind of relation each maintains toward sexual enjoyment. If the avowed ambition of Lacan's *Ethics* seminar is to remove the discussion of ethics from "the starry sky" and place it where it belongs, "in our bodies, and nowhere else," that is, if its ambition is to define an ethics of the *embodied* subject, then its crucial first step is to foreground the relation between work and the body as the site of pleasure, in order to distinguish the act of Antigone from the action of Creon on this ground.

Before embarking on an analysis of these relations, it will be useful to take a look at Hegel's reading from a different perspective, one that will eventually complicate the notion of pleasure. What makes Antigone and Creon equally guilty, in Hegel's eyes, is the fact that in choosing one course of action they thereby lose something that is not merely not expendable, but that sustains, or is the necessary condition of, the very thing they choose. Antigone and Creon act on behalf of the particular and the universal, respectively, but since there is no particular without the universal, and vice versa, each choice ends in a betrayal of that in the name of which it is made. Thinking, of course, of Hegel, Lacan termed the either/or structure of such choices the "*vel* of alienation" and cited the mugger's offer, "Your money or your life," as illustration of its lose/lose possibilities.[10] Once the choice is offered, you're done for—no matter which alternative you take. Between these terms, clearly the only real choice is life, but from the moment of your decision, yours will be a life severely limited by the loss of your wealth.

Now, it would seem that the revolutionary slogan, "Freedom or death," offers a choice with the same alienating structure. If you choose freedom and thereby invalidate the threat of death, you have no way of demonstrating your independence of the life situation, as Hegel argued in his essay on "Natural Law"; that is, you have no way of demonstrating that your choice is free. So in this case the only real choice is death, since it alone proves that your choice has been freely made. But once this decision is taken, you lose all freedom but the freedom to die. This is what Hegel called the "freedom of the slave."

If you attend closely, however, you will notice that the second or *ethical* choice between freedom and death does *not* conform to the first. The description of the first choice as a mugging is meant to underscore what is at stake here; it suggests that this particular choice is a game played entirely in the Other's court. Stumbling into its preprogrammed scenario, you, its victim, might have been anyone at all, and you must react, if you are rational, in a purely formal way, by making an *analytical* judgment, and surrendering your purse. Kant's moral law, "Act in such a way that the maxim of your action may be accepted as a universal maxim," would be sufficient to get you through this urban dilemma; it would prescribe the correct choice. But this only underscores the problem with this statement of the moral law: it still imagines a choice prescribed by law, however formal it may be, and reduces the notion of the *universal* to that of the *common* (*SVII* 77). In this case, everyone must act in the same way, but "must" loses its ethical connotation, since it is now guided by, rather than independent of, external sanction.

In the second example, however, by choosing one does *not* automatically lose what is not chosen, but *wins* some of it, instead. Lacan attributes the difference between the two examples to the appearance of death in the second. It is through the introduction of the "lethal factor," as he puts it, that the revolutionary choice opens the possibility of an act about which it is improper to say that it sacrifices freedom, loses it to the structure of alienation. The choice of death gains freedom. This point is utterly incomprehensible unless one assumes that the death one opts for in the second example is not the same one that is avoided in the first. That is, at the point at which death intersects freedom—which is to say, at the point at which it intersects the *subject*—it ceases to be conceivable in literal or biological terms. The authority for this observation is, again, Freud, who argued that death is for the subject only "an abstract concept, with a negative content."[11] For this reason it does not enter psychoanalysis as such, but only in an altered form, via the death drive. We must assume, then, if we are speaking of the embodied rather than the abstract subject, that what is at issue in the intersection of freedom and death is not biological death, but the death drive. It is to the latter that we owe the possibility of an ethical act which does not alienate freedom nor incur additional guilt. More specifically, it is to *sublimation,* which is strictly aligned with the drive as such in Lacan's account, that we owe this possibility.

My argument, in sum, is that Lacan attacks Hegel's argument by (1) sexualizing work, and (2) debiologizing death in an effort, in both cases, to corporealize the ethical subject. I understand that this appears to give rise to a contradiction: to declare ethical action, as such, a sublimation would seem to purify action of all reference to the body and pleasure. But this apparent contradiction arises from a common, yet faulty definition of sublimation. If one were successfully to show that "sublimation is not, in fact, what the foolish crowd thinks . . . [it] doesn't necessarily make the sexual object disappear—far from it" (*SVII* 161), then the contradiction would be dispersed.

Immortality in the Modern Age

Let us focus our attention, finally, on the act of Antigone. What precisely does she do? Hegel's version is the following: she buries her brother, Polynices, in order to elevate him to the status of "imperishable individuality"; she makes him "a member of the community which prevails over . . . the forces of particular material elements . . . which sought to . . . destroy him" (par. 452). This is Lacan's version: "Antigone chooses to be . . . the guardian of the criminal as such. . . . [B]ecause the community refuses to [bury Polynices, she] is required . . . to maintain that essential being which is the family *Ate,* and that is the theme or true axis on which the whole tragedy turns. Antigone perpetuates, eternalizes, immortalizes that *Ate*" (*SVII* 283). The two versions may appear to be roughly equivalent, but a striking difference (and one which will lead us to observe others) occurs in Lacan's introduction of a word that draws attention to a notion which not only Hegel, but the entire modern period is loathe to look at too directly or closely, a notion that has, since the Enlightenment, become more obscene even than death; this is the notion of immortality. What does it mean to "immortalize *Ate*"? In modern times, it is not only the Greek word *ate,* but also "immortalize" that strikes us as anachronistic.

Yet, although one might have expected the notion of immortality to perish completely, to become a total casualty of the Enlightenment's secularization of reason and its dissolution of the links to its past, the truth turns out to be more complex. For while officially we moderns are committed to the notion of our own mortality, we nevertheless harbor the secret, inarticulable conviction that we are *not* mortal. Indeed, as Hans Blumenberg announces in his monumental book *The Legitimacy of the Modern Age*, not only does the idea of immortality not disappear, it is even "pushed forward by Lessing, Kant, and Herder to the point of the idea of reincarnation."[12] And in his essay "The Death of Immortality?" Claude Lefort similarly exposes the insistence of the notion of immortality within the modern period, remarking that "after the Bonapartist coup d'etat in the middle of the last century . . . the question of immortality [took on] . . . a political import. Astonishing as it may seem to us, in order to be a true republican, a true democrat, or a true socialist, one either had to deny or affirm a belief in immortality."[13] Blumenberg and Lefort both stress that this notion is not a simple holdout from a superseded past, the survival in the present of an old religious idea; it is, rather, a new product of the break from our religious past. But though they concur generally on the need to differentiate the classical from the modern notion of immortality, they are at odds on the question of how the distinction should be made.

According to Lefort's account, the classical notion named a kind of mortal ambition to participate in everlastingness through the accomplishment of great works or deeds, although the deed itself was not thought to have any chance of enduring, ultimately. Since every human effort was conceived as time-bound, none could hope to elevate itself above the temporal flux in order to install itself within the timeless realm of eternity. Thus, while the deed could win for its doer some measure of *immortality*, it could not win *eternity*, which meant that it was worth relatively little. The modern notion of immortality benefits from the collapse of our belief in an eternal realm. Where formerly every deed (and the active life, in general) was thought to fail insofar as it was unable to elevate itself *out of time*, into eternity, in modernity the deed was reconceived as affording one the possibility of transcending historical time *within* time. This is what is new; this idea that the act could raise itself out of impotence, or out of the immanence of its historical conditions, without raising itself out of time. It is at this point that the act—or work in this specific sense—took on a value it could not have had in the classical era. The valorization of work helped to forge, Lefort argues, a new link between immortality and "a sense of posterity" ("DI" 267). The great social revolutions at the end of the eighteenth century may have severed all ties with the past, but they did so, paradoxically, in order to establish a permanence in time, a durability, of human deeds, that was not possible previously. In other words, the "sense of posterity" took place across a historical *break;* what was thus brought forth was "the idea of a conjunction between something that no longer exists and something that does not yet exist" ("DI" 270).

In the argument presented by Blumenberg, the notion of posterity is not linked to that of immortality, but opposes or replaces it instead. This argument is embedded in a larger one, which states that the attainment of complete knowledge by any individual has in the modern age been rendered strictly inconceivable. Within modernity, knowledge is objectified through scientific *method,* which means that it ceases to be a matter of individual *intuition;* that is, methods of objectification transform the process of acquiring knowledge into one that extends infinitely beyond the cognitive compass, and even ambition, of any single inquirer. Along with this objectification, the sheer speed with which knowledge comes into being is superseded and—discarded as useless—threatens to turn the curious into functionaries of the process of knowledge and to render the possession of knowledge irredeemably fleeting and incomplete. For these reasons, no individual, only a generational series of them, can become the subject of modern knowledge.

It is in order to clinch this argument that Blumenberg introduces Ludwig Feuerbach's notion of immortality into the discussion. According to Blumenberg's summary, Feuerbach "extracted the anthropological core" hidden within our modern notion of immortality to produce the following definition: "immortality extrapolated as the fulfillment of theory is the product of the difference . . . between the 'knowledge drive,' which relates to species man, and its unsatisfied actual state in the individual man" (*LMA* 441). In other words, once the rapid and conspicuous progress of modern knowledge makes the individual's limited share in this progress unbearable, the notion of immortality arises as a way of healing the wound between the species and the individual, of assuaging the structural dissatisfaction that emerges from their difference. A kind of error of prolepsis, immortality negates history in order to posit a *spatial* beyond where the future is already waiting to bestow itself on the individual. This error is *modern* because its anticipation of reward is based on the perception of the actual, temporal progress of man rather than on the presumed munificence of an eternal being; it is *mistaken* in that it unjustifiably converts some as yet-unrealized temporal progress into a spatial paradise.

To correct this mystification, Feuerbach argues, man needs to *surrender* the notion of immortality and confront the finality of his own death. This will allow man, unimpeded by otherworldly distractions, to concentrate his energies into the pursuit of his "knowledge drive (*Wissenstrieb*)," which is, for him, a *biologized* curiosity, through which "the interests of the species are imposed on the individual as an obligation, but through which at the same time the individual lays claim to a counterinterest" in his own happiness (*LMA* 444). What this says, in brief, is that only the species is able to accomplish the destiny of man and this destiny is man's happiness on earth. The knowledge drive—which Feuerbach also calls the "happiness drive"—aims at happiness by seeking to know not the answers to metaphysical questions, but only those things that will help satisfy the material needs of man; it thus places man within the cooperative machinery of the human pursuit of knowledge without reducing him to a mere cog, since this machine is specifically designed for *his* earthly benefit, for the benefit of his mortal existence.

While these conclusions are Feuerbach's, one looks in vain in the discussions of Kant and Freud that precede and follow this one in *The Legitimacy of the Modern Age* for some word of dissent from Blumenberg. One encounters instead the dubious implication that there is a *continuity* among these thinkers on the notion of the knowledge drive. If anything, Feuerbach is shown slightly to improve on Kant, for the former not only takes over the latter's position—that there are certain suprasensible ideas which are unsuited to human reason, which we cannot and should not strive to know—he also removes the last vestiges of the spatial metaphor of limits still discernible in Kant. Feuerbach thus allows us to view reason's limits as purely temporal; he teaches us finally that man has no "supernatural knowledge drive" (*LMA* 442). And though Freud's knowledge drive (*Wissentrieb*) is presented as similar to Feuerbach's in many respects, we are warned that in the study of Leonardo da Vinci, Freud does not pay sufficient attention to "the historical conditions affecting [Leonardo's] individual biography (*LMA* 452).

The distortions this continuity thesis precipitates are considerable; I will cite only the most basic. Kant's solution does not, as Blumenberg alleges, wipe out the tension between self-knowledge and salvation, or the immanent and transcendent destinies of the subject, quite the reverse. For in Kant, the suprasensible is not simply eliminated from the realm of knowledge and thought, as it is in Feuerbach; it is instead retained as the very condition of thought. That is: no thought *without* the suprasensible. As far as the criticism of Freud is concerned, that he does not dwell on Leonardo's historical conditions is no indication of a weakness in his theory, but of its positive contribution. For Freud, the knowledge drive is bound up with the solution of sublimation, the problem being to explain how thought manages to escape compulsion and inhibition, or how it escapes being a mere symptom of its historical conditions.

So far I have argued that the difference between Lefort and Blumenberg (or Feuerbach, since on this matter no discernible distance separates the commentator from the author on whom he comments) hinges on the fact that Lefort links immortality and posterity while Blumenberg opposes them. But there is another crucial difference that affects their respective notions of posterity, which also turn out to be dissimilar. The conjunction of immortality with posterity in Lefort takes place through a notion of singularity, which is absent in Blumenberg.[14] Here is Lefort's most concise statement: "The sense of immortality proves to be bound up with the conquest of a place *which cannot be taken,* which is invulnerable, because it is the place of someone . . . who, by accepting all that is most singular in his life, refuses to submit to the coordinates of space and time and who . . . for us . . . is not dead" ("DI" 279).

Someone dies and leaves behind his place, which outlives him and is unfillable by anyone else. This idea constructs a specific notion of the social, wherein it is conceived to consist not only *of* particular individuals and their relations to each other, but also *as* a relation to these unoccupiable places. The social is composed, then, not just of those things that will pass, but in relation to these places that will not. This gives society an existence, a durability, beyond the changing makeup of those relations and the things that come to fill it. If, with the collapse of eternity, the modern world is not decimated by historical time, it is because this unoccupiable place, this sense of singularity, knots it together in time. Singularity itself, that which appears most to disperse society, is here posited as essential rather than as antagonistic to a certain modern social bond. Not only this, but another paradox seems to define it; singularity is described both as that which is "localized in space and time" ("DI" 270) and as *universal,* as that which refuses the coordinates of space and time, which endures throughout time. (Quite clearly, "singularity" is distinct from "particularity," which is also localized, but which we commonly and rightly associate with things that fade with time and distance, with the ephemeral, things that do not endure.)

This notion of singularity, which is tied to the *act* of a subject, is defined as *modern* because it depends on the denigration of any notion of a prior or superior instance that might prescribe or guarantee this act. Soul, eternity, absolute or patriarchal power, all these notions have to be destroyed before an act can be viewed as unique and as capable of stamping itself with its own necessity. One calls "singular" that which, "once it has come into being, bears the strange hallmark of something that *must be,*" and therefore cannot die ("DI" 279). The *must* of this sentence—and thus the immortality of the act—is dependent on its *not* being determined by contingent historical conditions. Significantly, this notion of singularity, which gives rise to our obscure, one might even say *unconscious,* sense of immortality, is associated by Lefort with the writer, that is, with sublimation.[15] For my thesis is that it is through the psychoanalytic concept of sublimation that we will be able to clarify exactly how singularity is able to figure and not be effaced by the social bond.

However incomplete the notion of sublimation remains at this point, it is nevertheless clear that it is *meant* to bridge the gap between singularity and sociality. So the immediate question becomes: what allows Feuerbach to do without it? Or: what *blocks* the emergence of any sense of singularity or temporal immortality in his theory? Recall that Feuerbach entertained (and rightfully rejected) a *spatial* concept of immortality only; no temporal version of the notion (whereby one could conceivably transcend time *within* time) presented itself to him as it does to Lefort. Why not? What Feuerbach sets out to do is to eliminate every trace of transcendence by incarnating the notion of eternity in the finite and forward movement of time, that is: in progress. Yet as we have already suggested, the elimination of eternity presents a unique problem for the modern age; it risks the dissolution of society in a temporal vat. Something has to endure, it would seem, for progress to be even conceivable. In fact, Kant made this very argument: "[I]nfinite progress is possible . . . only under the presupposition of an infinitely enduring existence . . . of . . . rational being."[16] But while he offered this argument in defense of the postulate of the immortality of the *soul*, commentators have pointed out that what his argument actually requires, if it is to make any sense, is an immortal *body*.[17] Feuerbach tacitly acknowledges the problem, as well as the corporeal requirement for its solution, in his proposed notion of posterity as an infinite *succession* of bodies—which nicely avoids the seemingly self-contradictory notion of an immortal *individual* body.

The nub of this solution is sheer and continuous succession. None of the bodies by itself possesses or actualizes immortality in the way the body of the Monarch was thought to during the ancien régime, for example. Succession alone allows the individual inquirer to be taken up and included within the whole without limits of humanity and saves society from the pulverization of time. This solution also soothes the structural unsatisfaction, the unbearable gap, between the individual, whose share of progress is minuscule, and posterity, which "possesses in abundance" the happiness the individual seeks. Finally, this solution allows one to argue that the limits of human knowledge are merely temporal and thus capable of being gradually eliminated.

The Death Drive: Freud's Thesis on Feuerbach

Feuerbach is right to want to snatch life back from eternity in order to insert it into historical time. The problem is, however, that for him, this insertion means that life is only conceivable in biological terms, that is, as *finite,* or as defined by its temporal limit: death. His description of the relation between the human individual and his or her posterity resembles, one could say in this context, Aristotle's description of an animal's relation to its species, which relation, Aristotle argues, renders the animal eternal, a part of ever-recurring life: "Nature guarantees to the species their being forever through recurrence (*periodos*), but cannot guarantee such being forever to the individual."[18] But the irony such a comparison would entail (with Feuerbach's taking *flight from* eternity only to settle on a definition of life that *depends on* it) is ultimately undone when we stipulate that by the *biological definition of human life* we refer not *simply* to its reduction to some ahistorical "animal dimension," but rather to a conception of bodily life that is specifically modern—and highly problematic.

To which conception do we refer, and why is it problematic? At the end of his essay "Critique of Violence," Walter Benjamin isolates this conception when he mentions with disdain the familiar proposition that "higher even than the happiness and justice of existence stands existence itself." Judging this belief in the sacredness of life itself, that is, in the sacredness of "bodily life vulnerable to injury by [our] fellow men," to be "false and ignominious," he speculates that it is probably of recent origin, "the last mistaken attempt of the weakened Western tradition to seek the saint it has lost in cosmological impenetrability."[19]

In *Homo Sacer: Sovereign Power and Bare Life,* Giorgio Agamben follows up on Benjamin's suggestion by tracking the emergence of this dogma, wherein *bare* life, or life itself denuded of any political form or "protective covering," is deemed sacred. While in classical Greece, *bios* (a *form of life,* or way of living, defined within the political sphere) could be, and systematically was, distinguished from *zoe* (the simple *fact of life,* common to animals, men, and gods), in modern society, he argues, *bios* and *zoe* became conflated, making bare, biological life the very matter of modern politics. Agamben thus adopts Foucault's thesis that in the middle of the nineteenth century—or at the "threshold of biological modernity"—natural life became the primary concern of the State and, as a result, politics, as such, was transformed into *biopolitics.* With the development of the "life sciences," the old "territorial State" (in which power asserted itself through the possession and control of geographical territory) gave way to the "State of population" (in which power reigns less over land than over life itself): "the species and the individual as a simple living body become what is at stake in a society's political strategies."[20] It is against this backdrop that Feuerbach's notion of the biologically based "happiness drive" must be understood; it is in this context that its political profile assumes its ominous shape.

If modern political power becomes coextensive or *conflated with,* as was said a moment ago, the life over which it assumes sovereignty, it does so paradoxically by declaring bare life to be *separable from* forms of life, that is, from the political sphere wherein the living individual is accorded certain rights and powers. That is to say, it is only by declaring a (permanent) state of emergency, triggered by the emergency bare life poses, that modern power is able to suspend its self-limiting laws and assume absolute power over that same denuded (or, now, politically vulnerable) life. But if bare life in this way becomes barely distinguishable from the political power that invents it as simultaneously excluded from it and the very territory over which it reigns, *Homo Sacer* remains more interested in exploring the strategies of power than the notion of bare life they construct. The book's references to Foucault are therefore limited to *The History of Sexuality* and *Dits et ecrits,* where the focus is primarily on these strategies of power, rather than on the emergence of the biological definition of human life or, as Foucault puts it, the conceptual "bestialization of man." When Agamben faults Foucault, then, for failing to demonstrate how political techniques and technologies of the self ("by which processes of subjectivization bring the individual to bind himself to his own identity and consciousness and, at the same time, to an external power")[21] converge to produce that form of "involuntary servitude" which characterizes the modern subject, we recognize a need to know more about the biological definition of life if we are ever going to be able to explain how modern power is able to sink its roots so thoroughly—so *inexhaustibly*—into bare life. What is it about this definition of life that allows power to assume such an extensive, even capillary hold over it?

Though not a response to this question, *The Birth of the Clinic,* particularly the chapter "Open Up a Few Corpses," in which Foucault fittingly characterizes biological modernism as a "mortalism," might begin to provide an answer. Placing the French physiologist Bichat in the conceptual vanguard of this modernism, Foucault describes the former's innovation thus:

> [I]n trying to circumscribe the special character of the living phenomenon Bichat linked to its specificity the risk of . . . death—of the death which life, by definition, resists. Bichat relativized the concept of death, bringing it down from the absolute in which it appeared as an indivisible, decisive, irrecoverable event: he volatilized it, distributed it throughout

life in the form of separate, partial, progressive deaths, deaths that are so slow in occurring that they extend even beyond death itself.[22]

The "medical gaze" of which Foucault speaks throughout *The Birth of the Clinic,* the gaze, in Agamben's terms, of sovereign power, is an eye that sees death everywhere immanent in life, sees everywhere this threat to life, and finds in this very ubiquity the excuse for its own insidious and equally ubiquitous control. To the exact extent that life becomes defined by death, is permeated by death, it becomes permeated by power.

To return to Benjamin's formulation, from the nineteenth century on, "*bodily life*" is defined essentially as *that which is "vulnerable to injury,"* by processes of disease as well as by our fellow men. To measure the novelty of this notion, Benjamin asks his readers to reflect on the fact that this essential vulnerability, which we now choose to label *sacred,* bore in antiquity the mark of *guilt,* that is, it was a sign of abjection.[23] Human life has always been known to be vulnerable to disease and death, of course, but only in the nineteenth century did this vulnerability become sacralized, by the discourses of power, as its essential aspect. Agamben, however, departs from Foucault and Benjamin by seeing this notion of bare life not simply as a rupture with previous thought but as the culmination of a gradual solidification, throughout history, of the link between nude or bare life and sovereign power. Thus, when he declares, for example, that "*Not simple natural life, but life exposed to death (bare life or sacred life) is the originary political element,*" it is in the midst of a discussion of Roman law, which is in this sense not so different from that of the modern legal-juridical order.[24]

"Politicizing Death," the penultimate chapter of *Homo Sacer,* opens with a reference to a 1959 study of what two French neurophysiologists termed *coma dépassé* (overcoma), a degree of coma, or of death's incursion into life, involving a much greater loss of vital functioning than that which had previously been allowed to pass for life. The argument of the chapter is that advances in life-support technology have led medical science to redefine death by pushing its limits beyond those set by earlier standards. And as the limits of death are extended, so too are the reaches of sovereign power, which now begins to decide on the fate of a new class of citizens, the "neomorts," or *faux vivants,* that is, the new "living dead," over which power assumes a unique sort of control. What Agamben asks us to bear witness to is the fact that this recent extension of life beyond the cessation of its vital functions and the consequent increase of State power are enabled by the emergence of the life sciences in the nineteenth century, wherein death was conceived not as an absolute and unique event, but as a multiple phenomenon, immanent in life, dispersed through time, and extending "beyond death itself." Yet one of the most original aspects of Agamben's argument, as hinted, is the linkage of the historical account with a metaphysical one. It is, in the end, a certain metaphysical tradition that Agamben wishes to indict for the high crimes of biopolitics (in his narrative, the Nazi concentration camp comes to replace the city as the paradigmatic sociopolitical unit of this politics) because, he argues: by the way in which it isolates its proper element—bare life—biopolitics reveals its fundamental collusion with the metaphysical tradition. That is to say, he views the positing of *bare life* as strictly equivalent to the positing of *pure Being*, insofar as both issue as responses to the encounter with an "unthinkable limit" beyond which these elements are then supposed to dwell, "indeterminate and impenetrable."[25] According to this analysis, a logic of exception or of the supplement has been in place *ab urbe condita*, positing a limit and a beyond to the order of political life; this logic eventually provided support for the notion and construction of the camps. Thus, while divisions may have flickered momentarily in the classical City, Antigone may once have rebelled against Creon, these divisions and that rebellion were always placed at risk by the logic of exception that nourished sovereign power. And now, "we no longer know anything of the classical distinction between *zoe* and *bios*, between private life and political existence, between man as a simple living being at home in the house and man's political existence in the city."[26] Moreover, the current models by which the "social sciences, sociology, urban studies, and architecture . . . are trying to conceive and organize the public space of the world's cities without any clear awareness that at their very center lies the same bare life . . . that defined the biopolitics of the great totalitarian states of the twentieth century," are in danger of simply *perpetuating* this politics of bare, bodily—or bestial—life.[27]

In fact, it is almost impossible to imagine—not only for the reader but, one suspects, for Agamben himself, whose final pronouncements are irredeemably bleak—a model that would *not* risk perpetuating this politics. Ironically, the persuasiveness of *Homo Sacer*'s analysis adds another hurdle to the already difficult task of formulating an alternative. For by focusing, however productively, on historical continuities, Agamben is led to downplay the rupture the nineteenth-century "life sciences" represented, and it is precisely the notion of rupture, of a thought or act that would be able to break from its immanent conditions, which is needed to restore power to life. The most insidious difficulty confronting us, however, is the fact that we remain dupes of the dogma embedded within life; that is, we remain victims of the theme of bodily finitude, or of bare life, which these sciences cultivate. Alain Badiou, in an interview in *Artforum,* makes this important point: "The real romantic heritage—which is still with us today—is the theme of finitude. The idea that an apprehension of the human condition occurs primordially in the understanding of its finitude maintains infinity at a distance that's both evanescent and *sacred.* . . . That's why I think the only really contemporary requirement for philosophy since Nietzsche is the *secularization of infinity*" (my emphasis).[28]

Stated thus and affixed to Benjamin and Foucault's disparaging analyses of the modern sanctification of bestial life, this statement strikes one as a long-overdue correction of certain contemporary commonplaces. Yet its judgment will remain out of reach to cultural theorists who continue to misrecognize bodily finitude as the sobering fact that *confounds* our Romantic pretensions. For these theorists—for whom limits are almost always celebrated, insofar as they are supposed to restrict the expansionism of political modernism and its notions of universalism and will (this is only slightly a caricature)—the body is the limit, par excellence, that which puts an end to any claim to transcendence. What Badiou is here proposing, however, is that our idea of bodily finitude depends on assuming a point of transcendence. Death becomes immanentized in the body only on condition that we presuppose a beyond.

What is needed is not an abandonment of current interest in the body, but a rethinking of it. This rethinking would not have to entail a radical reinvention, for, in truth, another notion of the body has already been proposed, precisely as a challenge to the one offered by the (bare) life sciences. The notion to which I refer is the one suggested by psychoanalysis, where the body is conceived not "biopolitically," as the seat of *death* but, rather, as the seat of *sex.* Contrary to what Foucault has claimed, the sexualization of the body by psychoanalysis does not participate in the regime of biopolitics, it opposes it. Borrowing Badiou's phrase, one could put it this way: through its definition of the sexualized body, psychoanalysis provided the world with a secularized notion of infinity. Or: the concept of an immortal individual body which Kant could not quite bring himself to articulate is finally thinkable in Freud.

Yet notoriously, Freud's conclusion, stated in *Beyond the Pleasure Principle,* that *the aim of life is death*—seems on its face to contradict my assertion. Limited to this statement alone, Freud's theory would appear to be in harmony with the bio-theory of his day, insofar as his theory places the death drive at the very core of life and its various ambitions. Not flinching from this conclusion, even buttressing it by arguing that for Freud there are no life drives, that *all* the drives are death drives, Lacan nevertheless calls into question that simplistic interpretation of the death drive which perceives it to be nothing more than an explanation for the fact that a subject often chooses death or unhappiness rather than her own well-being. Why do people commit suicide or act against their own interests? Because of the death drive. If this were all there were to it, the drive would not have met Freud's own standards for a conceptual validity. Faced with the proliferation of drives invented to account for almost every definable activity ("the drive to collect," "the drive to build," and so on), a querulous Freud insisted that a concept which did nothing more than assign a substantialized cause to a specific, known effect without adding anything new to our knowledge was empty and useless. While one of the effects of the death drive may be the free choice of death, this is by no means the drive's only or even assured result.

The paradoxical Freudian claim that the death drive is a speculative concept designed to help explain why life aims at death, in fact, tells only half the story; the other half is revealed by a second paradox: the death drive achieves its satisfaction by *not* achieving its aim. Moreover, the *inhibition* that prevents the drive from achieving its aim is not understood within Freudian theory to be due to an extrinsic or exterior *obstacle,* but rather as part of the very *activity* of the drive itself. The full paradox of the death drive, then, is this: while the *aim* (*Ziel*) of the drive is death, the *proper and positive activity* of the drive is to inhibit the attainment of its aim; the drive, *as such,* is *zielgehemnt,* that is, it is inhibited as to its aim, or sublimated, "the satisfaction of the drive through the inhibition of its aim" being the very definition of sublimation. Contrary to the vulgar understanding of it, then, sublimation is not something that happens to the drive under special circumstances, it is the proper destiny of the drive. This alignment of the drive with sublimation clarifies a commonplace misconception about sublimation, namely that it substitutes a more socially respectable or refined pleasure for a cruder, carnal one. The common view is hereby amended so that the only substitution involved in sublimation becomes the substitution of something, *jouissance,* for nothing. Lacan summarizes this complex argument by referring to the death drive several times in the *Ethics* seminar as a "creationist sublimation." Significantly, in *The Four Fundamental Concepts of Psycho-Analysis,* in the midst of his discussion of the drive, Lacan quotes the following Heraclitean fragment, appropriating it for psychoanalysis: "To the bow (*Bios*) is given the name of life (*Bios*) and its work is death" (*FFC* 177). The Greek pun is emphasized in order to place the proper accent on life, as it were—specifically, on the form of life. Life may be joined here to death, but not, we will soon see, in the same way it is in biopolitics.

Historically situated at the very "threshold of biological modernity," as a contemporary of Bichat and the rest, Hegel considered

Antigone's act from the point of death. Her deed, he argued, concerns not the living, but the dead, "the individual who, after a long succession of separate disconnected experiences, concentrates himself into a single completed shape, and has raised himself out of the unrest of the accidents of life into the calm of simple universality" (par. 452). That is, Antigone's act may be considered ethical, in Hegel's terms, inasmuch as it involves universal being rather than a particular aspect of it, and it concerns universal being inasmuch as it is undertaken on behalf of a dead and therefore completed being. A problem arises, however, because the universality, or completeness, brought by death is merely *abstract:* it is the product of a natural biological process, not of a self-conscious subject. Antigone's task, then, is to redeem her brother from this first, biological death and this abstract universality by consciously performing a "second death" through her act of *burial.* She must complete for her brother the reflexive circuit of self-conscious life which he, whose life has been finally shaped by death, can no longer accomplish himself. But what is it she is able to reflect back to him, except his own particularity, his own corporeal finitude, now *consecrated* by her act, raised to the dignity of "universal individuality," which can only mean here a communally recognized individuality? Polynices is by this forever entombed in his own "imperishable individuality," his own imperishable finitude. In this way bare, bestial life has been dignified, rendered sacred; Hegel's analysis, supposedly an account of classical ethics, turns out to betray more than a little the thinking of his own day.

For Hegel the fault—the reason Antigone's act is ultimately as compromised as Creon's and results in the sacrifice of universality for the sake of particularity—lies with death. It sunders the journey out from the journey back, divides the circuit of self-reflexivity into mere biological or bodily life (a "mere existent," in his vocabulary), represented by the *corpse* of Polynices, and a bodiless act, purged of desire; the body, divorced from the deed, appears, in Hegel's discussion, only as dead. And the act is powerless to do anything more than enshrine corporeal finitude. In Lacan's estimation, the fault lies with Hegel's ceding too much to biological death, his reduction of the fact of human embodiment to the inevitable fact of death. Indeed, the whole of *The Phenomenology* is structured as a successive series of attempts to master bodily finitude and death, which has at this historical moment, according to Philippe Ariès's massive study, been newly rendered obscene.[29] Henceforth, death must be "civilized," taken up and transformed from the unique and traumatic event it once was to a normal and ongoing part of life. But this means that life itself becomes "finitized," "mortalized," and infinity—which is thus maintained at a distance (to recall Badiou)—taunts life with its shortcomings.

Once again: Lacan's interpretation turns on his recognition that the body is, rather, the site of infinity, of immortality, and his substitution, as we have said, of the "dialectic of the bow"—of the death drive, which sexualizes the body—for the dialectic that enfolds death in life. These are the corrections that lead him to describe Antigone's deed not as a bestowal of "imperishable individuality" on her brother, but as an "immortalization of the family *Ate*." But what does this difference signify in regard to Antigone's relation to the dead, to her familial past, or to the City? And what does it signify, to return to the terms of an earlier discussion, in regard to the relation between the *"individual organism,"* which may be looked at, as Freud put it, "as a transitory and perishable appendage to the quasi-immortal germ plasm bequeathed to him by his race," and the *species?*[30] Finally, how can our argument—that Lacan reconnects body and act, the very terms Hegel's analysis sunders—be reconciled with Freud's contention that sublimation pries the act, whether it be a physical act or the act of thinking, from the body's grip?

Let us begin at the most basic level: death, and only death, is the aim of every drive; this is the Freudian proposition. Where the aim of the sexual *instinct* (which is to be found only among animals) is sexual reproduction, the aim of the *drives* (which Freud sometimes calls the *libidinal drives*) is death.[31] This means to say not only that there is *no original life instinct* directing the subject outward toward an other of the species for purposes of copulation, but also that there is nothing directing her toward the outside world for reasons of simple curiosity, as Feuerbach believed, for example. There is no drive impelling the subject toward any sort of fusion with others, toward "vital association," which would allow "the community of [subjects to] survive even if individual [subjects] have to die"; a notion Freud dismisses as the "Eros of the poets and philosophers."[32] Freud claims categorically that *"there is unquestionably no universal instinct toward higher development"*; we must, then, definitively reject the "benevolent illusion" that there is among men a drive toward perfection or progress (*SE* 18:41; my emphasis). Drive pushes away from or against the stabilization of unities or the dumb progress of developments. But before thoughts of Schopenhauer's philosophy ("death is the 'true result and to that extent the purpose of life'") spring to mind and lead us astray, we must recall that the involuted death drives are described by Freud as working *against* the teleology of a system such as Schopenhauer's and as working instead toward winning for the subject "what we can only regard as potential immortality" (*SE* 18:40). How so?

Directed not outward toward the constituted world, but away from it, the death drive aims at the past, at a time *before* the subject found itself where it now is, embedded in time and moving toward death. What, if anything, does this backward trajectory, this flight from the constituted world and biological death, discover? It will surprise many to learn that Freud does not answer this question negatively by designating the nothing of death or destruction as the actual terminal point of drive, but argues instead that drive discovers along its path something positive, certain "'necessary forms of thought' . . . that time does not change . . . in any way and [to which] the idea of time cannot be applied" (*SE* 18:28). Freud rather surprisingly, but explicitly, quotes Kant in this passage. Why? Is it to bolster the philosopher's thesis regarding the conditions of the possibility of thought, which are not subject to temporal alteration or decay and cannot be absorbed within the temporality of thought itself? Not exactly. Freud does conceive his notion of drive as an intervention in Kant's philosophy, but this notion does not lend credence to the "Kantian theorem that time and space are 'necessary forms of thought'" not thinkable in themselves; rather, it significantly revises that theorem. As we shall see, the psychoanalytic theory of Freud replaces the transcendental forms with an irrecoverable, lost, or separated object.

The aim of the drive, we have already said, is death—or, as Freud alternatively puts it: "the restoration of an earlier state of things," a state of inanimation or inertia (*SE* 18:37). This state exists, according to the theory, only as a retrospective illusion, never as an actual state; but its purely mythical status does not prevent it from having had a long history. Plato's Timaeus, for example, depicted centuries earlier a similar inanimate past when the Earth, created as a globe and containing all things, had no need of sense organs or, indeed, of organs of any kind: "[T]here would not have been any use of organs by the help of which he might receive his food or get rid of what he digested, since there was nothing that went from him or came into him, for there was nothing besides him."[33] Psychoanalysis, it is well known, rewrites this mythical state as the primordial mother-child dyad, which supposedly contained all things and every happiness and to which the subject strives throughout his life to return.

If this were the end of it (and unfortunately, too many think it is), the death drive would be a pure will to destruction or a "will to nothingness," in Nietzsche's sense of the term. For since this original state is mythical, the search for it is vain and would, through its endless and unsatisfiable pursuit, result in the annihilation of heaven and earth; the death drive would always inevitably end in death, in suicide and devastation. But this error forgets two essential facts: (1) that there is no single, complete drive, only partial drives, and thus *no realizable will to destruction;* and (2) the second paradox of the drive, which states that the drive inhibits, as part of its very activity, the achievement of its aim. Some inherent obstacle—the *object* of the drive—simultaneously *brakes* the drive and *breaks it up*, curbs it, thus preventing it from reaching its aim, and divides it into partial drives. Rather than pursuing the Nothing of annihilating dissatisfaction, the now-partial drives content themselves with these small nothings, these objects that satisfy them. Lacan gives to them the name "objects a"; they are, as it were, simulacra of the lost (maternal) object, or as Freud and Lacan both refer to it, of *das Ding*. "Object a" is, however, the general term used by Lacan; specifically he calls them "gaze," "voice," "breast," "phallus." In other words, he gives them the names of bodily organs. Let us clarify why the objects are given these names and how they displace Kant's "necessary forms of thought."

The first thing to note is that Freud's analysis of the subjective constitution of knowledge of reality is concentrated on a genetic account of what takes place, while Kant's is more concentrated, at least in the first two *Critiques*, on a description of the conditions of thought.[34] It is as part of his genetic orientation that the mother-child dyad is privileged in Freud from the beginning. In the 1895 *Project for a Scientific Psychology*, specifically in the section on "Remembering and Judging," this dyad makes an early appearance with the primordial mother appearing in the form of the *Nebenmensch* ("fellow human-being" in Strachey's translation). This *Nebenmensch* is described as "the first satisfying object," and the child's ability "to cognize" is said to depend on its relationship to her. There is from the start, it seems, a structural disturbance of this relation, which is here theorized by Freud as a splitting of the *Nebenmensch*/mother into "two components, of which one makes an impression by its constant structure and stays together as a *thing* (*als Ding*), while the other can be *understood* by the activity of memory—that is, can be traced back to information from [the subject's] own body."[35] In his gloss of this text, Lacan designates the two components of the subject's experience of the *Nebenmensch* as (1) *das Ding*, that part which "remains together as a [*Fremde*, alien] thing" and thus, as Freud says, "evades being judged" (*SE* 1:334); and (2) *Vorstellungen*, ideas or representations through which the *Nebenmensch* can be cognized or remembered. The act of judgment falls then into two parts, as Freud will elaborate more extensively in his essay on "Negation," and the sense of reality is said to be constructed through the "specific action" of reexperiencing or refinding the first satisfaction with which the *Nebenmensch*/mother was synonymous. The various aspects of the mother, what she was like, will be captured by the *Vorstellungen*, the system of representations or signifiers that form the relatively stable and familiar world we share in common with our "fellow human-beings" or neighbors. But some aspects of the primordial mother cannot be translated into these representations, since they are, Freud says, "new and non-comparable" to any experience the child has of itself. A hole thus opens in the system of signifiers, since those that would enable us to recall these new and noncomparable, these singular, aspects of the mother are simply unavailable, they simply do not exist. The *Ding*-component is this alien, untranslatable part of the *Nebenmensch,* which is thus forever lost to the subject and constitutes, as Lacan puts it, "a first outside" (*SVII* 52).

Up until this point it is possible to think simply that the maternal Thing is lost for want of a signifier, that is to say, that the fault lies only with the signifiers. Representation fails, by its very nature, to capture the being of the Thing, which is thus inaccessible to the former. A Kantian analogy would thus suggest itself: the *Ding*-component of the *Nebenmensch* is to the *Vorstellungen*-component as the noumenal Thing-in-itself is to the idea we have of it, its phenomenal appearance. This would make the two components of the *Nebenmensch* a psychoanalytical endorsement of the philosophical separation of thinking and being: as we gain access to language and thus thought, we lose our access to that being which is the maternal Thing. Numerous passages from Freud's texts spring to mind in support of this thesis, including this famous one from *Three Essays on the Theory of Sexuality:* "At a time at which the first beginnings of sexual satisfaction are still linked with the taking of nourishment, the sexual instinct has a sexual object outside the infant's own body in the shape of the mother's breast. It is only later that the instinct loses that object, just at the time, perhaps, when the child is able to form a total idea of the person to whom the organ that is giving him satisfaction belongs."[36] The child is able to form an idea of the mother through thought, but it is precisely thought that forces the child to forfeit its link to the mother.

The radicalization of Freud by Lacan constitutes a refusal to be seduced by this analogy. At the core of this matter of the unforgettable, but forever lost Thing we find not just *an impossibility of thought,* but *a void of Being.* The problem is not simply that I cannot think the primordial mother, but that she no longer exists. Or, it is not that the Other/Being does not exist in representation or thought; more radically, there is no Other, no Being that "stays together as a *thing,*" to recall Freud's phrase. It is this void of Being, this radical *absence* of the Other (and not the Other itself), then, that constitutes the "first outside." But why continue to insist on the unforgettableness of this Other/Being, why not say curtly, "There is no Other," and leave it at that? Why do we not just forget this Being that stays together as a thing? Because we do manage to retain, to apprehend in thought, some trace of its loss.

The point is this: Freud did not rest content with the division of the *Nebenmensch* into two parts, but effectively added a third. In his work on the drive he introduces a term that can only be properly understood if thought in relation to this earlier division. This term is *Vorstellung-repräsentanz,* or "ideational representative" in Strachey's translation. Lacan is captivated by this concept, which he defines in the following way, "*Vorstellungrepräsentanz . . .* is a matter of that which in the unconscious system represents, in the form of a sign, representation as a function of apprehending" (*SVII* 71). Represents representation as a function of apprehending—what? Lacan answers this time, "the good that *das Ding* brings with it," even though a page earlier he insisted that the primordial loss of *das Ding* entails a loss of that Sovereign Good which had once been the goal of classical ethics. There is no longer any Sovereign Good any more than there is a Being that "stays together as a *thing,*" as a "constant structure," or as One. Lacan now informs us that representation, or thought, can "apprehend," can by itself grasp hold of some good. Not some of *das Ding*—this possibility is foreclosed as the subject finds itself perched over *the void of das Ding,* of its perpetual absence—but some good, something in place of *das Ding.* Freud's concept of *Vorstellungrepräsentanz* leads Lacan to formulate his own concept of the object a as that object or thing which is available in lieu of *das Ding.* Object a marks the point of intersection between thinking and being; not an intersection between thinking and Being-as-unified, but being as mercurialized and multiplied and as manifested by small fragments, as it were, of *jouissance.* Let me explain.

The object a is the aim of the drive, that aim being the drive's own satisfaction. In short, the drive is an act of autoaffection, it serves no purpose other than the repetition of its own trajectory. It is, however, very easy to misunderstand this point. Often it is claimed, for example, that the drive is indifferent to external objects, that virtually any object will serve as well as any other to satisfy it. Any object will do the job of satisfying the drive's true object—*jouissance,* object a—which lies beyond the ordinary, external object that happens to have been selected by the drive. A similar misconception forms one of the prejudices against sublimation, which is repeatedly accused of indifference toward the existence of its object. These claims are the precipitates of the same imprecision. The point is not that drive/sublimation is indifferent to external objects; on the contrary, what it is indifferent to, what is of no concern to it, is a beyond, a Being behind appearances. With reference to the scopic drive, Lacan makes a point that is applicable to the drive in general: "In my opinion, it is not in this dialectic between [the thing and the thing itself, the phenomenon and the noumenon] the surface and that which is beyond that things are suspended. . . . I set out from the fact that there is something that establishes a fracture, a bi-partition, a splitting of . . . being" (*FFC* 106). Now, if we disband the old dialectic between phenomenon and noumenon, surface and beyond by insisting that *das Ding*, or the "total idea of the mother," or the All of being, is not just transcendent, not just out of reach to a finite subject, but forever lost, where will we be able to locate the fracture, the splitting of being of which Lacan speaks? If the fracture occurs not between its appearance and that which is beyond it, it can only occur within the order of appearance itself. That is, we must be able to detect a "minimal difference" within a particular appearance or between two or more appearances of the same thing if we are to speak of the splitting of being in the sense Lacan intends.[37]

When Lacan defines the drive/sublimation as the "elevation of an ordinary object to the dignity of the Thing," he does not mean that the drive deigns to include an ordinary, external object in its trajectory as a means to its real end, the sublime *jouissance* it receives as byproduct of its circumnavigation. Nor does he mean that the ordinary object becomes the temporary repository of higher values or the symbol of something greater than itself. In each of these cases the drive would be viewed as aiming not at but past the object, thitherwards. Rather than elevating the object, this would on the contrary demote it relative to the true aim lying on its far side. To raise the object to the level of *das Ding* means to aim for the ordinary object rather than the Thing. This is why an alternative definition of sublimation is the creation of something ex nihilo. There is no Thing, only the void left by its absence; sublimation raises an object out of this void.

Let us dwell a little longer on the dignity of the object. In what does the extraordinariness of this ordinary object consist, then, given the voidance of the transcendental dialectic? The little extra attaching to its ordinariness stems from that minimal difference—the difference that appears in appearance not between what appears and what escapes appearance—mentioned a moment ago. We have been arguing that Lacan's designation of *jouissance* as the aim of the drive does not demote the external object to the status of a mere alibi. Quite the reverse, it is meant to proclaim the object's dignity. It would be preposterous, of course, to speak of the dignity of the instinct's object, which is unceremoniously gobbled or used up once found. Instinct is satiated by the object, but also extinguished by this very satiety. The instinct and its object finish each other off, as it were, as the former quickly has enough of the latter. The drive, on the other hand, does not easily finish with its object, though it is precisely this which is often confused theoretically with getting too little of what the object represents, what it stands for. This confusion takes frustration as the motive of the drive's repetitions, its drivenness, when in fact it is appreciation of the object's self-difference that keeps the drive going.

Since an illustration of this point will no doubt be useful, I would like to consider the work of Jasper Johns. It is not only a particular work—*Target with Plaster Cast,* with its anatomical fragments, or partial objects: hand, heel, ear, foot, penis painted and primly placed in boxes atop a painted canvas target—that brings this artist to mind in this context, it is also his enlightening yet matter-of-fact answers to a series of questions put to him by the critic Leo Steinberg. Steinberg observes that the commonplace objects which are the subject of Johns's work are chosen precisely because "they are nobody's preference, not even his own."[38] For instance, the clothes hangers that appear in some of his pieces are not fine-crafted wooden ones such as might have been selected to connote, derisively or admiringly, values of elegance or wealth, nor the pastel-colored plastic ones one might find in the closet of a teenage girl; they are rather the plain, wire hangers one gets back from the cleaners and to which no one ever really pays much notice. "No attitude of anger, irony, or estheticism alters the shape" of the objects Johns transcribes, rather "it's the way things are that is the proper subject [of his] art" ("JJ" 31). The American flags for which he is perhaps most famous do not "stand for" any specific American values, they are not the flags of a chauvinist or a flag-burner. Yet Steinberg keeps pressing, trying to find some preference to explain Johns's choice of objects. Finally the critic asks for this minimal explanation, "Do you use these letter types [commercial stencils] because you like them or because that's how the stencils come?"—to which Johns replies, "But that's what I like about them, that they come that way" ("JJ" 32). Bull's-eye! This answer hits its mark and Steinberg, recognizing this, uses it to summarize Johns's relation to his objects: "He so wills what occurs that what comes from without becomes indistinguishable from what he chooses."

There could not be a better description of drive/sublimation: *it so wills what occurs that the object it finds is indistinguishable from the one it chooses.* Construction and discovery, thinking and being, as well as drive and object are soldered together. The drive's creation, ex nihilo, of a being, a thing in the very place where unified Being, *das Ding,* is absent, is evoked in this description but without calling up along with it the Romantic image of the artist-creator. On the contrary, Johns seems to disappear, leaving his objects to stand by themselves, "without any human attitude whatsoever surrounding [them]," Steinberg remarks. The objects stand alone; they do not stand for anything else, reflect anything else, not even Johns's attitude toward them. The will that chooses these objects is absolutely Johns's and yet absolutely impersonal. Lacan sheds some light on this paradox when he speaks of the "headless subject"of the drive. If the ordinary objects of Johns's work are somehow disturbing, it is not exactly correct to say with Steinberg that they are "relieved of man's shadow" or "insinuate our absence." What they insinuate is the absence of that egoistic self-consciousness which leads the subject to bow to external circumstances, to the wills and desires—the preferences—of others or to be moved to pity by their pains and sorrows. Johns's work is affectless in the sense that it does not lavish on its objects any of this ricocheted feeling. But this is not to say that there is no subject, no will or passion discernible in the work which, on the contrary, displays a remarkable passion for the plain object. The same objects keep reappearing, as if their ability to fascinate Johns were inexhaustible. The works target a few commonplace objects or, better, they target that difference from itself which makes each object what it is.

The accusation that psychoanalysis is a determinism attacks Freud's core thesis that the subject is driven to reproduce an initial state, to recapture or find again its first satisfying object. Responding to this thesis, Jung concocted the notion of the archetype. This was his way of elaborating what he took to be a basic psychoanalytic belief, namely, that we can find in the psyche of each individual subject "some archaic relation, some primitive mode of access of thoughts, some world that is there like some shade of an ancient world surviving in ours" (*FFC* 153). This will permit us to dub Lacan's object a the "object anti-archetype," for to propose that the object a is what the drive seeks is thoroughly to dismiss everything the Jungian archetype implies about the subject's relation to a primordial past. It is not the past that insists, but its loss.

It is by remembering this, this hole in the symbolic, that the individual subject is able to establish some relation to its "species," to use the term Freud employs in *The Ego and the Id:* "No external vicissitude can be experienced or undergone by the id [or: by the drive] except by way of the ego, which is the representative of the external world to the id. Nevertheless, it's not possible to speak of direct inheritance in the ego. *It is here that a gulf between an actual individual and the concept of a species becomes evident.* "[39] Freud here marks his distance from Aristotle's description of the eternity of animal existence in which the gulf between individual and species is abolished through the obedience of the individual animal to the instinctual dictates of the species. Freud is also far from Feuerbach's description of a purely finite existence in which individual researchers acquire knowledge from those who have gone before and pass it on to others in the future to form a continuous sequence of laboring (and lapsing) bodies which effectively eliminates the gap between individual merit and recompense, virtuous hard work and happiness. For Feuerbach, the species whole reaps the profit the individual is prevented from collecting. Freud articulates a different position precisely because he does not try to close the gap between individual and species which he knows will never be reabsorbed. There can be no direct inheritance in the ego, no continuous line of progress, because the primordial past is not tributary to but that which has been subtracted from the ego's regime. One "inherits" the archaic past only by breaking free of those ties that knit us to current conditions, only by inventing-finding a passionate attachment to a new object-idea. Every such invention necessarily overturns the old order of passions. This is why the act of sublimation will never receive its just reward: it destroys the very possibility of a fixed sphere where accounts could conceivably be kept and from which debts might be paid out. Through the notion of primordial loss, Freud permits us to think the modern subject not as merely mortal nor as eternal, but as corporeally immortal.

The Obdurate Desire to Endure

Antigone exemplifies, we said, that which Freud designates under the term *Haftbarkeit*—or "perseverance"—with all the ethical connotations the word conjures up. She steadfastly persists in carrying out her implacable resolve to bury her brother, despite the remonstrations of the pliant and conservative Ismene and the wavering indecision of her community, that is, the chorus, which is swayed by the merits of both sides to the conflict, just as Hegel will be. In fact, a significant difference between Hegel and Lacan is their respective relations to the chorus. While Hegel places himself roughly in their moderate, pacific role, Lacan exposes this role as merely spectatorial, that is, as one of inaction and he thus disqualifies, or reports on the way they disqualify themselves, from any engagement with the real. Moreover, while Hegel focuses on the merits of Antigone's act of installing Polynices as "a member of the community . . . which sought to . . . destroy him," Lacan views the act of the loving sister as a definitive break with her community: "because the community refuses to [bury Polynices, she] is required . . . to maintain that essential being which is the family *Ate*." In other words, the deed Antigone undertakes traces the path of the criminal drive, away from the possibilities the community prescribes and toward the impossible real. That she is "required" to do so testifies to the *Zwang* or compulsion of

drive, which is indifferent to external criteria, such as the good opinion
of others. It will not be for Lacan a matter of setting another place at the
table, of making room for the one brother who was formerly excluded
from the rites of the community, but of destroying that community in
the name of what is impossible in it. This is not to say that the polis of
Thebes is founded on the forbidding of certain ideas or actions, on declaring them off-limits. The impossible is impossible even to conceive
under existing conditions—how then could it be forbidden? Ismene's
primary role in the drama is to mirror what is currently possible and to
mark the unthinkable nature of her sister's decisive deed; she goes so far
as to express skepticism that Antigone will be able to carry off her outra-
geous plan. Informed by her headstrong sister that she *would* do so, Ismene replies, "*If* you can do it. But you are in love with the impossible"
(ll. 104–5). And when Antigone persists, Ismene's skepticism switches to
warning, "It is better not to hunt the impossible at all" (ll. 107–8).

Lacan rejects Anouilh's portrayal of Antigone as a "little fascist"
hell-bent on annihilating everything in her path. What Lacan opposes is
not the thesis that her deed destroys, but that it is conducted out of a
pure will to destruction, for such a characterization overlooks the affirmation and the satisfaction from which her act derives its unstoppable
force. That which Antigone affirms in no uncertain terms is her love for
her brother which, she insists, must be proclaimed, must be exposed to
the light of day. Ismene is willing to go only this far in aiding her sister:
she will remain silent and not tell anyone of Antigone's crime. It is this
offer which provokes Antigone's greatest ire: "I will hate you still worse
for silence—should you not proclaim it to everyone" (ll. 99–101). This
small exchange goes to the heart of the matter: the singular truth of
Antigone's love for her brother must have a universal destiny, must be
openly declared. The proclamation of love occurs in a passage that has
struck several critics as so strange as to provoke the wish that it would
one day be found to be an interpolation: "If my husband had died, I
could have had another, and a child by another man, if I had lost the
first, but with my mother and father in Hades below, I could never have
another brother" (ll. 908–12). This is the sentiment we express when we
say of someone, "They broke the mold after they made him." Antigone
lets us know that her brother is unique, irreplaceable. There will never
be another like him. His value to her depends on nothing he has done
nor any of his qualities. She refuses to justify her love for him by giving
reasons for it, she calls on no authority, no deity, none of the laws of the
polis to sanction the deed she undertakes on his behalf. She says only,
tautologically, "from my point of view, my brother is my brother." Lacan
summarizes her stance this way: "Antigone invokes no other right than

that one ['this brother is something unique'], a right that emerges in the language of the ineffaceable character of what is ['my brother is my brother']. . . . What is, is, and it is to this, to this surface, that the unshakeable, unyielding position of Antigone is fixed" (*SVII* 279).

Some readers of Lacan may be tempted to turn Antigone's stance into a demand for a certain type of community, one in which the "otherness of the other" would be respected, differences tolerated, a community of "singularities," where by "singularity" is meant that which cannot make itself public, that which is in retreat from publicity and thus inaccessible to others. But the argument Lacan advances does not support such an extrapolation. The point of his reading is not to insist on the radical, unplumbable otherness of the other, quite the contrary. The singularity of the brother is not in doubt, it is his "otherness," his inaccessibility which is in question. That Antigone does not give reasons for her love does not imply that her brother is unfathomable to her but that she is, as even the chorus perceives, autonomous. She gives herself her own law and does not seek validation from any other authority. In other words, it is not the otherness but the nonexistence of the Other on which Lacan's interpretation turns.

Antigone's affirmation of love is, I am arguing, similar to Jasper Johns's affirmative declaration, "But that's what I like about them, that they come that way." Like Antigone, Johns declines to offer reasons for his fascination with targets or American flags or a particular set of commercial stencils; he, too, attests, in Lacan's phrase, to the "ineffaceable character of what is." We are invited once more to taste the tautologism of love, and perhaps now we can say in what it consists, namely: the coincidence, or near coincidence, of the drive with its object. This is what Lacan sometimes called the "illusion of love": one believes the beloved is everything one could hope for without recognizing the role one's love for him or her plays in one's satisfaction. Though her love for her brother does not depend on any of his qualities, Antigone is not indifferent to them; she accepts them all, lovingly. For love is that which makes what the other is loveable. This is not to say that Antigone overlooks part of what he is, that she fails to see that he is a traitor to Thebes or that he has any personal flaws. It means she loves him as he is, the way he comes. This is quite different from saying she loves something ineffable, unfathomable in him. To be sure, the Lacanian phrase "I love in you something more than you," taken alone, lends itself to either interpretation. Everything depends on how one interprets the "something more." Advocates of absolute otherness will see it as an "inaccessible more"—I love your inaccessibility, what I cannot reach in you—while Lacan means to say that this "something more" is accessed through love. If one were to

receive identical gifts or identical reports of an event one has unfortunately missed both from an acquaintance and from a beloved friend,
one would get more, a surplus satisfaction, from the latter. A gift given
by a beloved friend ceases to coincide with itself, it becomes itself plus
the fact that it was given by the friend. The same is true of everything I
get from the beloved, all the qualities, everything he or she is. That is,
the "is" of the beloved is split, fractured. The beloved is always slightly
different from or more than, herself. It is this more, this extra, that
makes the beloved more than just an ordinary object of my attention.

I spoke above of a "near coincidence." The theory of the drive
seems to issue forth in a series of such near coincidences: not only of the
drive with its object, but also the drive with sublimation, and the external object with the object a. It is as if the very element of the drive were
this continuous opening up of small fractures between itself and itself.
Immediately after noting that Antigone's proclamation of love is expressed in the "ineffaceable character of what is," Lacan adds that this is
ineffaceable "in spite of the flood of . . . transformations." Here again
the being, the "what is" that is the object of the drive, is described as ever
so slightly different from itself, as indistinguishable from a flood of
transformations. The singularity of Polynices, what he is, is synonymous
with these *surface* transformations, the ruptures in the order of his appearance. The drive continues to circle the object because the latter is
never identical to itself, is split from itself.

The claim which Lacan makes is not that Antigone immortalizes
her brother, erecting a monument to his memory, but that she immortalizes the family *ate,* that point of madness where the family lineage is undone or overturns itself. "Immortalize" does not mean here to preserve
in memory, but to continue not to forget that loss that permits one to "go
mad," to dissolve oneself in a transforming act. One must not confuse the
fact that Antigone is unyielding in carrying out her deed with a rigidity of
being. If she is able to undertake such a fundamental break with the existing laws of her community, this is only because she has first been able
to unloose herself from the fundamental law of her own being. It is not
only the object of the drive that is split from itself; the subject, too, is fractured through the drive's repetitions. Because the play begins only after
the critical events of her brother's death and Creon's cruel edict, some
readers have been persuaded to see her as simply intransigent, unchang-
ing in the very core of her being. But Antigone is portrayed on the
contrary as a figure of a radical metamorphosis, whose terrifying transformation we are not permitted to witness but are required to imagine.
For the most part this metamorphosis must be supposed to have taken
place just before the play begins, but some trace of it remains in the mes-

senger's report of the screeching, birdlike cries which Antigone emits upon learning that her brother's body has been reexposed after the first burial. It is this wild tearing away from herself, this inhuman rather than heroic metamorphosis that is the subject of Lacan's analysis. For the ethics of psychoanalysis is concerned not with the other, as is the case with so much of the contemporary work on ethics, but with the subject, rather, who metamorphoses herself at the moment of encounter with the real of an unexpected event. Lacan's ethical imperative, "Do not give way on your desire," proposes itself as anything but an insistence that one stubbornly conform to one's own personal history.

In short, the ethics of psychoanalysis filiates itself with Kant's argument that ethical progress has nothing to do with that form of progress promoted by modern industry, or the "service of good," but is rather a matter of personal conversion, of the subjective necessity of going beyond oneself. What psychoanalysis contributes to Kant's basic argument is an account of the psychic mechanisms by which such conversions are effected. The theory of drive-sublimation is the theory of the process through which the subject is able to give itself its own laws of thought and action. This helps explains how Freud, in *Beyond the Pleasure Principle,* happens to cross paths with Kant, specifically with his idea of "necessary forms [or conditions] of thought." But rather than endorsing the Kantian theorem that time and space are the necessary forms of thought, psychoanalysis will propose that thought—that is, actual or fresh thought—always requires new sublimations, new satisfactions of the drive. Antigone's love for her brother or Johns's targets replace Kant's "necessary forms of thought." We could call these drive-objects, or objects a, maxims, or even axioms and say that they are the axioms of Antigone's act and Johns's art.[40] Like an ordinary axiom, the object of the drive is not the product of any prior reasoning, nor does it define the goal of thought or action; the object or aim of the drive, recall, is that which inhibits its goal or final cause. But if the axiom or aim of the drive does not determine its goal, it does assure that the subject will not be indifferent to what the act accomplishes, the results it produces in reality. Antigone's love for her brother does not itself determine what she must do; it supplies the compulsion to act or is that which "convinces" her that it is time to act, to conclude. That is, the aim exerts a pressure toward action, not just any action, but one that is in accordance with the real of her desire. Lacan's intent is not to raise the specific conclusion of Antigone's act—the burial of Polynices—into an ethical principle of psychoanalysis: honor the dead or respect the otherness of the other. He proposes rather, as the sole imperative of psychoanalysis: "One must conclude! Act! Do not wait for the Other who will never arrive."

Antigone's *Haftbarkeit,* her perseverance to the end or to the momentous conclusion of an act that will necessarily overturn her, is contrasted to the *Fixierarbeit* of Creon as conversion, or self-rupture, to modern progress. This contrast lets us observe the difference between "acting in conformity with the real of desire" and acting in a self-interested way, or acting to preserve one's own continuity with oneself. The principle of *Fixierarbeit* is articulated by Lacan as, "Carry on working. Work must go on . . . As far as desires are concerned, come back later. Make them wait" (*SVII* 315). "Work" here signifies something different, something opposed to the act insofar as work never concludes, it keeps going—or rather waiting. What is it that holds progress back, on what is Creon fixated?

To answer this one must refer to the concept of inhibition. In *Inhibitions, Symptoms and Anxiety* Freud offers as a memorable example of inhibition the hand of the obsessional which is suddenly incapable of performing the simple act of writing. To release his hand and the flow of his thoughts the obsessional, it is often said, must first de-eroticize the process of writing and thinking. This theory has no doubt contributed to some of the confusion surrounding sublimation, which is assumed to spring from a separation of knowledge from sex or *jouissance.* But our account of sublimation paints a different picture; sublimation separates *jouissance* not from knowledge, but rather from the supposed subject of knowledge, that is, from the Other. For, the satisfaction of the drive by sublimation testifies to the autonomy of the subject, her independence from the Other, as we have argued. But if the *inhibition of the drive* by the achieved aim of its satisfaction bears witness to the loss of the Other, the *inhibition of the obsessional's hand and Creon's fixation* on the laws of the State betray a linkage between *jouissance* and a supposed subject of knowledge. This does not mean that enjoyment becomes proscribed, that pleasure is forbidden by the Other, but that *jouissance* is now prescribed: "Henceforth you will find your enjoyment in the following way!"

This thesis garners support from something Freud says in *Beyond the Pleasure Principle.* Quoting a phrase from *Faust's* Mephistopheles, he speaks of a "driving factor which will permit of no halting at any position attained, but, in the poet's words, '*ungebandigt immer vorwarts dringt* (presses ever forward unsubdued)'" (*SE* 18:42). This phrase seems to apply to the intransigence of Creon and Antigone, both of whom appear to be, in the technical sense, driven. But Freud then distinguishes this particular "driving factor" from that which produces sublimations. To what does Faustian drivenness owe its unsubduable pressure? This is Freud's answer: "it is the difference in the amount between the pleasure of satisfaction which is *demanded* and that which is actually *achieved* that provides the driving factor which will permit of no halting."

While Antigone is driven by the satisfaction afforded by her love for her brother, which provides the pressure or tension necessary to act, Creon is driven by an idealization of the difference between the satisfaction demanded and that which can be achieved through work. In psychoanalytic terms we would say that Creon is driven by his superego, which is that psychic agency that fosters in the subject a distaste for mundane, compromised pleasures and maintains us in a state of dissatisfaction. Creon's fixation on the lost object causes him to be relatively indifferent to all others available to him. He remains glued to an ideal he will never attain, since it is derived from his nostalgia for what he never possessed. One often hears it said that the superego is an internalization of the laws and ideals of the culture or community; this simplification misses the fact that the laws and ideals of the community are themselves fabricated only on the basis of an idealization of dissatisfaction. If the superego always demands more sacrifice, more work, this is because the ideal it sets in front of the subject is kept aloft by a loss which the subject is unable to put behind him. The superego attempts to mask the loss of the Other by posing as witness or reminder of that absolute satisfaction which can no longer be ours. The stubborn unity of purpose Creon displays is indistinguishable from the aggressivity he unleashes toward everything—even his own ego—that falls short of this ideal. This stubbornness is thus not inconsistent with his failure of nerve toward the end of the play, his bending to public opinion. The egoistic unity produced by such a fixation does not always manifest itself as consistency of character. Since the ideal pursued is formed wholly from a harboring of dissatisfaction, that is, wholly negatively, it can be sought under a series of different banners, as defined by the vicissitudes of public opinion.

The superego thus maintains a rigorous division between that satisfaction available to us and the one that lies beyond. It is possible to argue that there where Agamben has observed the notion of "bare" or "nude" life emerging out of the metaphysical positing of a realm of pure Being, "indeterminant and impenetrable" and located beyond an "unthinkable limit" that separates us from all it offers, there, too, one can recognize the handiwork of the superego. If, as Lacan argues, Creon represents a sovereign law that knows no limit, if he seeks "the good of all without limit," this is because his superegoic positing of a pure satisfaction or absolute goal is founded on the prior positing of an external limit to the world. This limit decompletes, empties out, all his endeavors, all his satisfactions, causing him to strive fruitlessly toward a goal he will never attain. Creon's hounding of Polynices beyond the limit of death prefigures modern science's hounding of the subject beyond death, apparently without limit, into infinitely extendible states (in principle, at least) of *coma dépassé*. When she covers the exposed body of her brother, Antigone raises herself out of the conditions of naked existence.

Notes

1. Jean-Pierre Vernant, "Greek Tragedy: Problems of Interpretation," in *The Structuralist Controversy,* ed. Richard Macksey and Eugenio Donato (Baltimore and London: Johns Hopkins University Press, 1972), 278, 288.

2. Vernant, "Greek Tragedy," 278–79.

3. This is the place to note that anachronism formed part of the very substance of Athenian tragedy; as Vernant remarks, "the surprising fact, often pointed out, is that there are more archaisms in Greek tragedy than, for example, in the epic" (ibid., 283). While the chorus, which was made up of Athenian citizens, responded to dramatic situations remarkably similar to their own, they did so in a lyrical, elevated language that appeared antiquated in comparison with normal speech. Contrarily, the dramatic protagonists of the tragedies represented legendary figures from the past, but who spoke in the rhythms and idiom of the current day. This curious anachronistic stuff of tragedy is precisely what the films of Pier Paolo Pasolini and Jean-Marie Straub and Daniele Huillet attempt to redeploy.

4. A history of the relation of the German idealists to Sophocles' *Antigone* can be found in George Steiner, *Antigones* (Oxford: Clarendon Press, 1984).

5. G. W. F. Hegel, *Aesthetics: Lectures on Fine Art,* trans. T. M. Knox (Oxford: Clarendon Press, 1975), 464.

6. G. W. F. Hegel, *The Phenomenology of Spirit,* trans. A. V. Miller (Oxford: Clarendon Press, 1977), par. 468; this edition will hereafter be cited in text by paragraph numbers.

7. Sophocles, *Antigone,* ed. and trans. Hugh Lloyd-Jones (Cambridge: Harvard/Loeb Classical Library 1994), 45.

8. Jacques Lacan, *Seminar VII: The Ethics of Psychoanalysis,* ed. Jacques-Alain Miller, trans. Dennis Porter (London: Routledge, 1992), 88; hereafter cited in text as *SVII.*

9. Sigmund Freud, *Civilization and Its Discontents,* in *The Standard Edition of the Complete Psychological Works of Sigmund Freud,* vol. 21, trans. James Strachey (London: Hogarth Press, 1957), 80n. (This edition will hereafter be cited in text as *SE.*) Mary Ann Doane, in her fascinating essay, "Sublimation and the Psychoanalysis of the Aesthetic," in *Femmes Fatales* (New York and London: Routledge, 1991), also highlights this footnote.

10. Jacques Lacan, *The Four Fundamental Concepts of Psycho-Analysis,* ed. Jacques-Alain Miller, trans. Alan Sheridan (London: Hogarth Press, 1977), 210–15; hereafter cited in text as *FFC.*

11. Sigmund Freud, *The Ego and the Id,* in Freud, *Standard Edition,* 19:58.

12. Claude Lefort, "The Death of Immortality?" in *Democracy and Political Theory* (Minneapolis: University of Minnesota Press, 1988), 256; hereafter cited in text as "DI."

13. Hans Blumenberg, *The Legitimacy of the Modern Age,* trans. Robert M. Wallace (Cambridge, Mass.; and London: MIT Press, 1983), 443; hereafter cited in text as *LMA.*

14. An examination of the Blumenbergian concept of the "reoccupation of positions" would be a good way to explore the contrast with Lefort further. My own sense is that Blumenberg's notion is a functionalist one, but I will not argue that here.

15. In "What Is an Author?" (*Language, Counter-Memory, Practice,* ed. and trans. Donald Bouchard and Sherry Simon [Ithaca: Cornell University Press, 1977]), Michel Foucault reserves for two authors, Marx and Freud, this singular and immortal status. One might answer the essay's question this way: an author is a writer who, for us, does not die, to whose text we continue to return and whose place is not occupied by any intellectual successor.

16. Immanuel Kant, *Critique of Practical Reason,* trans. Mary Gregor (Cambridge: Cambridge University Press, 1997), 102–3.

17. See Lewis White Beck, *A Commentary on Kant's Critique of Practical Reason* (Chicago: University of Chicago Press, 1960), 270–71; and Alenka Zupancic, "Kant with Don Juan and Sade," in *Radical Evil,* ed. Joan Copjec (London and New York: Verso, 1996), 118–19.

18. Aristotle, *Economics,* 1343b24; quoted by Hannah Arendt in *The Human Condition* (Chicago: University of Chicago Press, 1958), 19.

19. Walter Benjamin, "Critique of Violence," in *Illuminations,* ed. Peter Demetz, trans. Edmund Jephcott (New York and London: Harcourt Brace Jovanovich, 1978), 298–99. Benjamin then adds, in order to forestall any ahistorical objection: "The antiquity of all religious commandments against murder is no counterargument, because these are based on other ideas than the modern theorem."

20. Giorgio Agamben, *Homo Sacer: Sovereign Power and Bare Life,* trans. Daniel Heller-Roazen (Stanford: Stanford University Press, 1998), 3.

21. Agamben, *Homo Sacer,* 5.

22. Michel Foucault, *The Birth of the Clinic,* trans. A. M. Sheridan Smith (New York: Vintage Books, 1975), 145.

23. Benjamin, "Critique of Violence," 299.

24. Agamben, *Homo Sacer,* 88.

25. Ibid., 182.

26. Ibid., 187.

27. Ibid., 181–82.

28. Alain Badiou, "Being by Numbers," interview by Lauren Sedofsky, in *Artforum,* October 1994, 87. Badiou further summarizes his own mathematical, and resolutely atheistic, project by stating: "The philosophical destiny of atheism, in a radical sense, lies in the interplay between the question of being and the question of infinity. . . . Mathematics secularizes infinity in the clearest way, by formalizing it. The thesis that mathematics is ontological has the double-negative virtue of disconnecting philosophy from the question of being and freeing it from the theme of finitude." The covertly theological theme of the

"finitude of man," epitomized by the Heideggerian phrase "being-towards-death" and vaunted by deconstruction, is rigorously challenged by Badiou, who remains faithful (in his carefully theorized sense of this term) to Lacan on this issue.

29. Phillippe Ariès's *Essais sur l'histoire de la mort en Occident, du Moyen Age a nos jours* (Paris: Seuil, 1975) is one of the sources on which Lefort draws for his analysis of immortality in the modern era.

30. Sigmund Freud, "Instincts and Their Vicissitudes," in Freud, *Standard Edition*, 14:125.

31. The contrast is never stated this starkly. Instead, instinct is described as an innate, biological "knowledge"/pressure toward sexual reproduction, while the drive is said to be a kind of derailment of this trajectory; drive then becomes a kind of failed instinct. This description is misleading because it (1) allows a normative viewpoint to take hold, even as it attempts to counter it; (2) obscures the true aim of the drive, which is away from rather than toward the empirical world; (3) muddies the conceptualization of human sexuality; and (4) effaces the double paradox of the death drive. My restatement of the contrast is a strategic intervention designed to help rectify these problems.

32. Sigmund Freud, *Beyond the Pleasure Principle*, in Freud, *Standard Edition*, 18:121–22.

33. Plato, *Timaeus*, 33 b–d.

34. See the essay by Gilles Deleuze, "The Idea of Genesis in Kant's Aesthetics," *Angelaki* 5, no. 3 (December 2000).

35. Sigmund Freud, *Project for a Scientific Psychology*, in Freud, *Standard Edition*, 1:331.

36. Sigmund Freud, *Three Essays on the Theory of Sexuality*, in Freud, *Standard Edition*, 7:222.

37. Alenka Zupancic has brilliantly developed and illustrated this Lacanian argument in an unpublished paper, "Signs and Lovers"; there she makes use of Deleuze's phrase "minimal difference" to describe the splitting of appearance from itself. I am indebted to her fine analysis.

38. Leo Steinberg, "Jasper Johns: The First Seven Years of His Art," in *Other Criteria* (New York: Oxford University Press, 1972); hereafter cited in text as "JJ."

39. Sigmund Freud, *The Ego and the Id*, in Freud, *Standard Edition*, 19:56.

40. Jacques-Alain Miller has stated that he operates from Lacan's texts not *dogmatically*, but *axiomatically*, and the term "axiom" crops up similarly in the work of Alain Badiou.

The Confession of Augustine

Jean-François Lyotard

Blazon

Thou calledst and criest aloud to me; thou even breakedst open my deafness: thou shinest thine beams upon me, and hath put my blindness to flight: thou didst most fragrantly blow upon me, and I drew in my breath and I pant after thee; I tasted thee, and now do hunger and thirst after thee; thou didst touch me, and I even burn again to enjoy thy peace (X, xxvii).[1]

Here, in the middle of book X, we have been hearing him complain, he has been listening to himself groan, has continued to moan, has apologized, has accused himself for being late, for always being behind you. For being delay in person, for never being on time for the encounter with you. He has been accusing you a little: you left me by the wayside, why did you abandon me? The late ones' lamentation, confessing their distraction, they beg to be given another chance.

O thou Beauty, how late came I to love thee, both so ancient and so fresh, yea how late came I to love thee. But behold, thou wert within me, and I out of myself, where I made search for thee: I ugly rushed headlong upon those beautiful things thou hast made. Thou indeed wert with me; but I was not with thee. These beauties kept me far enough from thee: even those, which unless they were in thee, should not be at all (X, xxvii).

Infatuated with earthly delights, wallowing in the poverty of satisfaction, I was sitting idle, smug, like a becalmed boat in a null agitation. Then—but when?—you sweep down upon him and force entrance through his five estuaries. A destructive wind, a typhoon, you draw the closed lips of the flat sea towards you, you open them and turn them, un-furling, inside out.

Thus the lover excites the five mouths of the woman, swells her vowels, those of ear, of eye, of nose and tongue, and skin that stridulates. At present he is consumed by your fire, impatient for the return to peace that your fivefold ferocity brings him.

Thine eye seekest us out, he protests, it piercest the lattice of our flesh, thou strokedst us with thy voice, we hasten on thy scent (XIII, xv) like lost saluki hounds. Thou art victorious; opened-mouthed he gapes at your beatitude, you took him as a woman, cut him through, opened him, turned him inside out. Placing your outside within, you converted the most intimate part of him into his outside. And with this exteriority to himself, yours, an incision henceforth from within, you make your saint of saints, *penetrale meum*, he confesses, thy shrine in me.

The flesh, forced five times, violated in its five senses, does not cry out, but chants, brings to each assault rhythm and rhyme, in a recitative, a *Sprechgesang*. Athanasius, bishop of Alexandria, invented the practice, from what Augustine says, for the Psalms to be read in this way, a modu-lation of respectful voices, in the same pitch of voice, to whose accents the community of Hebrews swayed.

The Inner Human

But is the poem of the five torments a psalm? Or the blazon of a body in ecstasy? The flesh tempers fright, cushions the shattering visit that con-verts it into its truth. Does the flesh have an idea of this shedding of skin, an idea that this shedding reveals its true being? It has no means to think; it feels. It feels, in one, agony and joy. The most repugnant and the sweetest Christian mystery, infinity made flesh, bread and wine, is accomplished without the concept, next to the flesh, in a convulsion. This spasm is the sole witness of grace. It cannot be submitted as evi-dence to the tribunal of ideas, which declines comment: confession does not come under its jurisdiction.

The verse concerning the theme of your visit relates it to the past perfect. Was it the first, the only one? Has it passed? This tense in Latin, *rupisti,* you have broken up, you break up, *fugasti,* you have chased away, you chase away, can also hold for the present. A fore-echo, at the begin-ning of book X, has anticipated the event. In like manner the stretto in a contrapuntal piece can imitate the theme before this theme is entirely laid out, overturning the order of consequents.

The announcement here describes before the event the after-event of your fivefold assault, point by point and in perfect congruence with it.

Before and after collapse, a trait common to all violent affection. The shrine that you have set up in the most intimate part of his person is not a consequence of your visit. The ecstatic pleasure provided by it, that it constitutes, has no history. This is how he speaks of it:

Whenas I love my God, I love a certain kind of light, and a kind of voice, and a kind of fragrance, and a kind of meat, and a kind of embrace—embrace, taste, fragrancy, voice and light which are of the inner human in me, *interioris hominis mei:* where that light shineth into my soul there no space can receive, where that voice soundeth there no time is taken, where that fragrancy exhales there no wind scatters; where that meat tasteth there eating devours not, and there the embrace clingeth to me that satiety divorceth not. What I love whenas I love my God, this is it, *hoc est.* (X, vi)

May the soul, soul-flesh, be thrown out, smitten enough, taken from within, thrown in, inconvenient, free of its aesthetic composure, no more space, no more time, no more limits to sensibility, to sensuality! The assault that bears down upon the soul does not stop transfixing it. The visit is both an encounter and not. Since the trance never draws to an end, it did not begin. The soul, cast out itself in its home, out of place and moment, intrinsically, what could it place, fix, have memorized of an avatar that abolishes the natural conditions of perception and therefore cannot be perceived as an event? Supposing that the syncope takes place once or that it is repeated, how would the soul know— since the syncope deprives the soul of all power to gather together the diversity of instants in a single length of time? Where can an absolute visit be situated or placed in relation, in a biography? How can it be related?

When it is visited, oc-cupied, in the Latin sense of *ob-*, seized by and turned toward what falls upon it, the soul-flesh passes into a phantom state. It invites a fairy-story, a fable, not a discourse. Augustine's *stilus*, to be in keeping with vibrant weakness, bends to the *timbres*, the movement of assonance and dissonance, the rhythms of poetry. Coming from the farthest Near East, reaching out to us, to Rimbaud, through the courtly *canto*, the ancient figure of the erotic blazon lends itself to words, that they may confess holy copulation.

Witness

Not memory, then, but the said inner human, who is neither man nor inner, woman and man, an outside inside. This is the only witness of the presence of the Other, of the other of presence. A singular witness, the poem. The inner human does not bear witness to a fact, to a violent event that it would have seen, that it would have heard, tasted or touched. It does not give testimony, it is the testimony. It is the vision, the scent, the listening, the taste, the contact, each violated and metamorphosed. A wound, an ecchymosis, a scar attests to the fact that a blow has been received, they are its mechanical effect. Signs all the more trustworthy since they do not issue from any intention or any arbitrary inscription, they vouch for the event since they remain after it. Augustine's *Treatises* abound in these analyses of semiotic value: the present object evokes the absent one, in its place.

The inner human does not evoke an absence. It is not there for the other; it is the Other of the there, who is there, there where light takes place without place, there where sound resounds without duration, etc. Explosive and implosive, it is the *plosum,* the plosion canceling the a priori forms of inscription and hence of possible testimony. A witness in proportion to there being none, and there can be no witness of this blow that, we repeat, abolishes the periods, the surfaces of the archive. The tables of memory fall to dust, the blow has not passed. The inner human attests *ab intestat.*

A present oxymoron, in one blow a serene erection and a tumultuous abyss, what was taken for life dies in it, and from out of this death there shines forth true life: *coruscasti,* you have shone, you shine. This classic inversion of the dead and the living weaves its motif through the whole of the *Confessions,* as is the case in the writing of the revelation, in the Psalms, Exodus, Genesis, in John and Paul.

I was tarrying, Augustine confesses in book VIII, the very moment that the repeated words *Tolle, lege, tolle, lege,* take up and read, borne by a child's voice from some neighbor's house, will decide for him what he wants, I was still tarrying, dying unto death or living unto life (VIII, xii). He was hesitating before the abyss of elation.

Cut

Conversion, reversion, inversion, or perversion, however one wishes to speak of it, it is a shedding of flesh, the body is suddenly transformed into soul-flesh. When I asked the appearances of the world, they replied: we are not God, he made us. But that, I the inner human, the soul, I learnt it *per sensus corporis mei,* through the senses of the body and the ministry of the outer human (X, vi). With this body being punctured and penetrated by the other sense, the soul can assume bodily form, be incarnated, flesh find its soul, your presence reside in the inner human.

I sought thee with my animal body, it laboured, *laborans, aestans,* foamed, starved of the true. I fed the brute spadefuls of hungerstoppers, morsels of nonsense, heresies, the fabrications of pagan theater, the masquerades of the Manichean sect. I rolled with it into the depths of gullibility. And yet, thou, thou wert more inside me than my inmost part, *interior intimo meo,* higher than the topmost part that I could reach, *superior summo meo* (III, vi).

The meeting overturns the natural seat of the body, exceeds its great axis at both extremities, origin and head. But this is still little. In truth, the blow is a *cut,* in the sense of the *n*-dimensional space theory. An *n*-dimensional space-time folds around the naturally three-dimensional volume of the body: what would cut into the latter body, a plane for example, which indeed separates two regions of space, loses this property when inserted into four-dimensional space. Its function becomes that of a line in ours or that of a point in a plane, either of which cut nothing.

To conceive the logic of these transformations of space, Augustine cannot rely on Dedekind and Poincaré geometry. For want of this, seeking to represent to himself how you, Lord, are present at your creation, he has the following image: the totality of bodies, including those places occupied by pure spirits if they were bodies, forms one very great mass, as big as I thought convenient, for I could not come to the knowledge of its true expanse, a mass in every part surrounded and penetrated by thee *ex omni parte ambientem et penetrantem eam,* for thou art infinite in whatever aspect thou art grasped. It is, he adds, as if there were supposed to be a sea, which everywhere and on every side by a most unmeasurable infiniteness should only be a sea; and that sea should contain in it some huge sponge, but yet finite; which sponge must needs be everywhere and on every side filled by that unmeasurable sea (VII, v).

Such is flesh visited, co-penetrated by your space-time, disturbed and confused with this blow, but steeped in infinity, impregnated and pregnant with your overabundant liquid: the waters of the heavens, he says. The body, sponge-like in its permeability to the other space-time, exceeds its *sensoria.* Lifted are the blindness waiting for vision from the other side of the visual field, the deafness at the edge of hearing, the anorexia threatening taste, the anosmia smell, and the anesthesia touch. If the human, thus bestowed with grace, is declared to be inner, it is simply because the secret of such an ecstasy remains kept, because the words to express it are lacking. Not easily does grace let itself be revealed.

The confessing I looks for words and, contrary to all expectation, those that come to him are those that make physiology work to the point of pushing the body's sensorial and hence sensual powers to the infinite. The inhibition that naturally overtakes him is lifted, it is metamorphosed into generosity. To deliver the soul from its misery and death, grace does not demand a humiliated, mortified body; rather, it increases the faculties of the flesh beyond their limits, and without end. The ability to feel and to take pleasure unencumbered, pushed to an unknown power—this is saintly joy.

Grace rarely takes a less dialectical turn, less negativist, less repressive. In Augustine, flesh bestowed with grace fulfills its desire, in innocence.

Resistance

Does this mean to say that everything is accomplished, felicity procured with the inner human, life forever vouching for true life? Has the sinner jumped, bags and all, onto the other side of the firmament? Has the dreadful delay that makes the creature run after its truth in vain been filled in, has the accursed time in which the encounter with the absolute is incessantly put off been abolished? No, the pagan, at thirty-two years of age, indeed later, has not finished taking his cup of pleasure as the sun shines and the snows fall on the Aures; not finished either with the games he played with friends in Thagaste, with the rhetorical exploits at Hippo or Carthage, and with the drinking-bouts; and he has by no means finished with seducing pretty girls and mounting his mistress. For appetite is resistant, in the tense body of the African, a pebble polished by the wind, tanned by the sun, broken in to racing, ball-games, and the ways of the bed. And indefatigable remains the rhetor's concupiscence for argument and persuasion, forever vivacious in Rome, Milan, and again at Cassiciacum when, after the said conversion, he retired from the practice of law. Sure of their means as they are, indifferent to their ends, muscle stiffens against the Other's hold, neck refuses to let pass the word that is not its own.

What a scandal, the other flesh, the other voice parasiting his own voices, what an aversion, the conversion! His body and speech, brought up to dominate and to exude sensuality, do not bend unprotesting to a regime whose *rex* is not him and whose rule lies beyond his grasp. The course of real life, biography, gives lasting resistance to the improbable event of your coming.

At the end of the book of hours page after page of which the will runs out of breath from confiding itself to the Other, that his will be done, the very last words of the *Confessions* repeat, hammer out in vain the promise. For they still exhale the bitterness of the unaccomplished:

Thou being the Good, needing no good, art at rest always, because thy rest thou art thyself. And what man is he that can teach another man to understand this? Or what angel, another angel? Or what angel, man? Let it be begged of thee, be sought in thee, knocked for at thee; so shall it be received, so shall it be found, and so shall it be opened (XIII, xxxviii).

You will open your door, it will be crossed, entry will be had, for certain, it's a promise—for those at least who are of the elect. But it's for tomorrow, it still lies in the future, one has to be dead already, once time is over.

On the point of resting his *stilus* after thirteen books of contrition and celebration of grace incarnate, the penitent finds himself on the threshold of your door, still stuck in the thick pall of affairs, pulling in every direction on the harness of the before, of the after, wishes, sorrows, pleasures. He has aged in vain, the young master, the brilliant seducer, old in matters of devotion, an eye always watching the seeds of evil growing everywhere. It is as if, encysted in the folds of the bishop's holy soul, the sexual—for it is it—turns out to be of such stamina that, next to it, the small change of chance encounters of ecstasy, the parsimony of secret meetings with the Other count for nothing.

You will have not brought the stray one to your step, a step that never advances. Futile history continues, the world of death is not dead. The other time, without duration, the other field without horizon, yours, cannot be measured by the *gnômon,* the compass of living creatures. As your years do not end, your years are always the day of today. But thou art the same still. And all tomorrows and so forward, and all yesterdays and so backward, thou shalt make present in this day of thine; yea, and hast made present (I, vi).

Distentio

It is scarcely as if the assault of your eternity signs itself, with a syncope, with what is, after all, a nothing, in the calendar of days. A tiny wing, come from elsewhere, brushes him very lightly with your presence, it does not take him away from the concerns of his dead life. Your visitation is almost indiscernible when compared to the slow beat of habit and the dissipation of desire.

The euphoria of a drunken beggar encountered in the street, Ambrose, his open door, him reading in silence, the fresh voice from the neighboring house reaching the fig-tree in the Milanese garden where Augustine cries prostrate on the ground—this makes for a highly discreet, not to say impish signaling of the absolute. These few signs, threaded within the tissue of the things of life, are rarely made out by him, and certainly never immediately, as signs with a calling value, smoothly coated in the facile evidence of reality.

Only after the event, when the uneasiness will have prevailed, when the worry of having gone astray concerning the direction of his life will have driven him to scrutinize the past in order to tear from its loquacious silence what this past perhaps meant, or means for him now, only then, through memory, or rather through anamnesis, will he recompose the hidden semiotics bestrewing his history. Yet he will have been blind, hurriedly thrown, without him knowing, upon paths unbeknown to him, right to the end.

Strange misrecognition, a distraction, a leading astray more essential, more archaic than your truth, one would say. For time itself, the time of living creatures, the time that he calls created, is the child of this permanent self-absence. To go blank is what we say for a lapse in memory, but what falls out into the three temporal instances is the oblivion inherent to existence itself. Past, present, future—as many modes of presence in which the lack of presence is projected.

The delay that throws the confessing I into despair is not due to a failure in its chronology; no, *chronos,* at once and in its entirety, consists in delay. Even the shattering visit of the Other, even the incarnation of grace, if ever it truly arrives, from the fact that this visit subverts the space-time of the creature, it does not follow that it removes this creature from the hurried, limp course of regrets, remorse, hope, responsibilities, from the ordinary worries of life.

But it's worse than that. Delighting with your presence in such sudden ecstasy, he feels more in dissociation with himself, cleaved, alienated, more uncertain of what he is than usual. But thou, O Lord my God, hearken, behold and pity and heal me, thou in whose eyes I am now become a question to myself, *mihi quaestio factus sum et ipse est languor meus,* and that is my languor (X, xxxiii).

Lagaros, languid, bespeaks in Greek a humor of limpness, a disposition to: What's the point? Gesture relaxes therein. My life, this is it: *distentio,* letting go, stretching out (XI, xxix). Duration turns limp, it is its nature. But more so from the fact or phantasm of the Other's visit. The everyday ego tries willy-nilly to gather the dispersion of what befalls it under the unity of a single history. Broken, sundered by the blow of your encounter, it grows anxious: Where am I, who am I? And the languor lulls to sleep the straying of a: But, after all, so what?

The Sexual

The endurance of the sexual is its *flaccidity*. It bends, it slips, it does not confront. Its flights of anger are, precisely, flights. The sexual is not sub-jected to time if Freud is to be believed, and on occasions dispatches in its course offspring who disorganize it and are remarked within it. Au-gustine's confession is still inspired by another motif which, together with the preceding trait, confers upon the power of the sexual a more fearful inconsistency, that of structuring the entire course of experience. A-temporal as it is, enemy as it is of chronological order, this powerless power would also be, so to speak, the agent, the bearer of what is recur-rently deferred, making the triple instance of time, or temporal exis-tence what it is: the not yet, the already no longer and the now. From book XI of the *Confessions* Husserl reads off the phenomenology of the internal consciousness of time. In this book Augustine sketches out from below a libidinal-ontological constitution of temporality.

The sexual continuously surprises, takes from behind, works from the back. Upright resolutions, probity and the honest promise—the sex-ual lets all things go; it will pass. Somnolence is its accomplice, much stronger than vigilance. Representations, *imagines,* lascivious things, fixed by sheer habit, if they assail me when I am awake, they are without force, but when I am asleep, they take me off into pleasure and, what is more, to consenting to pleasure and to experiencing it, as if it were real. So powerful is the error induced in the soul and in the flesh by these im-ages that the scene which, feigned in sleep, seduces me is unable to do so when I am awake. Does that mean, the confessing I worries, that I am not myself, O Lord my God, when sleeping? (X, xxx).

The other of the I, the *ipse,* is indeed awake when I sleep. But is not thine hand that can do all, he pleads, able to cure the languor, *sanare languores,* of my soul, *lascivos motus mei soporis extinguire,* and quench the lascivious motions of my sleep (X, xxx). Sleep does not belong to I. An-other principle, another prince exercises at its own pace on the stage of the dream the langorous and lascivious illusions. When the master's lieutenant, controlling the passions and upright in chastity, is on leave, what can the master do? Has he not given the conjurer the reins?

So great is the sovereignty of artifices that the dreamer has trouble distinguishing them from dreams that you have sent him. Monica, the mother, was so happy to be able to tell, from whatever relish it was, she said, which she could not put into words, those dreams where your pres-ence was revealed from those of her own spirit (VI, xiii). Happy are they, he exclaims, who, seized by an unexpected motivation, contrary to every rule, know that it was thou who gave the command (III, ix). Your signs are deciphered by Monica whatever state she is in, awake or asleep. The wooden rule on which she sees herself in a dream perched with her son near, she knows it to be the rule of faith, and Augustine, then sunk in debauchery, will not fail to embrace it (III, xi).

As for him, it is not that he hears your call, he does not want to hear it. Like a sleeper after whom one urgently calls: Arise, here is true joy! And he persists in playing with his fantasies. Ears open, members deaf. A little more of not yet. The languor of the later excites the immediate.

He is told of sudden conversions: that of the very pagan Victorinus, *iam me esse christianum,* would you have said that I am already a Christian? (VIII, ii); that of two young wolves from the entourage of the emperor— at the sight of a *Life* of Anthony lying open in a wooden hut, what is one doing with one's eye still upon the favors of Valentinian, while to be the friend of God, however little I may wish it here, I am even now, *si voluero, ecce nun fio* (VIII, vi). These edifying narratives reach him with clarity; misted over with the charm of the magical, they add to his impatience, but also to his patience. He clearly hears the Arise thou that sleepest that Paul shouted at the Ephesians, but he cannot get up (VIII, v). Much better were it for me to give myself up to thy charity than to give myself over to my own covetousness, but notwithstanding that former course pleased and convinced me, yet this latter seized me and held me confined (VIII, v).

Two attractions, two twin appetites, almost equal in force, what does it take for one to prevail upon the other? A nuance, an accent, a child humming an old tune? Who speaks here of transcendence when divine grace is placed at the same level as a charm? Evil is perhaps not substantial, as the Manicheans believe, just a matter of willing, asserts the repentant, of, that is, desire. But evil is to desire the good just as one desires evil.

Consuetudo

See, here I come, just a moment more. But the moment does not pass, there is no sequel (VIII, v). Laziness prevents even the deciphered signs from being put to work, a sluggishness concerning change, which he names *consuetudo,* the quietude of *ipse* close to *ipse.* A stagnant energy, *lex enim peccati est violentia consuetudinis,* since the law of sin is the violence of custom, a law without law, the customary law of what is done, what has always already been done (VIII, v).

It is neither that concupiscence balks at undergoing too severe a treatment, nor that it is threatened by the practice of faith with an awesome castration, in the manner of Tertullian's radicalism. No, the taste of pleasure can find its happiness in the Christic *caritas*. And the blazon has made us hear with what stunning sensual exultation—fantasized or real, where is the difference if one is used to sleeping?—with what ecstatic pleasure is enacted the rape perpetrated by the Other. This ravishment is also undergone in surprise, there is no need to get to one's feet, to confront the Other head on, to experience the delights of torment—rather the contrary.

To the being lying in custom nothing must happen but from the back. Just as he is on the verge of agreeing to get up, the old girlfriends, the amusing toys, the adorable vanities pull him back, hold onto him fast: And shall we no longer accompany thee from this time for ever? And what were those things which they suggested to me in that phrase this or that? This and that, O my God, you know well, he entreats, what impurities, *sordes,* what most shameful things, *dedecora,* did they suggest to me, muttering as it were softly behind my back *a dorso mussitantes* (VIII, xi). As if, he feigns believe, they wanted him to turn around toward them. Nothing of the sort, however—he and they are used to being taken by surprise, only to being themselves by surprise, for dirty habits have no need of a contract, they are contracted *a tergo.* With *consuetudo violenta,* the custom of being violated by custom, turpitude is so violent that it need only murmur: Thinkest thou to be ever able to live without all that? (VIII, xi)—women, concubines, the unclean world of the other sex, it takes but a faint whisper to keep him on the bed a little while longer.

Concupiscence waits for it to be too late, temptation lingers on, pleasure will come in a catastrophic rush, the I will have been able to do nothing to ward off the rout. This future anterior in the negative sets the future upon a powerlessness that is always already accomplished. And the *ipse* comfortably nestles its fatigue into this time of lifeless relapse. Giving itself up to it, in the course of Augustine writing, the *ipse* eludes the cruelty of a real beginning, of adieus, of fright.

The *ipse* is unable to face the adventure of an unknown future, to envisage it in itself, by itself, for itself. Sedentary. The *ipse* ought at least to be wrung out, to be shown its behind from the front, completely naked, abject, presented to the horrified look of uprightness. While listening to the story of Ponticianus that tells of the conversion of ambitious courtiers, Augustine experiences, he says, the inverse torture, that of being pulled up straight. Lifted up from his back while asleep, he is cast straightaway before his own eyes: turpid, unsound, sordid, bespotted, ulcerous, the arse of a turned-over carrion, a sight to be abhorred. The Lord's grip holds him fast, with his nose over the filth, that he may loathe it, that he may decide to flee that self, *ipse,* and cast off the moorings, bound for you.

In vain, however, yet again the straightening effect that the example of the true departure was meant to create, soon fades, however tormenting it was; it is cushioned, absorbed within the elasticity of the constant return to the same. It is not, he says, that I did not know my infamy, I had dissembled it, had winked at it, and forgotten it (VII, vii).

Oblivion

Oblivion, the great concern of the *Confessions,* if it is true that to confess has as task to hide nothing any longer, to shed light upon what has remained crouched in the night of life and to offer it up and return it to you, the giver. At the beginning of the fifth book: Receive here the sacrifice of my confessions, *de manu linguae meae,* from the hand of my tongue which thou hast formed and stirred up to confess unto thy name (V, i). In true sacrifice, the confession gives back to him who first gave and gives forever. In the event, the reciprocity of roles appears so close that the writer leaves unsettled whether it is he, the sacrificer, who is the author of the offering, or you. If your Word or his tongue will have written these memoirs. He will not know, and you are silent.

Since to confess is to bring into language, to language what eludes language, the object to be sacrificed, the most precious possession that one has, as must be the case, is here silence. To confess explicitly to that which has said nothing and says nothing, to give what one has not been, what one is not, is the exorbitant work to which Augustine harnesses himself: a working-through, we would say today.

It is, then, childhood that is brought first to the altar, which not having the use of linguistic signs, *in-fantia,* has left no traces for which I can answer before you. For what have I to do with it, whereof I can no vestige recall to memory? (I, vii). Beginnings absolutely unknown, conception, uterine life, birth, breast-feeding, crib-rage, senseless gesticulations, jealousy towards the suckling-brother at the breast, this period of my life that I did not live, and that has been reported to me.

Is it a sin? It is the sin of time, delay. The encounter with the act is missed from the beginning. The event comes before writing bears witness, and writing sets down when the event has passed. Confession reiterates this condition of childhood measured against the scale of full presence: I will have always been small with regard to Your greatness. You, you who had no childhood, you are not transported into the oscillations of too soon and too late. Thus forms, infantile, the imago of the perfectly erect, pure act, word absolved from antecedent and consequent. The little one honors the great one with tiny names, with *hoc,* with *id,* with *id ipsum,* this, that, that itself: that—a deictic without object, bearing in ontology the name of that which has none, eponym, anonym (VII, xvii; IX, x; X, vi; XII, vii).

The small child undertakes to learn and make known what he does not know, confident, with Matthew, that it is to little children that thou hast revealed, and from the learned that thou hast hidden (VII, ix). Confession is written posthumously, in search of the *anthume,* in *distentio* then. And *distentio* recurs, returns in the quick of confessive writing. The delay that this writing seeks to fill in, to retrace through running after you, through running after the act—this delay is not to be caught up. The very time taken for the proclamation of the instant of your actuality to be written down, the time taken to go through the delay again, to obtain pardon for misspent time, the raised hand of pagan sequestration, the pardon for heresy, absolution for debauchery—confession aggravates the belatedness of this time lost in gaining time over time.

Is the confessing I innocent in all this?—Is there not a little pleasure afforded in deferring, in squandering, in diverting urgency into childish pursuits? The great wealth of style deployed in petitions and celebrations, the courtly figures of speech dispensed in abundance with the pretext of persuading a judge who has no need of persuasion (since he already knows all there is to know), the flowers of poetry sampled here and there, the falsely wise arguments aiming to give substance to a metaphysics that is, after all, nothing but a hazardous allegoric and one, what is more, that is lax in its interpretation—one is led to suspect that such decorous language, a language so full of pathos, is yielding to the pleasure of length, to its being drawn out, to the languor found in the very avowal of the sin of languor. From behind his back, as ever, the old young female partners in sin, dispensers of this and that, murmur to their denouncer the supreme vanity—to play the great writer. Of scorning vainglory, he brazenly writes, one can provide oneself glory all the more vainly (X, xxxvii). What a way, indeed, of asserting the fact that he is worth nothing! He had to write to save himself from oblivion, and yet through writing he forgets himself . . .

Temporize

But, all the same, will it be said, memory is his main weapon against forgetfulness? One can even remember having forgotten, he remarks (X, xvi). Before reviewing each concupiscence, he sets out in book X to explore the vast *praetoria* of memory, its palaces, its treasures. He draws up a systematic inventory of memories stocked on the shelf, each by category: images of corporal sensations, catalogued according to which sense, easily available; then, a little to one side, but retrievable through study, the elements of thought, its tools, the problems, the notions; finally *affectiones*, the affects, which memory retains but, like a stomach that holds its food, deprived of taste. The memory of a joy is not joyous, emotion is something actual, nothing is retained from it but the tasteless occurrence. That the affective quality is lost is at least not lost.

What is the balance of this inventory: that memory is solid, trustworthy, that it is in truth mind itself, all *animus?* Not at all. He comments: memory, what energy it has, what energy it is! It exceeds my forces, those of me, the ego, it is a field of hindrances and sweat from my labor, something horrifying, folds upon folds, dens of them, innumerable, a life so various, so full of changes, vehemently immense, *immensa vehementer* (X, xvi). I turn and flit about from one to another, mining into them as far as I am able, and *finis nusquam,* and there is no end in sight, nowhere. So great is the energy of memory, so great the energy of life, he concludes, in this man who lives of mortal life, *in homine vivente mortaliter* (X, xvii).

These last words say it: the overall balance is actually disastrous. The I can try as it likes to reassure itself, putting finishing touches to the lucid taxonomy of memories. The contents of memory, however, all that can happen to the *ipse* in the course of life, reverberate with a chaotic dynamic that condenses, displaces, topples over their images into each other, disfigures them endlessly. Behind the guardian of time, supposed to watch over its order, under the wing of memory, the work of the drives persist in turning languid the seizure of events. The clear phenomenology of internal temporality covers over a strange mechanic, a grammar of the ways in which concupiscence conjugates essential frustration.

It is not of mind itself, as it is written, *ipsius animi,* that time turns out to be a threefold *distentio,* but, within the mind, of the desire that bears three times the mourning of its thing (XI, xxvi). When he expects it, *expectat,* the *distentio* pre-poses and proposes to come; when he seeks to apprehend it, by dint of attention, *adtendit,* it is ex-posed and supposed in the present; when he gives it to himself in such a way that it is retained, *meminit,* it is deposed and reposes in the past. These object positions are never posed, but indisposed, apt to slip away, since it is dispropriation that gives them birth. The object is only there to the extent that it is not there, it passes in transit, its present nickname does nothing but streak with the tiniest of flashes the interface between two clouds of nonexistence, the not yet and the already no longer. Impatience, boredom, haste or suffering lengthens time, pleasure or surprise shortens it. Time is measured by *affectio,* in the singular mode in which things touch us in their eclipse, *affectio quam res praetereuntes in nos faciunt* (XI, xxvii).

The *ipse* shall not have, does not have and did not have what it desires. It lacks being, and drugs its privation in temporal mode. It lives a mortal life, it survives, outlives itself, arranges it such that it is never on time for its objects, it *temporizes.* Temporality is its settling down, to *ipse,* its way of getting on with the unaccomplished, with custom, with the deferment of the act. The times decline deception, time bows and relinquishes presence.

Immemorable

And the Other, then, the true? You, where does he find your trace in this disorder of muffled deceptions? He reasons thus: time is disastrous? But, precisely, the essential frustration that gives birth to him receives his seed with a constant, universal appetite, one that does not tolerate laziness, that is uncompromising towards any transaction: the desire to be happy. Now you alone, being perfect, can give the *vita beata. Gaudere ad te, de te, propter te,* to rejoice concerning thee unto thee and for thy sake: this is the happy life, and there is no other (X, xxii). He encounters, or believes he encounters, this mad, perfect joy when you come to visit him, crushing his skin and soul. But, then, who is he at that moment, what is that that he loves when he loves his god? Does he remember?

The I that holds the *comput* of his life asserts its rights: the memory of the perfect does indeed figure, he claims, in the archive. See now, how many spaces I have run over in my memory seeking thee, Lord; and I found thee not outside it. For I find nothing at all concerning thee but what I have kept in memory, ever since I first learnt thee: for, he insists, he swears it is so, I have never forgotten thee, since the time I first learnt thee. Since therefore I learnt to know thee, hast thou always kept in my memory; and there still do I find thee, whenever I call thee to remembrance, and delight myself in thee (X, xxiv).

Note, however, the restriction: from the moment that you were known to me. The avowal is enough for the soul-flesh to appeal to the authority of the mind: where, then, did I find thee that I might learn thee? (X, xxvi) The soul-flesh objects: For in my memory thou wert not before I learnt thee! And concludes: In what place therefore did I find thee, that so I might learn thee, in what place but *in te super me,* in thee, far above me? (X, xxvi) Supposing that the mind could have miraculously kept trace of an encounter that does not take place in its place or time, its memory would still be worth nothing. Just as the succulence of a morsel of meat held in the mouth is lost when digested by the stomach, conscious memory would, at best, only retain from the encounter an episode purged of the formidable emotion that metamorphoses flesh and soul.

How would such a *memorandum,* without body, testify to the presence of the Other? Not upon the standing of the I, well-trained to think, nor in the soft tissue of the spongy *ipse,* but in those *vacuomes* full of you, in you, then, on the hybrid edge that you weave, in a web of sophistry, for me above my head; there alone you fall upon me, you despoil me, you transport me away. True life, happiness jump like flying fishes in my lapses of memory, pockets for your ocean, breaks in the clouds for your sky.

Differend

Dissidio, dissensio, dissipatio, distensio, despite wanting to say everything, the I infatuated with putting its life back together remains sundered, separated from itself. Subject of the confessive work, the first-person author forgets that he is the work of writing. He is the work of time: he is waiting for himself to arrive, he believes he is enacting himself, he is catching himself up; he is, however, duped by the repeated deception that the sexual hatches, in the very gesture of writing, postponing the instant of presence for all times.

You, the Other, pure verb in act, life without remainder, you are silent. If he encounters you, the I explodes, time also, without trace. He calls that "god" because that is the custom of the day, theology also being a work of custom. And, here, the differend is such, between your vertiginous visitation and thinking, that it would be as smug as the last, as false and as deceptive, to explain that not the name of god but that itself, *id ipsum,* far above me, the mad joy, proceeds from the sexual. Who can take the common measure of something incommensurable? A form of knowledge that vaunts it can do so, in bestriding the abyss, forgets the abyss and relapses. The cut is primal.

Notes

This chapter is reprinted with permission from Jean-François Lyotard's *The Confession of Augustine,* trans. Richard Beardsworth (Stanford: Stanford University Press, 2000), 1–36.

1. Augustine, *Confessions,* trans. William Watts, 2 vols., Loeb Classical Library, Cambridge, Mass. (Harvard University Press: 1989). (The translation will be revised where appropriate—Translator.)

The Limits of Ethics and History

Joseph Margolis

1

The human condition is a strange hybrid, an indissoluble mix of the biological and the cultural, not a compound of separate layered natures. It may be characterized as an initial potentiated nature (what we know as *Homo sapiens*) transformed and emergent under conditions of enculturation as a history incarnate in that nature: a *self*, in short, and such only among a society of similarly apt enabling selves. There is no compelling reduction of the cultural to the biological or the physical. There is, therefore, no reduction of the cognitive or the ethical or the historical. We understand ourselves under a condition of endogenous limitation; since, for one thing, nothing else in nature understands itself; and, for another, the conditions of understanding make sense only at that level at which the infant members of *Homo sapiens* first become selves, the functional sites of languaged thought and judgment, of the capacity to report experience and perceived events, the capacity to share a culture, to communicate in its terms, to plan and act in the way of choice. All this falls within the bounds of nature without being "naturalizable" in the sense now favored in Anglo-American philosophy: that is, the sense of describing and explaining whatever belongs to languaged thought and history in causal terms restricted to whatever explains nature "below" that level.[1]

This, therefore, is not a neutral report about the peculiarity of human history. It is, rather, a characterization that could not have been offered persuasively or comprehendingly before the work of that boldest period of modern Western philosophy, the post-Kantian, which, primarily through Hegel, descends through Marx and Nietzsche down to our own age. For, at the end of that descent, both in evolutionary and historical terms, we understand ourselves, as selves, as artifacts of history.

But if so, then history cannot be confined to what is merely ephemeral in the human world: for we ourselves are histories. Correspondingly, what is constant in the way of human understanding is such only in historied terms. We occupy a niche in nature in which we know, because we make, the sui generis order of the cultural world that makes us in turn. In that sense, what is constant is not invariant but only legible to ourselves—what, relative to an interpreted past, may be construed as an evolving innovation that fulfills that past's potentiality. For this reason, none of the forms of intelligible order correctly assigned to nature apart from culture can be counted on to be descriptively or explanatorily adequate, except in the sense, top-down, of potentiating the emergent world it incarnates.

Every other thread of theory about history produces paradox. For if, as Aristotle seems to suggest, history collects no more than the ephemera of human lives, then history barely has significance at all; and if history is genuinely important, then the supposed "accidents" of history cannot be confined to the transient appearances of essential human nature drawn from one contingent vantage or another, that is, subordinated to one or another form of an ahistorical science.[2] The Greeks had a sense of history, of course. It's palpable in Aeschylus and Thucydides. But for such intelligences, as indeed for Aristotle, the meaning of history lies outside of history, in the sense in which the supposed fixed norms of human life bring the contingencies of time and causality into line with what no such contingencies can alter. History, for the Greeks, is the narrative form of the meaning of human life, which history alone cannot possibly discern: it waits to be recovered through the distraction of such ephemera.

In the Christian world, history is assigned its hidden telos in the unfathomable purpose of God's creation. Hence, as in Saint Augustine's tireless letter explaining the sack of Rome, we come to know enough of history to understand that; and, knowing that, we understand that if we learn to love God we may do as we will and nothing in history or the judgment of our lives will significantly change. Hence, history is even more ephemeral than for Aristotle, for its meaning lies beyond natural life itself. In this regard, Vico is an odd upstart, the first of a tentative breed that thinks of man as a lesser god.

The puzzle of history invites us to link Vico and Hegel in construing telos as the endlessly contrived narrative of self-reflecting selves. Anything more robust would consign the meaning of history to an order of reality beyond mere history—in Aristotle's or Augustine's way. For the only alternative conception of history (beyond Aristotle's and Augustine's) that could possibly escape paradox would concede that everything distinctive of a society of encultured selves is the work of those same mortal selves (ourselves, of course), themselves the artifacts of enabling histories. History, as the representation of real histories, is the reflexive work of historied selves, the only agents history could possibly claim.

To admit this much is to constrain telos within those modes of interpretation and judgment that issue from our own constructed aptitudes. There is in fact no other discerning competence to name, even where another is imputed to Divinity or Nature. Historical and ethical judgment are the same, therefore; alternative expressions of self-understanding offered under the only condition of autonomy that counts—the willingness of the human mind to bear witness to the meaning of its own invented world. History makes no room for historicity if God or an implicit telos in Nature is admitted. And even there, we could never trust the categories of reason or revelation if we could not trust the invented categories by which we grasp them to be such.[3]

History in the sense of historicity is, then, a sufficient condition for the emergence of apt selves. Any reasoned opposition requires, somewhere, an explanation of how natural-language aptitude arises by purely "naturalized" means. There is no such compelling explanation. Deny, for cause, the naturalizing alternative: you cannot then deny the historicity of human nature—the historicity of history, of practical judgment fitted with historied norms. Every resisting formula will prove arbitrary and wedded to one or another form of unearned privilege.

Against essentialism and revelation, then, historicity claims no doctrinal hegemony of any kind. It offers no more than a genuinely presuppositionless beginning to the study of history. This radical, this third, notion takes form haltingly, for the first time, in western Europe at the end of the eighteenth century. But of course, to ensure the acceptance of its own validity, it fell back instinctively to the hegemonic possibilities of the narrow culture in which it first emerged. At the end of our own millennium, we can no longer rely on any such unearned privilege, although saying so vouchsafes nothing. We can, however, begin to offset the pretensions of that small corner of the Eurocentric world by endorsing the following theorems at least: (1) the real standing of artifactual selves, (2) the denial of a natural telos in human history, (3) the sui generis emergence of human culture, (4) the constructed nature of the narratives and norms of societal life, (5) the denial of doctrinal privilege, (6) the unrestricted ubiquity of historical and ethical rationalization fitted to any society, (7) the eligibility of all actual forms of life as a basis for the work of history, and (8) the denial of any principled disjunction between theoretical and practical reason. These are, surely, the minima of historicity.

Still, taken singly or together, none of these eight themes defines historicity itself; they presuppose it rather. "Historicity" signifies that encultured or enlanguaged thought *is history:* a process formed and transformed in real time, through actual use, so that whatever belongs to a society's understanding of itself is a changing function of the continually transformed conditions of understanding under which it succeeds in doing that. But if languaged thought *is* the paradigm of thinking, then *historicism* (in the modern sense)—the thesis that the intelligible = the historicized—*is* effectively a constructivism (a form of constructive realism) under the condition of opposing all forms of modal necessity, modal invariance, and privilege.

There is no danger here of losing intelligibility in yielding fixity. For the actual discernibility of change must accord with whatever conserving pace human language can sustain. Too rapid a pace disables language altogether, in a sense not far from that of Hume's insistence on differences of meaning produced by the least discernible change in qualities experienced; and too great a reliance on the fixity of culturally formed meanings finally requires the impossible resources of Platonism or more.[4]

2

Of course, all of this will seem quite pointless if we fail to recover a working sense of the objectivity of history and practical judgment. The solution in the abstract is plain enough: objectivity must be a construct of some sort; but if so, then it can be such only on the supposition that the norms of rationality or legitimation on which it depends will be as much a construct as the other—also, reciprocally dependent on their discovered benefits. To say that there are no epistemic or ontic priorities in the human world is to say that any would-be rule or ground or criterion or sense of objectivity must be open to being continually transformed (if not dismissed) by passing beyond some prior stage of consensual understanding.

Once you grant this, you realize that it must be constructivism all the way down; for if the human self is itself spontaneously constituted by enculturing history, then the constructed objectivity of history and science and practical judgment cannot fail to be "historicized" as well. Whatever is convincing in the way of the consensual or tacit tolerance of the collective life of an actual society—I do not say "true"—will be a continuing function of its own historical career, though not of course criterially.

In the West, the clearest, most general, most plausible sketch of what is needed (notably underdeveloped, I'm afraid, indifferent to all the complexities of history) appears in Wittgenstein's conception of "language games" within the human *Lebensform*.[5] If you read Wittgenstein's post-Tractarian work as committed, metonymically, to replacing everything concerned with knowledge and rationality and understanding that accords with the indefensible optimism of the correspondence theory of truth offered in the *Tractatus* (what is now generally called objectivism), then the converging upshot of the entire inquiry that runs from Hegel to Foucault and that assesses the import of dismantling the objectivisms of so much of Western philosophy—the benefit of which Wittgenstein collects too sparely (though usefully enough) in his *lebensformlich* way—comes to a conclusion that easily absorbs Wittgenstein.

To abandon correspondentism in the grand Tractarian sense is to concede at a stroke that objectivity must be grounded in the ongoing practices of inquiry (and life) of viable societies. The argument is simplicity itself, but the consequences are distinctly radical. They need not embrace skepticism, of course, but they preclude any principled disjunction between descriptive sources that would "save" the objectivity of the sciences and the historicized interpretive features of history and practical judgment that call into doubt all the older canons of neutrality and direct discovery. (I admit I am using Wittgenstein for my own ends here. For Wittgenstein's conservative goal would never have been hospitable to historicism. Nevertheless, that *is*, I believe, the final import of "language games." There is no other conclusion to draw.)

Until quite recently, most efforts made to assure us of the coherence, amplitude, and adequacy—even the humanity—of the constructivist account of objectivity have been too difficult to cast in a compelling and conformable brief. But the thorough dismantling of objectivism, which by now is remarkably advanced (if we recall the original authority of the tradition that runs from Frege through Russell and Carnap down at least to Quine), now confronts us with a palpable need for alternative conceptions—fairly begs for a better sketch of constructivism. What's needed is a pointed account of what it means to say that the human self is a historicized artifact—a sketch at least fluent enough to explain its fresh conception not only with respect to history and practical judgment but to the objectivity of science as well. You would not, for instance, be wrong if you supposed that Foucault's return, toward the end of his life, to the question of the "care" of the "technologies" of the self signifies his awareness that he had himself neglected to construe the selves of his genealogies as robust enough to serve as responsible agents of history and judgment.[6] That is still constructivism's lack.

Foucault was, to some extent, a structuralist manqué, malgré lui. Let that serve as the mate of the discerned weakness in Wittgenstein's *lebensformlich* theme, which, together, I venture to say, count as a strong sign of the need, but a very weak philosophical impulse, to recover and explain the promising themes of Hegel's original vision of historical *Geist,* too densely compressed (by Hegel himself of course) to be of much use to us now, long after their first appearance. We must recover the best of Hegel by other means, if we are to recover Hegel at all. I mark a great sea-change in philosophical conviction here, poised uneasily for the time being between a return to objectivism (which many would applaud but is surely past reclaiming) and the full articulation of constructivism itself (which no more than a handful would ever champion against the hegemony of the other).

The fact remains that, now, against all odds, a frank constructivism ranging over the principal ontic and epistemic questions—historicist rather than transcendental—has pressed its way into mainstream philosophy. The failures of objectivism are too well known to require a catalogue at this late date, though correspondentism and cognitive privilege have already been noted. Other weaknesses might be mentioned that would not require the analysis of history, but they effect (as Hegel realized) the parity of history and the sciences. Kantian transcendentalism affords, for one, a natural motivation for favoring such a parity, because its own constructivism rests on alleged necessities of thought and experience that it cannot possibly secure.

In fact, objectivism's failure suggests a natural declension of constructivism from transcendentalism to historicism. For example, it is clear enough that there cannot be an algorithmic solution to the problem of reference and denotation[7]; there is also no way of treating predicative similarity algorithmically if Platonism is inaccessible, as it obviously is;[8] and, again, there is no algorithmic way of fixing the sufficient context of empirical truth-claims. Once you grant the insuperable difficulties of the older objectivisms, you see the point of replacing the entire conception in every inquiry—as much in the sciences as in history and practical judgment.[9]

That was, in fact, the essential lesson of Thomas Kuhn's ultimately failed project regarding the sciences. Kuhn touched on the decisive puzzle, but he was unable to meet the rearguard worries of the objectivists.[10] If you concede the conceptually benign holism of the human world (which includes of course both science and history), then, although those inquiries are hardly the same, the conditions of their respective objectivity and validity surely depend on the same constructed aptitudes. That is why the absence of an adequate theory of the self in Kuhn and

Wittgenstein and Foucault anticipates the seeming failure of constructivism at the very moment of discerning the deeper failure of objectivism.

If you grant all that, you will find that you cannot easily elude adopting something akin to Wittgenstein's *lebensformlich* maneuver—or the historicizing of same. But if the recovery of objectivity is constructivism's and historicism's proper goal, the effort must still convince all those willing to entertain the notion that the would-be replacement need not be arbitrary or paradoxical at all. On the argument, it must be the same society of artifactual selves who undertake the explanation of nature, the interpretation of history and art, and the defense of ethical and political judgment.

Here you glimpse easily enough the patent failure of the dampened Kantianism of John Rawls and Jürgen Habermas, which straddles the West's entire moral vision: for neither ever bothers to explain what we should now mean by the self's rational powers or how those powers may be reconciled with the conditions of enculturation.[11] Lapses of these sorts count as philosophical carelessness. By parity of reasoning, to recover scientific objectivity in the constructivist's way (as Thomas Kuhn should have realized) is to make provision for cognate answers in history and interpretive and practical settings. Closet objectivist that he was, Kuhn believed a change of paradigm—a change of interpretive theory—was incapable of rational defense. There you have the fatal clue to Kuhn's repudiation of his own important guess at historicism's promise. For every new conception is bound to address its own legitimation.

3

All the correctives for making good the lapse (in Kuhn and Wittgenstein and others) are surprisingly close at hand. It only looks as if abandoning objectivism, essentialism, revelation, Platonism, fixities or necessities *de re, de dicto, de cogitatione,* cognitive privilege, extensionalism, reductionism, eliminativism, and the rest of the exotica that belong to the Jurassic phase of philosophy (what is nearly philosophy's entire modern history) must signify the grossest sort of arbitrariness. But nothing could be further from the truth.

Bear in mind that, on the thesis before us, the self and its enabling society are hybrid creatures, sui generis emergents, aggregated individual histories whose proper "natures" are only predicated histories indissolubly incarnate in a certain natural-kind nature (*Homo sapiens*). Grant only that, and you realize that the structure of historical narrative and the norms of ethical judgment must be drawn from that same hybrid condition and must be congruent with one another; also, that the provisions made possible by that history must, from the side of nature and culture both, be presuppositionless. To reclaim all that is to provide the minima of a thoroughgoing constructivism, which, as far as I know, has never been explicitly worked out, in the last century, against the dominant objectivism.

The single clue by which the arbitrariness of objectivism may be offset—everywhere—rests with the strategic discovery (Hegel's, I should say) that the mind/body problem cannot ultimately be different from the culture/nature problem and that neither can be solved without solving the other. Constructivism is the opponent of every Cartesian vision and every Kantian transcendentalism, which, after all, are the principal sources of objectivism. To oppose all that, you have only to insist that the emergence of what distinguishes the self obtains, sui generis, in an indissolubly incarnate hybrid.

Paradigmatically, thought is the enlanguaged aptitude of human speakers embedded in a way as yet inadequately understood in the potentiating biology of *Homo sapiens;* so that even if all the languages of the world did not originate from a single ur-language, which seems reasonable enough, their divergences must be constrained by the weighted saliencies of human neurophysiology. That alone probably would account for the ubiquity of bilingualism among peoples that have no pertinent history in common, or would account, more radically, for the ability of the members of utterly unrelated cultures to cooperate and exchange thoughts and goods of every sort, or the ability of professional scientists, committed to utterly disparate theories and ways of describing and appraising the technical work and equipment they share, to share their common undertaking.

I see no reason why the same should not be true of the consensual ground of all forms of inter- and intra-societal understanding, without the least pretense of criterial or privileged fixities. Communicative success—of every sort—is at least as easily reconciled with a constructivism of a *lebensformlich* cast as with the dubious objectivisms that we know.[12] To speak of enlanguaged and encultured selves is already to speak of tacit commonalities in terms of which human understanding has never been known to fail massively. But here, I must warn, success is a constructed artifact, hardly enough to ensure Descartes' or Kant's or Husserl's (or Habermas's) universalisms.

The individuation of languages and dialects is never boundaried in a disjunctively principled way; no more are cultures, societies, histories, or any other collective ensembles involving selves. That explains why admitting the enculturing origins of our own particular emergence entails no privileged loyalty to the norms and categories of our "home" society. There are no fixities to find, nothing but practical fluencies that theory will do its best to inscribe in fixed ways.[13] Every language and every culture—*a fortiori,* every philosophy and every vision and practice—may be conceptually reconciled with "our own." But "our own" hardly counts as a fixed ground from which to identify "another" culture. Dispute is the same, epistemically, within and between societies.

You see, therefore, the asymmetries that must be admitted. For, from the side of cultural diversity, it is hardly reasonable to suppose that the categories of historical description or ethical and political appraisal can convincingly ignore the vulnerabilities and imputed animal interests of the species-specific creatures that we are. But then, from the side of biology, those same vulnerabilities and interests can hardly be correctly calibrated *for* the variably artifactual selves that we also are. To conflate the two is hardly more than to propose a false naturalism. Our animal nature only potentiates our cultural history—which we forever interpret and reinterpret. Hence, among ethical theories, hedonisms, utilitarianisms, evolutionisms are obvious specimens of the faulty kind.

Perhaps Aristotle's eudaimonism is not quite so simple; but then, even apart from its puzzling treatment of intellectual virtue and the barest recognition of Alexander's adventurism, Aristotle's rationale is much too inexplicit about the difference between biology and culture to be properly contested or defended. That is already more than a negligible charge, given Aristotle's immense authority. By a similar line of reasoning, that Kant manages, in the *Foundations of the Metaphysics of Morals,* to make moral judgment depend on a fixed (however conjectured) faculty of reason that is in no way tethered to the biology of *Homo sapiens* or the history of encultured selves, consigns Kant's account to little more than arbitrariness, though I concede that its arbitrariness takes an exalted form. The whole of transcendentalism fails for a similar reason. There is no explanation in Kant as to how *Vernunft* is related to specifically human thought or human history. In fact, the attraction of both Habermas and Rawls is largely the work of a weakly naturalized form of Kantianism; and the attraction of contemporary Aristotelians like Alasdair MacIntyre and Martha Nussbaum depends on an accommodation of historicity that, one way or another, each finally denies.[14]

4

In any case, the general strategy is clear: our culturally formed powers are "potentiated"—no more than that—by our biology; but how and in what specific normative regard that is true can only be imputed within the range of our reflexive competence—which we thereupon pretend to judge from the vantage of biology. Unless we are objectivists, we cannot deny that those potentiating dispositions are logically subaltern, subject to determinable histories, never independent enough to decide the right norms of science or historical narrative or practical appraisal. As a result, no reasonably imposed biological constraints are ever so strictly defined that alternative, even irreconcilable, proposals can be convincingly ruled out at the level of legitimating critique. No one has ever shown that that can be done.

Let me illustrate what I mean. It is certainly reasonable to suppose that our animal interests as members of *Homo sapiens* include—from the side of our reflexive powers—our mortality at least; creatures like ourselves "generally" act to prolong their lives. *But how long a life are we entitled to,* and *under what specific conditions?* Certainly, our expectations (our postulated norms) are bound to be congruent with the potentiating technology of our particular culture. But, then, there cannot be a fixed rule for determining what is ethically obligatory regarding mortality or longevity from the side of biology; and, from the side of historical culture, the question cannot fail to be self-serving.

I should say that what holds true of our biological nature vis-à-vis history and ethics is always interpreted (hence *sub*functional) with respect to such molar (cultural) functioning; or that what we "require" as members of *Homo sapiens* (either ethically or in some respect judged to hold objectively for history) cannot fail to be "anthropomorphized" via our conjectures. I see no viable alternative, but I also see no reason to think that that is philosophically fatal. It merely exposes the fatuousness of universalized moralities and objectivist histories.

From the side of our being the functional selves that we are, the picture is simpler and more interesting. For *to have been* formed as we are is to have internalized, in acquiring language and cultural habits, the *lebensformlich* practices and prima facie norms of the social life that belongs to our local world. We *begin* there, because initial resistance literally makes no sense; furthermore, resistance to any selected norms drawn from our local world is premised on our mastery of, and adherence to, the deeper practices that first formed us as the creatures that we are.

It's for this reason that the question of the meaning of life is culturally trivial, even if individually troubling; for the same reason, we cannot merely be arbitrary (even if we wish to be) in the way of understanding ourselves or assessing conduct. Both undertakings are at least initially *lebensformlich*.

There you have the single most important lesson of my brief: neither constructivism nor historicism leads to arbitrariness regarding objectivity. That comes as a surprise. Rightly read, it settles the lion's share of the argument. Let me say again, as clearly as I can, precisely what we have gained. We begin our reflections about what to count as a reasonable picture of objective inquiry—of *any* sort—presuppositionlessly: meaning by that no more than that we eschew all forms of objectivism, privilege, first philosophy, apodicticity, modal necessity, and similar baggage; we build, as we must, on the spontaneous, habituated, historically contingent and alterable aptitudes we take ourselves to manifest. The bare attempt to *say* what "objectivity" is (in science, in history, in practical judgment) cannot fail to be a second-order construct based on our contingently encultured practices, which, in their *lebensformlich* way, already entail viable, prima facie, first-order norms and practices consensually tolerated as objective enough for our conforming needs.

Merely to admit the reflexive powers of a society of selves is, therefore, to confirm the ineliminability of legitimative questions *and* their continuity, in terms of epistemic resources, with whatever (thus seen) count as our first-order powers. Hence, postmodernism, in the sense made notorious by Jean-François Lyotard and Richard Rorty, however unintentionally, cannot be more than a conceptual scandal.[15] Only the persistence of objectivism could possibly have made the postmodernist disclaimer plausible at all. But if, in the grand sense in which we act to avoid the classic forms of skepticism—in Kant as well as in Descartes— without denying a need to recover "objectivity," we see that any such would-be attempt must rely on some version of the familiar second-order work that we have always called philosophy. How could it be otherwise?

To admit that selves are cultural artifacts is already to admit the unavoidability of second-order questions. But that means that constructivism and historicism are perfectly capable of treating legitimative questions coherently. Postmodernism and objectivism deny that that is so. But they obviously have no argument.

In any case, the objective standing of truth-claims, whether descriptive, explanatory, interpretive, or normative, is plausibly taken to be grounded in the consensual fluency of what (adjusting Wittgenstein along historicized lines) I have taken the liberty of calling *lebensformlich*. (By that, as I say, I mean to suggest that Wittgenstein was himself a very thin, a very dampened sort of innocent Hegelian.) Since objectivity is grounded only in a holist way, it is benignly presuppositionless, never criterial: hence, not question-begging and not arbitrary either. On the cultural side, our practices are determinable enough, even where normative, along the lines of what (once again, with Wittgenstein) may be fairly described as our "savoir faire" (our "knowing how to go on"). On the biological side, judged according to what we admit (but cannot entirely fathom) as our encultured "perspective" or "horizon" or "prejudice" or "preformation," we make conjectures—again, hardly arbitrarily—about what to count as our needs and interests and vulnerabilities as the animals we are. Our cultural norms are relatively determinate in the *lebensformlich* way; but of course, there, they are never normative in more than a prima facie sense; correspondingly, every determinate "natural" or biological constraint on our normative pretensions is never more than provisional and subaltern, never more than imputed from the cultural side it sometimes pretends to govern. Read conformably, *any* further second-order projection of norms regarding truth, validity, confirmation, legitimation, propriety, rationality, coherence, consistency, relevance, fitness—in the way of fixing objectivity—is, so far forth, as eligible as any other.

I draw, then, the following conclusions: (1) that the question of objectivity cannot be entirely arbitrary if it is at least grounded in the *lebensformlich* way, because that is the condition sine qua non on which we first emerge as creatures capable of posing the issue; (2) that, if that is so, then the further attempt to test or strengthen our would-be norms by exploring all possible second-order rationales regarding what to count as objectivity (according to our lights) cannot be any more arbitrary than the first, because such conjectures will be submitted within the same *lebensformlich* constraints that are subject, through actual use, to historicized change; (3) that, eschewing objectivism, there can be no compelling a priori reason for supposing that there will always be a uniquely valid, or strongly convergent, rule of objectivity fitted to any and all culturally habituated forms of inquiry[16]; and (4) that second-order improvements in the very idea of what to count as objective, ranging over any and all of the usual kinds of inquiry and eschewing necessity, apodicticity, neutrality, uniqueness, exceptionless universality, and the like *must* produce insuperable paradox somewhere, or must inevitably be rejected for cause, and could never be convincingly confirmed, because, on the theory before us, whatever objectivity is imputed will be constructed, and because its own rationale will depend on disjunctive saliencies favored within holist conditions under which alone such undertakings make any sense at all.

There can be no principled bifurcation between science and history or ethics, because each is abstracted from within the same *lebensformlich* practice. To insist, for instance, on the validity of an exceptionless bivalence for the objective work of the natural sciences and thereupon to deny the propriety of assigning truth-values or truth-like values to historical interpretation or ethical judgment (because perhaps they cannot be made to conform with bivalence), or to insist that, in historical and art-critical contexts, bivalence can never give way (coherently) to a many-valued (even a relativistic) logic, is hardly more than to fall back to objectivism's illicit presumption. I say again: if we are to be constructivists, it must be constructivism all the way down. Historicism is no more than constructivism viewed in terms of pertinent change.

5

The threat of the arbitrariness of constructivism's treatment of science and history is easily turned, as I say. Arbitrariness cannot even meaningfully arise regarding our merely *lebensformlich* practices; nor, a fortiori, in the mere attempt to reform such practices. That is the stunning import of what I take to be Wittgenstein's discovery in the post-Tractarian writings, in *On Certainty,* for instance: namely, that even the rejection of cognitive privilege cannot provide an escape from a vicious regress, unless the validity of all our inquiries is ultimately grounded—holistically, by way of open-ended practices—in ways that require no more than the informal savoir faire of encultured selves. Doubtless, Wittgenstein would not have approved of my putting matters thus, or of my historicizing the conditions of a *lebensformlich* consensus. I am pirating Wittgenstein here, I admit. But Wittgenstein himself nowhere considers the artifactual nature of the self and would doubtless have opposed the notion. (Here, I dare suppose he would, if he would object, do so inconsistently.)

Objectivity is another matter. It presupposes an answer to the charge of arbitrariness in the face of abandoning objectivism altogether. But, as I say, it is easy enough to escape the charge (of arbitrariness) on constructivist grounds. I have also narrowed the gap between defeating objectivism and disciplining constructivism, by suggesting how the hybrid nature of the human self yields epistemic resources regarding objective history and objective practical judgment that may (and must) be fitted to what the sciences require but cannot secure elsewhere: notably with regard to the insuperable informality of effective reference and predication, contextual fixity, and constancy of meaning. Reference and predication make no sense, I claim, except in *lebensformlich* ways—which, once granted, confirm objectivism's untenability and legitimate constructivism. Grant that: you will have vindicated historicism in the strongest possible terms as well.

A further difficulty lurks, however. The objectivity of history and ethical judgment (also, the objectivity of science) cannot be merely *lebensformlich.* In fact, all such inquiries favor very different questions and very different forms of rigor. There is, we must concede, no definitive interest in history and ethical inquiry sufficiently compelling with regard to particular policies about appraising truth-claims and separable from all other inquiries, by reference to which we might assess (as we obviously do in the sciences, with regard to prediction and technological control) the relative success of competing second-order policies meant to satisfy such interests. The would-be norms of objective history and ethical judgment appear suspiciously to entrench our partisan convictions about first-order history and judgment, by way of self-certifying legitimative powers; we seem unable to segregate such considerations in ways that robustly match what is moderately convincing among the natural sciences. This helps to capture our sense of the difference between empirical science and history and practical judgment, without ever falling back to patent arbitrariness.

Reflecting on this difference, many would deny objective standing of any kind to history and ethics. But that would be no more than an expression of regret or preference; for now, the question demands a constructivist solution. The obvious solution is to favor a dampened measure of what to count as "objective," wherever ideology and doctrinal bias cannot be eliminated or sufficiently offset. Is such a policy viable? I see no reason why not. It would entail not only abandoning objectivism, but very probably replacing the usual marks of objectivism's declared rigor—in particular, restricting, even replacing, the scope of bivalence and excluded middle, and also conceding that we can do no better than appraise the reasonableness or plausibility of competing partisan histories or ethical judgments offered from the vantage of distinctly opposed convictions—entrenched of course in the interpreted practices they pretend to govern. These are bound to be the most contested ways of dampening objectivity. But no principled objection to such a strategy can be more than a vestigial form of objectivism.

Thus, whatever the narrative, historical, intentional, purposive, normative structure of human life may be thought to be, that structure must be reasonably congruent with the salient concerns of actual societal life and with what we conjecture are the needs and interests and vulnerabilities of *Homo sapiens*—a fortiori, selves. Whatever is elicited regarding our biology contributes to what may be called prudence on the cultural side: survival, for instance, the avoidance of pain and harm, the loss of security, family or community relations, food and shelter, sexual and social solidarity, and the like. These constraints are characteristically variable and variably determined, informal, inclined to err on the side of generosity (relative to social resources), approximate, merely plausible, never essential, not intrinsically moral, open to alternative or incompatible grading and ranking, and not infrequently denied, discarded, or overridden (without thereby clearly violating nature or reason). These are surely the common themes of history and practical judgment alike.

There are, of course, bound to be additional prudential concerns drawn from the side of cultural life alone or incarnate in our biology: for instance, property, respect, freedom, power, due process, well-being, and the like. These are usually cast in the form of rights—to signify their nonarbitrary standing. They cannot be easily universalized in any determinate form: think of property rights and liberty, for instance. But they are fair specimens of a "reduced" or logically weaker kind of objectivity that one expects in history, interpretation, practical judgment: the kind that accommodates reasonable bias and conviction and can never be merely neutral or uniquely confirmed.

I cannot see why, for instance, there must be in principle a uniquely valid history of great events—the French Revolution, say—if we assign such histories objective standing. It seems far more likely (far more reasonable) that a "valid" history would accommodate a run of seriously contending normative visions, without either being exclusionary or indifferent to their oppositional roles. And if it holds in history, it surely holds in practical judgment. Furthermore, to accept the argument cannot fail to affect the very ethics of pursuing ethics and history. For if the logic of ethics and history precludes an exclusionary bivalence, then it would be simply wrong to insist, say, on applying excluded middle to the puzzles of abortion and physician-assisted suicide and the Rwanda disaster. Frankly, I view the adjustment as inescapably relativistic.

You begin to see, therefore, what objectivity comes to. In the natural sciences, description and explanation are characteristically honed in the interest of prediction and explanation favoring predication and technological control, pursued under conditions of quantified precision and as much uniformity in nature as can be empirically claimed. Such executive concerns are not objectivist per se; nor do they become objectivist when, dialectically, we find that the "best" results may be had, in selected disciplines, by yielding pride of place (in description and explanation) to material forces that lack altogether the intentional and normative entanglements that we associate with human history. Science *is*, after all, a cultural undertaking and, *in* being a form of human inquiry, is as much affected by human "intervention" as is history itself. Ludwig Fleck, for one, has given us an unforgettable proof of that.[17] The fact is, the apparent objectivism of physics is itself a constructivist triumph. It would be troubling if it were otherwise.

It is also true, however, that there is no comparable interest obtaining in historical and ethical inquiry that could possibly adapt the special constraints that serve the physical sciences so well—*if "naturalizing" fails!* There's the single most strategic consideration bearing on what to count as "objectivity" in history and ethics. I've already offered reasons for thinking that objectivism fails among the natural sciences. There cannot then be any prospect of reclaiming correspondentism in history. The reason stares you in the face: the subjects and objects of history are one and the same—historically constituted selves reflecting on themselves and their evolving histories.

I don't for a moment concede that correspondentism works in the physical sciences; I don't concede that objectivism is defensible anywhere. But certainly, it is particularly difficult to reclaim "objectivity" in the cultural disciplines in objectivist ways. Even in the physical sciences, where the would-be laws of nature are said to be formulable in extensional and exceptionless ways, it is reasonably clear that their acceptance depends on idealizations that cannot be easily reconciled (perhaps cannot be reconciled at all) with the severe constraints that naturalizing would impose.[18] The same is obviously true of our general inability to translate high-level explanatory theories in directly testable materialist terms. Here, constructivist and historicist complications bearing on *what we should believe* regarding the nature of physical reality prove ineliminable—and as pertinent to sustaining the would-be rigor of our sciences as anything naturalizing might rightly insist on.

Nevertheless, "objectivity" in history and ethics does not answer to anything like the executive interests of the sciences, where it *might* indeed turn out that truth-claims regularly converge toward a single adequate vision of nature. Certainly, physicists are strongly drawn to the idea. But, however simpler it may be to legitimate objectivity in history and ethics (because their logic must be slacker, say), it cannot fail to be more quarrelsome and more unsettling.

The seeming paradox is this. In the sciences, we know well enough what work we want our notion of objectivity to serve: the best disputes concern what is finally true and false on the best evidence thus directed. But *what* "objectivity" comes to, metaphysically, remains even there a disputed matter, as the rise of constructivism attests. By contrast, we are very clear that objectivity in history and ethics is primarily *lebensformlich*—that there are no executive interests in either inquiry that match the predictive and technological concerns of the sciences. In a word, there is no principled disjunction between championing one or another second-order view of objectivity along historical and practical lines and pursuing whatever answers to our first-order doctrinal interests and conviction. That has always been the stumbling block. The idea that there *is* an objective account of historical events that we can progressively approach, or make relatively neutral additions to (as time goes by), is surely unresponsive on its face.[19] It is in fact little more than another vestigial form of objectivism.

6

The essential complication comes to this: (1) the interpretation of human events implicates a historically freighted perspective which the historian advances as objective (that is, the way events "appear" to him, as Raymond Aron insists)[20] but which cannot then preclude, as logically or necessarily indefensible or inadmissible, similarly freighted but opposed perspectives; (2) the contest between such differences cannot convincingly appeal to any deciding neutral "interest," such as predictive power; and (3) despite all that, even irreconcilable histories are regularly judged to be entitled to claim a measure of objectivity. It's not even a matter of prediction's being a neutral norm in the physical sciences; it's only that it's possible to agree on relatively "detachable" results in its name. Historical and ethical disputes cannot even yield detachable results.

This is not to confirm any particular conception of history or ethics as fully valid, but only to draw attention to the meta-legitimating considerations in terms of which legitimation may be thought to be "objective" at all. We surely cannot go beyond the legitimation of our legitimative practices. Partisans will hardly be satisfied with that; nor should they be. The fact is, normative passions *are* truly needed to power our lives, to motivate legitimation without excessive loss of ardor. History and judgment must bring past and future together effectively. Conviction tends to outstrip legitimation at any moment; but, over time and well after the fact, the two are more closely reconciled. This often requires the rewriting of history and the reassessment of norms. The Nuremberg Trials suggest the pattern. But if you required for a closed system of adequate principles the elimination of the ad hoc, you would never find it. We expect too much of narrative history and ethical judgment—in the old way of objectivism; and yet we know the futility of that. That is perhaps no more than the final pathos of the human condition.

How can we then discover history's valid interpretation or the valid judgment of how we should judge or act? I follow Plato's *Statesman* here in recommending a "second-best" conjecture, that is, a conjecture that seeks, dialectically, to escape, on all fronts, the untenable excesses of the "best" (objectivist) claims and, at the same time, proposes plausible gains against such claims and against all other second-best alternatives.[21]

In sum: objectivity is a human construct—in the sciences as well as in history and ethics. It remains grounded, therefore, in a *lebensformlich* way, as does truth, and for the same reason. But it is also a two-storied affair: meaning by that that we engage (as we must) the dialectical possibility that, within limits and in different ways for different inquiries, we continually reinvent our norms to catch our "better" possibilities. Such undertakings I call "second-best" because they and their legitimation are bound by the untenability of objectivism and the improvisational and nonexclusionary nature of our legitimative hopes.

Let me mention, very briefly, one final qualification that complicates matters enormously in ways I dare not address in a fresh way here. I think of "our" society as reasonably determinable, or boundaried, in the sense in which we actually first emerge, as selves, by way of a historically specific enculturing process. *Thereafter,* "our" society—or history or culture—extends to *whatever,* in the whole of human experience, may be viably assimilated to our originally encultured powers and which, thus assimilated, may alter those powers and make such further assimilation possible.[22] This catches up a small dictum mentioned earlier: namely, collectively construed, bilingualism = biculturalism.

Hence, the self-impoverishing loyalties of a postmodernist like Rorty count for nothing here; also, the dialectical possibilities of envisioned changes in second-best historical and ethical conjectures are now enormously enlarged. In the global society that we seem destined to occupy ere long, whatever will count as a reasonable history of our past, and a reasonable ethical judgment about our future, will implicate departures from a very narrow *lebensformlich* vision that cannot yet be easily fathomed or made plausible. But that *is* the human condition: the sense in which selves *are* artifacts; and history, the sense in which our practical demand for objective validation always exceeds the changing resources by which we try to satisfy any such demand.

Notes

1. The classic texts in favor of "naturalizing" include W. V. Quine, "Epistemology Naturalized," in *Ontological Relativity and Other Essays* (New York: Columbia University Press, 1969); and Donald Davidson, "A Coherence Theory of Truth and Knowledge," in *Truth and Interpretation: Perspectives on the Philosophy of Donald Davidson,* ed. Ernest LePore (Oxford: Basil Blackwell, 1986).

2. Aristotle, *Poetics,* trans. Ingram Bywater, in *The Complete Works of Aristotle,* 2 vols., ed. Jonathan Barnes (Princeton: Princeton University Press, 1984).

3. Radical Protestant theology converges here with the claims of historicity. See Karl Barth, *The Epistle to the Romans,* trans. Edwyn C. Hoskyns (London: Oxford University Press, 1933), 88, 202; cited in Van A. Harvey, *The Historian and the Believer: The Morality of Historical Knowledge and Christian Belief,* with a new introduction (Urbana: University of Illinois Press, 1996). The second phrase is Harvey's. See also Harvey, *Historian and the Believer,* xvi–xxviii.

4. The full defense of historicity in this sense appears in my *Historied Thought, Constructed World: A Conceptual Primer for the Turn of the Millennium* (Berkeley: University of California Press, 1995).

5. See particularly Ludwig Wittgenstein, *On Certainty,* ed. G. E. M. Anscombe and G. H. von Wright, trans. Denis Paul and G. E. M. Anscombe (Oxford: Basil Blackwell, 1969); and Wittgenstein, *Culture and Values,* ed. G. H. von Wright with Heikki Nyman, trans. Peter Winch (Oxford: Basil Blackwell, 1980).

6. See Joseph Margolis, "Foucault's Problematic," in *Foucault,* ed. Robert Nola (Ilford: Frank Case, 1998).

7. See W. V. Quine, *Word and Object* (Cambridge: MIT Press, 1960), §§37–38.

8. See Joseph Margolis, "The Politics of Predication," *Philosophical Forum* 27 (1996).

9. If I understand him correctly, although we converge considerably on the characterization of history or historical interpretation, I cannot quite agree with F. R. Ankersmit, who finally holds to an objectivism regarding science but not regarding history. The disjunction cannot be maintained *if* the same human self is the agent of all these inquiries and *if* the self is itself an artifact of history. But see F. R. Ankersmit, "Six Theses of Narrativist Philosophy of History," in *History and Tropology: The Rise and Fall of Metaphor* (Berkeley: University of California Press, 1994), in the context of the rest of the book. From the side of the sciences, I may mention the recent, extremely detailed analysis—entirely hospitable to both constructivism and historicism—offered in Peter Galison, *Image and Logic: A Material Culture of Microphysics* (Chicago: University of Chicago Press, 1997), chapter 9. This may well be the most sustained attempt to date to provide the empirical evidence confirming the effective viability of "societies" of scientists committed to the most profoundly divergent, incommensurable, even incompatible conceptions of the technical import of high-level physics and of science and philosophy in general. Galison offers a vision much more radical than T. S. Kuhn's, but also much less vulnerable (and much less explicit) in conceptual terms.

10. Compare Thomas S. Kuhn, *The Structure of Scientific Revolutions,* 2d ed. (Chicago: University of Chicago Press, 1970); and his "Afterwords," in *World Changes: Thomas Kuhn and the Nature of Science,* ed. Paul Horwich (Cambridge: MIT Press, 1993).

11. See, for instance, John Rawls, *A Theory of Justice* (Cambridge: Harvard University Press, 1971); and Jürgen Habermas, "Discourse Ethics: Notes on a Program of Philosophical Justification," in *Moral Consciousness and Communicative Action,* trans. Christian Lenhardt and Shierry Weber Nicholsen (Cambridge: MIT Press, 1990).

12. This counts decisively against Davidson's influential opposition to plural conceptual schemes, which he brought to bear in a powerful, but unearned, way against Kuhn's original conception of a "paradigm shift." See Donald Davidson, "The Very Idea of a Conceptual Scheme," in *Inquiries about Interpretation and Truth* (Oxford: Clarendon Press, 1984).

13. You will find that Rorty's postmodernism fails to provide any convincing criteria for "ethnocentric" loyalty. It cannot be more than opportunism. See Richard Rorty, "Postmodern Bourgeois Liberalism," in *Objectivity, Relativism, and Truth*, vol. 1 of *Philosophical Papers* (Cambridge: Cambridge University Press, 1991); and "Private Irony and Liberal Hope," in *Contingency, Irony, and Solidarity* (Cambridge: Cambridge University Press, 1989).

14. See, for instance, Joseph Margolis, *Life without Principles: Reconciling Theory and Practice* (Oxford: Basil Blackwell, 1996), chapter 5.

15. See Jean-François Lyotard, *The Postmodern Condition: A Report on Knowledge*, trans. Geoff Bennington and Brian Massumi (Minneapolis: University of Minnesota Press, 1984).

16. See Allan Megill, " 'Grand Narrative' and the Discipline of History," in *A New Philosophy of History*, ed. Frank Ankersmit and Hans Kellner (Chicago: University of Chicago Press, 1995).

17. See Ludwik Fleck, *Genesis and Development of a Scientific Fact*, ed. Thaddeus J. Trenn and Robert K. Merton, trans. Fred Bradley and Thaddeus J. Trenn (Chicago: University of Chicago Press, 1979).

18. See, for instance, Nancy Cartwright, *How the Laws of Physics Lie* (Oxford: Clarendon Press, 1983).

19. I cannot think of any more telling way of dramatizing the issue than by inviting you to consider and compare the claims in Raymond Aron, *Introduction to the Philosophy of History: An Essay on the Limits of Historical Objectivity*, trans. George J. Irwin (Boston: Beacon Press, 1961), section 4; and Arthur C. Danto, *Narration and Knowledge* (New York: Columbia University Press, 1985).

20. Aron, *Introduction to the Philosophy of History*, 272, 274, 276, 278.

21. See, further, Joseph Margolis, *A Second-Best Morality* (The Lindley Lecture) (Lawrence: University of Kansas, 1998), 1–26 (published as a separate).

22. You will find versions of this idea in Gadamer's use of *Horizontverschmelzung* and Bourdieu's *habitus*, but I'll say no more than that. See Hans-Georg Gadamer, *Truth and Method*, trans. Garrett Barden and John Cumming (New York: Seabury Press, 1975); and Pierre Bourdieu, "Structures, *Habitus*, Practices" and "Belief and the Body," in *The Logic of Practice*, trans. Richard Nice (Stanford: Stanford University Press, 1990).

Part 3

History and Responsibility

Responsibility and Irresponsibility in Historical Studies: A Critical Consideration of the Ethical Dimension in the Historian's Work

Jörn Rüsen

> The aim of study is humanness, nothing else. . . . Humanness is the virtue through which heaven has a share in us.
>
> —Cui Shu

1. Responsibility as a Challenge of Historical Studies

Responsibility is a normative relationship between an actor and his or her activities. It is related not only to the actions of a person or a group but to their omissions as well. It is an essential notion of law, ethics, and morality. It confronts individuals and social units with expectations of what they should or shouldn't do or should or shouldn't have done. At the same time, it is a point of view in understanding and interpreting human agency. Saying that people are responsible for what they do or don't do implies an *authority* to which they feel responsible or which makes them responsible or claims their responsibility. This authority demands and grants justification. It may be a law court, a deity, or one's own conscience. In modern culture, history itself can play the role of such an instance of responsibility and irresponsibility and justification and condemnation. Such an authority of responsibility and justification renders someone guilty, after he or she has caused a damage to another person. Being guilty, one person owes the other compensation, or enables one to punish the culprit.

"Irresponsibility" has a double meaning: in an objective sense, it denominates an outcome of an action for which the actor is not responsible (e.g., for consequences of a condition he or she can't know and can't take into account). In a subjective sense, it expresses a negative evaluation of an action: a person or a group of people had done something for which they are responsible. My focus on irresponsibility will mainly be on this negative or "dark" side of human agency.

Speaking of the "responsibility" of a historian means to confront his or her historical work with certain values and norms and to put it into a normative relationship to others he or she lives with. Responsibility confronts the historian's work with an authority of justification, which judges it by a set of norms and values and even has the power to execute them by the reaction of those to which the historical work is addressed.

What are these values? To whom is the historian responsible and for what? And how are these values and this responsibility effective in the historical work? These questions cover the whole realm of historical activities and they can't be separated from any understanding of what historians do. But they get a certain tapering when being related to historical studies as an academic discipline. In this case, they are transformed into the question of objectivity and of the treatment of values, which are specific to the scientific character (in the broader sense of the word) of historical cognition.[1] Do the methodical rules of research, which stand for objectivity, dissolve historical responsibility? Or does the commitment to these rules and to the ideal of objectivity execute another responsibility than the above-mentioned one?

Historical objectivity can be described as a kind of truth brought about by methodical procedures of recognition related to the experience of the past. Historical responsibility can be described as another kind of truth, brought about by discursive procedures related to the cultural function of historical knowledge in social life. The first can be named "theoretical truth," the second "practical truth." The question is whether they contradict each other or whether they confirm or complement each other. In the case of contradiction, the disciplinary status of history has to be understood as an institutionalized irresponsibility of historical thinking. In the case of complementation, the methodical rules of research which place the obligation on the historian to strict neutrality in treating the experience of the past become dubious.

In order to come to terms with this uncomfortable alternative, I would like to start with an attempt to differentiate three dimensions of historical responsibility. One of them requires more extensive treatment, since it involves the difficult problem of historical responsibility concerning the past as such. Then I would like to check the place of the methodical principle of objectivity: does it belong to the realm of responsibility or does it push the work of the historian beyond it? Then he or she would lose the burden of ethical commitments in favor of a new status of historical knowledge, which now is ruled only by theoretical truth-claims. Finally, I would like to reflect on a possibility of mediating theoretical with practical truth, thus contributing a better understanding of the work of the historian beyond the gap between the responsibility of life orientation by historical memory and the value-neutrality of valid historical knowledge.

2. Three Levels of Responsibility

There are three dimensions of responsibility in the work of the historian. The first is apparent: historians are responsible to their contemporaries for the fulfillment of the specific needs of orientation, which are related to the commemoration of the past. They are the advocates of collective memory and responsible for its order.

The second complements the first responsibility for the present: historians are responsible for the future insofar as it is a matter of their representation of the past. There is no historical thought without a more or less hidden perspective of temporal change which leads into the future and serves as a factor in guiding human activity by intentions.

The third responsibility is related to the past: historians are responsible for taking over the heritage of the past. They have to do justice to the people of the past and they have to come to terms with crimes and horrors which belong to this heritage. It is this kind of responsibility which today draws the most attention, not only of metahistory but of practical politics in the field of historical culture as well.

1. The historian's responsibility for realizing the practical purposes of historical memory is evident: history is an integral part of cultural life orientation. It gives the experience of contingent temporal change a meaning which enables the people concerned to come to terms with it in their practical lives. Historical memory has to contribute to the validation and legitimation of the life order of today. (This is the simple reason why modern states have installed history instruction as a necessary part of the curriculum.) No competent member of social and political life is without history. Social and political competence in history in-

cludes the ability of sharing and bearing collective identity, contributing to it and at the same time getting a place for one's own personal identity in it. History is responsible for identity, i.e., for a balanced connection between the experience of the past and the expectation of the future in the relationships that persons and groups have among themselves and to others. It has to confirm (or—in certain cases of identity crisis—to criticize or to deconstruct) the values of self-esteem and the distance to and difference from others in personal and social perspectives. This is done with the corroborating force of the experience of the past. So, for example, the national historiography of the nineteenth century was shaped by historians' responsibility for a powerful national identity. It rooted the new and in many cases even revolutionary collective identity called a "nation" in the core of the moving forces of history. Heinrich von Sybel, a disciple of Ranke and prominent representative of the German historicism of the Prussian school, expressed this commitment to nationality in his inaugural lecture, "On the Status of Modern German Historiography" (1856):

> There were historiographers of all parties, but there were no longer any objective, impartial, blood- and nerveless historians. A highly relevant progress! Since it is obvious that no real historian can grow up without an ethical conviction, there is no genuine conviction without a certain relationship to the world-moving questions of religion, politics and nationality . . . [2]

Today many historians feel responsible for the liberation of national identity from its traditional constraints of uniformity and aggressiveness (inward and outward) in favor of a more open relationship to cultural difference in a comprehensive political system. The same is true for a wider scope of cultural identity: the ideological identification of mankind with the features of modern Western culture has received a radical postmodern critique which has led to a new awareness of cultural differences and particularity. This critique pursues the historians' responsibility concerning identity; it has set the principle of (mutual) recognition of differences at the very place where traditionally the universality of humankind took the uniform features of the West.[3]

But historical responsibility has a negative side: if historians fail to address the orientation needs of their time concerning the temporal framework of practical life and identity-building, one can speak of irresponsibility. This irresponsibility takes place when historians ignore the value system to be confirmed and brought to life, or when they apply it in a one-sided way to the experience of the past. On the other hand, it is irresponsible if historians ignore, overlook, or cover ambivalences or contradictions in the relationship between experience and values in historical memory. In this failure lies a specific irresponsibility which has to be considered more extensively, since it has recently become an important issue of metahistory.

Historical thinking is responsible for the ability of its addressees to act in correspondence to historical experience in a stable framework of self-understanding. Therefore it has to lift the burden of the past in favor of a free future perspective. Historical memory in general is highly selective and effective in forgetting; this is true for the historian's elaborated work as well. It represents the past in such a way that it remains relevant for the present and becomes an integral part of the cultural orientation of human life. But at the same time, the past is partly allowed to become forgotten if it can't pass the filter of relevance.

In elaborating and handling this filter, which consists of a system of values and norms, the historian might fall into the trap of irresponsibility. This trap is always open, if something of the past relevant for the present contradicts, opposes, or hinders the historical confirmation of the value system which constitutes the historian's society. Painful experiences which couldn't be mastered tend to be suppressed, but in their suppressive form they remain effective and out of mind at the same time. It is the contrary of historical responsibility to admit and allow, or even to support or pursue, such a suppression. In this case the historian's work prevents an articulation of historical experience which is effective in the life world of its time.

One has to conclude that it belongs to the historian's responsibility to reveal not only those features of the past which fit into the self-esteem of contemporaries, but also to reveal those hidden but effective disturbances in their self-esteem, which are grounded in a traumatic and suppressed historical experience. Historical responsibility includes the duty of disclosing and—if possible—of dissolving disturbances in the temporal coherence of life forms and identity concepts. In a metaphorical way, one can speak of a healing or therapeutic function of history for which historians are responsible.

2. The second dimension of historical responsibility is constituted in the future-relatedness of historical thinking. Historical orientation directly or indirectly includes a future perspective for topical activities. This inherence of the future in the representation of the past can be conceptualized in different ways: e.g., as a duration of tradition, as a critique of outdated life-forms, or as a prolongation of developments. Today we can observe a growing awareness of the responsibility of the people of today for their offspring's future life conditions. This awareness is initiated by

threatening environmental problems: a simple continuity and widening of the dominant industrial exploitation of nature will inevitably destroy the natural conditions for human life in the future. The responsibility of preserving nature for future generations has consequences for historical thinking, which have not yet been sufficiently discussed. The future is becoming an emphasized and elaborated aspect of treating the past in order to come to terms with present-day life.

Historical responsibility for the future perspective of human life is guided by a value system of hopes and threats. A commitment to these values allows the historical work in its practical function to disclose abilities and chances for activities by its representation of the past. It might miss this achievement if it fails to address its interpretation of historical experience to the spontaneity of human activity, i.e., to the mental point where actions get their intentional direction. Then every element of ethical commitment would be cast off the future perspective. This is the case if historians present the past as a closed predestination of the future, so that the future is no more than a necessary consequence or a plain extrapolation of conditions already given by the past or established by present-day activities. Then there is no need for further ethical commitment. In this case, a good deal of the potentials of human agency are excluded by its historical orientation: it only advises the actors to pursue the predetermined course of history. Examples of this irresponsibility are those concepts of development which are molded like laws of nature. Past and future are welded together in an unbroken chain of time, with no place for value-generated transformations or critical refutations of predetermined developments.

This irresponsible concept of the future as a necessary consequence of the past provides human activity with the conviction of being able to master the past in analogy to the mastering of nature by technology. This conviction may raise the self-esteem of the actors to fantasies of omnipotence: they may think they can govern the course of history by knowing its entire law of development. At the same time, this weakens their identity by depriving them of the freedom of negating and transcending the constraints the past has built into the possibilities of future life.

3. The third dimension of historical responsibility is related to the past itself. Here the value system of historical interpretation is related to the value system of the interpreted people and their actions or omissions of them. This seems to be an astonishing and unusual thought, since the past has gone, and its representation for orientation purposes of today is a matter of the value system of this orientation.

But my point is that this value system itself has a relationship to values and norms effective in the activities of the people who have passed away. This relationship is of concern for historians' responsibility because it is an integral part of the authority to which they feel responsible and which they use to justify their work.

A simple example of everyday modes of historical thinking is the pride people can feel concerning achievements of the past brought about by their ancestors. They think of these achievements as if they themselves had brought them about. Another example is the manifold procedures of cultivating traditions. In this case, the value system of the past embedded in the life-form of today is acknowledged as still binding. It is valid because it has already been valid; the past reaches into the value system of the present, and those who live according to this system feel responsible for the very past which is part of their present-day lives. Without this responsibility and the related activities of cultivation, the orienting force of tradition would fade away. A good deal of historians' work is committed to this cultivation—at least the production of knowledge which is an integral part of textbooks in general education.

An elaborated form of this commitment to and responsibility for the past is ancestor worship in archaic societies. Every commitment to origins (as they are to be found in many forms of community) implies a normative relationship to the past which keeps it historically present. Here it is not the value system of the present which gives the past the features of life, but it is the value system of the past which by cultivation gives the features of present-day life order, vitality, and the power of persuasion.

Usually this responsibility is related to achievements of the past which have become an integral part of the present-day life order. Responsibility is realized by affirmation. But there is another possibility of responsibility: the contrary of affirmation. In this case historians feel responsible for activities which negate their own value system and disturb the life order they are part of. Because of the prevailing function of the historian's work—to provide personal and collective identity with stability in the change of time—this responsibility can easily be overlooked and is very often missed in the effective practices of historical culture. But at least in recent times, one can observe a growing importance of this responsibility for the past in its dark and burdening side. One example is favoring the state of victimhood in presenting one's historical identity in the political struggle for power and recognition. Another example is the growing importance of official apologies for crimes or misdeeds one people or nation has done to another in the past. Such an apology has become a part of symbolic foreign and domestic politics.

What kind of historical responsibility can be seen here, and how is it possible to be responsible and to feel responsible for something in the past, which has not been done by those this responsibility is addressed to and who are even willing to take it?

This question leads us into the ethical realm of the historian's work, which is worthy of being considered closely, since it strictly contradicts the widely shared opinion of intellectuals (including, of course, metahistorians) that history is an invention and an ascription. In this opinion, nothing can be ascribed to us and no responsibility for what we ourselves never did and never intended to do can be felt.

But this message of the past delivered to those people of today with whom it is objectively connected may fail. Then we can speak of historical irresponsibility concerning a constitutive commitment of historians related to the normative dimension of past activities. Such an irresponsibility may occur in a twofold way: either the past is considered as an inevitable causality of fate not only for us, who are conditioned by it, but also for those who lived in it; or it is considered as insignificant and meaningless for the evaluation which the historians pursue in the aftermath. In both cases, any ethical qualification or morality of the past as an instance of historical responsibility has been dissolved—into a pure causal relationship or even into a meaningless accumulation of facts. Then any responsible evaluation takes place afterwards and is no more than a retrojection of meaning and significance by the historian. The past as such has become a reified or frozen factuality, and all its significance and importance for the orientation of present-day activities and practices of identity formation is an input from the present into the experience of the past. Historical irresponsibility, then, means that the people of the past have been deprived of their dignity of choice or freedom. The evaluative procedures of historically making sense of the past are done in a pure arbitrariness which completely neglects the fact that the evaluating historians themselves are culturally grounded on a fundament of sense and significance which has been laid under their feet by the people of the past. This irresponsibility can only be overcome when historians give back to the past the feature of chance and contingency, insofar as it conditions the circumstances of present-day life, to be met by responsible actions.

3. Temporal Intersubjectivity as a Ground for Historical Responsibility

Historians are, of course, not responsible for what actually happened. Their responsibility is related to the interpretation of the facts as a necessary condition for their effectiveness in the cultural orientation of present-day activities. In interpreting these facts they work out their critical meaning, and in doing this, they use criteria of historical sense which include values and norms. These values and norms constitute their responsibility. Historical responsibility for the past means that historians' set of norms and values is a part of the past they interpret with them. In this respect the past is a moral predetermination of the intentions of present-day activities. It is an ethical legacy, already inbuilt in the cultural framework of topical life. Historians have to pick it up in order to become aware of the cultural constitution of themselves and their world.

In this respect—of course only partly—the past determines the contemporaneousness of historians. If this is true, historians have to lift themselves to the normative height of this contemporaneousness of the past. And—in the case of negative values—they have to plumb the depths of the failures of the past which belong to the normative legacy of their own time.

There are several possibilities of coming up with this responsibility for the past: (1) by doing justice to the dead, (2) by accepting the normative heritage, the achievements and the offenses, even the crimes of past generations by later ones, and (3) by making oneself an addressee of expectations and threats of the people in the past. The latter possibility is expressed by Walter Benjamin's words: "*Wir sind erwartet worden.* (We have been expected.)"[4] Here the present has to pay off the past.

All three possibilities depend upon a fundamental relationship between the acting and suffering people of the past and the present on the very level where the normative commitments have been effective and their personal and social identity is in the making.

1. This relationship is in question when the demand to do justice to the dead gets a response in the manner of historicism. It says that the people of the past can only be evaluated according to their own value system. This is true in the sense that without referring to their own worldview and self-understanding, an evaluation is unfair; significantly, we would call it "ahistorical." But does this mean that, for example, the Nazi crimes lose their negative evil character since they were committed according to the Nazi ideology? There must be something in between the normative horizon and value system of the past and the present which mediates them in a way that justice to the dead is possible by taking their values into account as well as the values of the historians' time and life order.

History itself as a temporal development from past to present is this mediation. It unifies the different agents into a *temporal intersubjec-*

tivity (or a temporally comprehensive subjectivity) which knits together the two value systems into a normative and obligatory unit along the change of time.

A very simple example of this temporal connection and its normative coherence is the statement "*Nie wieder!* (Never again!)," which combines the past of the Holocaust with the presence of its historical evaluation.[5] The temporal extension of this judgment is implied in the word "again."

There are, of course, many more complex relations of value systems in their temporal intersubjectivity, such as:

> a continuity of validity of the same value system
> a supertemporal validity of general principles
> a genetical extension of change in values, such as a process of universalization or individualization of values[6]

Doing justice to the dead presupposes that two value systems, the one of the judged and that of the judging, are merged into a temporal whole which serves as the instance of responsibility and judgment.

2. Taking over the heritage of the past seems to be no problem as long as it is worthwhile for one's own life order. It is no problem to integrate the actors who have brought about this heritage into a comprehensive temporal "we." If the results of the past belong to the life order of historians, they ascribe the moral quality of these activities to themselves. The self of the offspring merges with the self of their ancestors into the temporal intersubjectivity of a historical identity.

Such an ascription is much more difficult if the heritage has a criminal character. Nevertheless, the term "historical responsibility," often complemented with the term "shame," is applied to such a case.[7]

This is the case for the Germans in respect to the Holocaust. The generations after 1945 can't be made responsible for the misdeeds of their parents and grandparents, but, nevertheless, the sensitive members of these innocent generations have an unclear feeling of responsibility and shame.[8] This application presupposes an intergenerational transference of responsibility, forging the different instances of responsibility for the former and subsequent generations into one entire subjectivity across the gap of guilt and innocence.

3. Benjamin's dictum that we have been expected is the other side of the same coin. Taking over the ethical heritage of the past in its conditioning of the present life order—either worthwhile or burdening—is a way of living the lives of the dead in the aftermath. It means struggling with their guilt, being moved by their hopes and fears and grounded on

their achievements. This transference is not a direct one, of course; it is mediated, broken, influenced, and changed by intervening incidents.

The assumption that it belongs to our historical responsibility to ascribe the hopes and threats, the achievements and failures of past generations to the orientation of our own life order can be expressed as the idea that the future can redeem the past. Concerning the specific work of historians, this idea and this responsibility can be made plausible in an epistemological argumentation: What the past—in Ranke's words— "*eigentlich gewesen* (actually was the case)" depends partly upon our interpretation, and in the light of ensuing times things look quite different from what they did for those who lived with them. "What actually was the case" is a subject matter not of a simple reproduction of facts but of the interpretation of them as well. In this interpretation, the knowledge of what has been the case later on and the value-guided intentions of remembering play an important role. In its core, history has an eschatological feature (beyond religion, simply by epistemology).

But only under the condition of temporal intersubjectivity does this change of the past after it actually happened have a chance of consolidation or even reconciliation. At least this change of later times has to be implied or even invested in the past by the intentions, interpretations, and by the sufferings and actions of those who brought about what was the case. And this implication and investment has to be identified as an anthropological feature in every change of the human world brought about by human activity and suffering.

Here we enter the realm of metahistory, where the ethics of the historian's work discloses the philosophy of history as its own condition of possibility—a philosophy of history in the form of an anthropology of temporal change, in which change and alteration and related differences and diversities stand for the unity of humankind and its internal subjectivity and the value of humanness.

It is not my intention to outline such an anthropology of history. But without at least some consideration of the possibility of temporal intersubjectivity, my whole argument concerning historical responsibility directed to past and future activities and their actors' intentions would lack a theoretical as well as an empirical fundament.

Is this concept of intersubjectivity only a projection, a fictional widening of the scope of one's own identity beyond the limits of birth and death? I would like to ask the question, whether there is something "real" in the temporal connection between the people in past, present, and future or not. Metaphorically one can formulate it in the following way: What kind of human entity corresponds to the temporal inclusion of past and future generations in historical responsibility? Can one speak of something like a time-comprehending mental "body" of human beings?

In order to approach this idea of a "body," I first have to separate the future dimension from it. There is no "real" future in the sense of a reality the past has in its empirical manifestation. The future as a mere extrapolation of pre-given conditions and a closed determination of development in the form of prediction with high probability is—as I have already shown—against the idea of responsibility. A future for which one can be responsible is an intentional value-directed dimension of activity: it can be made plausible with the argument that the projected course of development corresponds with a line of development in the past and with the experience of the power of human agency. One can say that the future dimension of temporal intersubjectivity is the open end of the connection of past and present. It is "real" to the extent that the direction of intended development—foreseen and started by one's activity in the name of unborn generations—corresponds with the "real" connection between past and present with its gravity of experience and real life.

So what is the reality of this connection in historical responsibility? I will answer this question by pointing at three historical examples, then discussing the topical concept of *Erinnerungsgemeinschaft* (community of commemoration), and finally by indicating the use of psychoanalysis to go a step further.

Temporal intersubjectivity as a ground for responsibility, which constitutes its "historical" character, i.e., its temporal character extension into past and future, is an established cultural phenomenon. In archaic societies it is defined by kinship and conceptualized as *ethnos,* which constitutes the responsibility of each member (in social differentiation) for the deeds of every other throughout the course of time. Feuds with a lot of bloodshed are well-known examples of this long-lasting responsibility of the offspring for their ancestors.

Another temporal intersubjectivity taking people of today into responsibility for a value system and its realization or failure is constituted by religious belief. In Christianity, for example, the natural limits of historical identity were transcended into a spiritual sphere of togetherness—*corpus mysticum Christianorum*—which for the believers has been a social reality to which they could sacrifice their lives or were willing to kill others.

My third example is a very modern one: it is nationality. A nation is a "body" of temporal intersubjectivity with an enormous power for identity-building and normative orientation of political life. Romantic philosophy attributed to this body a metaphysical entity, called *Volksgeist* (spirit or mind of the nation). This *Volksgeist* is an invisible equivalent for the archaic natural bonds of kinship, and like most other concepts of temporal intersubjectivity, it follows the logic of ethnocentrism with its power of life and death.[9]

The belief in this metaphysical entity today has faded away among intellectuals. But the concept of a mental body of people comprehending a long chain of generations is still alive, for example, in the usual idea of "the" Chinese or Indian or Western culture or in a more elaborated form of a "cultural deep code."[10] A more preferred successor of *Volksgeist* is the concept of *Erinnerungsgemeinschaft* (community of remembrance). This term confirms the mental or even spiritual character of the body of historical togetherness, but it fences it into the narrow borders of a mental procedure of today—past and future have lost their own weights (one could even speak of their dignity) in favor of a simple and fictional projection or "invention." What is overlooked is the fact that it is not memory which constitutes togetherness, but real incidents with normative importance and cultural power which constitute memory.

It is an open question whether there is a kind of substrate which mentally constitutes responsibility beyond the ethical and moral intentions of human activity and suffering and their instance of judgment and justification. But mental acts of taking over responsibility in an obligatory relationship to former and later generations are at least grounded in an intergenerational relationship of human subjectivity. This is a psychoanalytic commonplace. Psychoanalysis has told us (and metahistory is learning it) that the older generation always has already become a part of the mental organization of the younger one and that the feelings and convictions of commitment and responsibility are always constituted by this presence of the past. Freud himself even speculated on an archaic deed which constituted human culture and is mentally repeated by every generation ever since.[11] C. G. Jung developed a theory of archetypes which not only provides human agency with fundamental and comprehensive drives and patterns of interpretation common to all human beings (thus constituting humankind as a psychic entity) but at the same time even constitutes cultural change and development.[12] Here I see a starting point for gaining a sound concept of intersubjectivity along the lines of the intergenerational connection of culture and mentality. With the help of psychoanalysis it might become possible to get deeper insight into the psychic and spiritual nature of the body, in which historical responsibility has its vital force.[13]

4. Two Ways of Rendering History Irresponsible

Until now I have dealt with "the work of historians" without any specification concerning its cognitive status, and I have taken (a few) examples from various fields of historical culture. But modern historical thinking has got a specific character by the comprehensive process of rationalization: it has brought about historical studies as an academic discipline (or in German: as a *Wissenschaft*) with an elaborated claim of validity. This makes historical responsibility as I have hitherto dealt with it fundamentally problematic.

Rationalization of the historical work can be and has been understood as a change in its logic, which pushes responsibility as an ethical matter of historians' attitude towards the past out of their awareness. "Value freedom" and "objectivity" are the characterizing terms for this new logic. It consists of a cognitive procedure of gaining historical knowledge by a process of methodically ruled research. Historians' responsibility to realize culturally pre-given sets of values and norms in their interpretation and representation of the past is now replaced by their responsibility to follow methodical rules of research which give their work the logical status of intersubjective validity, which often has been called "objectivity." Historical knowledge has to be true despite and beyond different and contradicting standpoints in social and political life and their corresponding value systems and perspectives. Ethical commitment is an extradisciplinary matter of personal decision, social convention, and the cultural attitudes of historians and their audience. The emphasis on rational method points in a completely different direction: to use clearly defined notions, and even theoretical concepts, to relate historical statements in a systematic and checkable way to experience of the past (pre-given in the source materials), and to form historical narratives in an argumentative discourse.

Max Weber has given us a classic description of this new strategy of historical thinking: It remains related to values and norms, since its subject matter is constituted by them, but the scientific approach keeps them in the status of facts to be interpreted by analytical modes of explanation.[14] To speak of historians' responsibility for values and norms and corresponding standpoints and perspectives, including their cultural identity, is irrelevant for the validity of the historical work: "It is and remains true that a methodically correct argumentation in the field of the social sciences has to be accepted even by a Chinese, if it tends to reach its objective. . . ."[15]

In this concept of historical studies, value-commitment is pushed beyond the methodological rules of research. The shaping of the image of the past by values is no longer seen as related to principles of ethical responsibility and normative justification, but simply as grounded in an irrational act of decision. Now the instance of responsibility and justification has become a truth-claim which is logically placed beyond any ethical commitment; it is only a matter of solid information about the past and of an explanation to be checked by experience and logical coherence.

Understanding historical studies in this way changes the role of values and the narrative processes of sense-generation in dealing with the past. The process of transforming the incidents of the past into a sense-bearing and meaningful history for today takes place on the dark side of irrationality. This irrationalization has been confirmed and thus the irresponsibility of methodical rationality been justified by the linguistic turn of metahistory. It has picked up the nonrational and nonmethodical principle of sense generation by narration and explicated its poetic character. The features of history, in which the past becomes an integral part of the cultural orientation of human activity and of forming personal and social identity—these features are seen as a result of a poetic or aesthetic creation of the historian, an "invention" not at all related to an ethical instance of responsibility and justification. Truth-claims of methodical rationality are replaced by or deconstructed in favor of a sound narrative form.

Historical experience is cleansed of any normative power to be recognized in the work of historians. The ethical dimension of historical thinking is dissolved into its narrative form of representation. Objectivity is seen as a veil of epistemological self-deception spread over the only effective procedures of sense generation by exclusively linguistic means on this side of any control by experience and explanatory rationality. Here we have an irresponsibility opposed to the modernizing rationalism which has brought about history as an academic discipline and the professional competence of historians as scholars.

5. Pursuing Responsibility as an Act of Methodical Interpretation

Rationalizing historical studies into irresponsibility doesn't mean that the historian's work stopped fulfilling orientation purposes. On the contrary: it went on doing so as it went on to use narrative forms. What changed was the correspondence between the methodical rationality of treating the experience of the past, on the one hand, and the use of norms and values in shaping the image of the past and fitting it into the cultural framework of practical life.

The historian's work has gained a higher cognitive status of validity concerning its digestion of experience, its time horizon, and its explanatory complexity. On the level of metahistorical analysis, it has won a deeper insight into its linguistic, poetical, and rhetorical means of representing the past as history. The methodical strength of research and its undoubted success in bringing about solid historical knowledge have not yet been mediated with the use of norms and values in shaping the image of the past as history by the mental work of historical consciousness. Neither has this dimension of history been sufficiently recognized in the new awareness of the narrative procedures of historical sense generation. Thus responsibility as a conscious factor of historical work has vanished under the veil of research methodology and the linguistics of historical representation. How can it be brought back into the life of a reflected and knowing pursuit of historical consciousness?

The answer is: hermeneutics as a cognitive procedure. It reaches into the operations of research as well as into narrative procedures of shaping the past as history.[16] It is in the act of understanding where temporal intersubjectivity takes place and responsibility can be realized. In this act the understanding subjectivity merges with the understood subjectivity of past activities. In this merging the internal side of the historical chain between past, present, and (indirectly) future is disclosed. The "body" of time comprehending togetherness, the unity of generations within the difference of their distinguished life, becomes visible. Can this be done in a methodical way?[17]

My answer is yes, but only if we widen the concept of method. In premodern times, method meant the way of forming the knowledge of the past into a sound historical representation. Today we call this the narrative form. "Method" in respect to this form means that it has to be realized by the use of intersubjectively solid rules or principles. These principles can be identified: first, as principles of empirical and theoretical soundness guaranteed by research, and second, as ethical principles of responsibility. Questions of principles are a matter of reason. So I would like to call these principles of the historian's work *theoretical and practical reason*. They coincide with the sense criteria of historical narration. As a matter of treating the experience of the past, they work as rules of understanding. (They include the analytical reconstruction of conditions and circumstances of human activity in the past and their unintended change as well.) As a matter of representation, they work as rhetorical rules of addressing those who need history to come to terms with their world, with themselves, and with the others with whom they live.

It is short-sighted to understand only linguistic tricks of taking people into a normative direction by these rules. As principles of persuasion, they include the rationality of argumentation. To explicate, reflect, and justify the norms and values concerned belongs to this rationality, and if the work of the historian stands for elaborated truth-claims, this reflection should lead to a theoretical conceptualization as a framework of rhetorical argumentation. Research as a methodical treatment of the experience of the past has always been done in such a framework. And it belongs to its methodical rationality to use it in an explicated way by theorization. The same should apply to the framework of rhetorical argumentation. Both frameworks will reveal a large realm of intersection; they will not contradict each other but, on the contrary, they are necessary complements. I suppose that the already mentioned anthropology of the temporal intersubjectivity of human agency in the change of time can serve as such a framework. Here theoretical and practical reason in doing history become visible as two sides of the same coin.

Notes

The epigraph for this chapter is a quotation in Michael Quirin's "Kein Weg außerhalb der sechs Klassiker oder doch? Bemerkungen zum Verhältnis von gelehrter Tätigkeit und persönlicher Wertpraxis bei Cui Shu (1740–1816)," *Monumenta Serica* 42 (1994): 389.

1. Compare Jörn Rüsen, *Historische Vernunft. Grundzüge einer Historik I: Die Grundlagen der Geschichtswissenschaft* (Göttingen: Vanderhöck und Ruprecht, 1983), 85; Rüsen, "Narrativität und Objektivität," in *Metageschichte,* ed. Jörn Stückrath and Jürg Zbinden; Hayden White and Paul Ricoeur, *Dargestellte Wirklichkeit in der europäischen Kultur im Kontext von Husserl, Weber, Auerbach und Gombrich* (Baden-Baden: Nomos, 1997), 303–26.

2. "Es gab Geschichtsschreiber von allen Parteien, aber es gab keine objektiven, unparteiischen, blut- und nervenlosen Historiker mehr. Ein höchst erheblicher Fortschritt! Denn so gewiß der echte Historiker nicht ohne sittliche Gesinnung heranreifen kann, so gewiß gibt es keine echte Gesinnung ohne ein bestimmtes Verhältnis zu den weltbewegenden Fragen der Religion, der Politik, der Nationalität . . . " (Heinrich von Sybel, "Über den Stand der neueren deutschen Geschichtsschreibung," in *Kleine historische Schriften,* 3rd ed. [Stuttgart, 1880], 354).

3. Compare Jörn Rüsen, "Vom Umgang mit den Anderen—zum Stand der Menschenrechte heute," *Internationale Schulbuchforschung* 15 (1993): 167–78.

4. Walter Benjamin, "Über den Begriff der Geschichte," in *Gesammelte Schriften,* vol. 1 (Frankfurt am Main: Suhrkamp, 1991), 694.

5. Compare Theodor W. Adorno, "Erziehung nach Auschwitz," in *Stichworte. Kritische Modelle*, vol. 2 (Frankfurt am Main: Suhrkamp, 1969), 85.

6. Compare Jörn Rüsen, "The Development of Narrative Competence in Historical Learning: An Ontogenetical Hypothesis concerning Moral Consciousness," in *Studies in Metahistory* (Pretoria: Human Science Research Council, 1993), 63–84.

7. Compare Irmgard Wagner, "Arbeiten am Schamdiskurs. Literaturkritik der Nachkriegszeit in psychoanalytischer Perspektive," in *Die dunkle Spur der Vergangenheit. Psychoanalytische Zugänge zur Geschichte (Erinnerung, Geschichte, Identität)*, vol. 2, ed. Jörn Rüsen and Jürgen Straub (Frankfurt am Main: Suhrkamp, 1998), 375–96.

8. Compare Jörn Rüsen, "Holocaust-Memory and Identity-Building—Metahistorical Considerations in the Case of (West-)Germany," in *Disturbing Remains: Memory, History, and Crisis in the Twentieth Century*, ed. Michael S. Roth and Charles G. Salas (Los Angeles: Getty Research Institute, 2001), 252–70.

9. A recent example of this kind of thinking in historical studies is Daniel J. Goldhagen's interpretation of the Holocaust. He vitalized this ethnocentric concept with his idea of a "cultural code" which predestined the political activity of the Germans as a nation to become a collective murderer of the Jews. He combines this concept of German cultural intersubjectivity with a strong ethnocentric (in a broader sense of the word) approach to identity politics: confirming one's own identity by strictly demarcating one's own belonging to the civilized world, differing from the world of the "others" ("the Germans") as a barbaric one.

10. Compare Jörn Rüsen, "Some Theoretical Approaches to Intercultural Comparison of Historiography," *History and Theory*, theme issue 35 (1996): 5–22.

11. Sigmund Freud, *Totem und Tabu* (Vienna, 1913; reprinted Frankfurt am Main: Fischer Taschenbuch Verlag, 1964).

12. Compare C. G. Jung, "Zur Psychologie der Tricksterfigur," in *Archetypen* (Munich: Fischer Taschenbuch Verlag, 1990), 171–72; see also Erich Neumann, *Ursprungsgeschichte des Bewußtseins* (Frankfurt am Main: Fischer Taschenbuch Verlag, 1986).

13. Compare the theoretical discussions of intergenerational relationship by Christian Schneider, Cordelia Stillke, and Bernd Leineweber in *Das Erbe der Napola: Versuch einer Generationengeschichte des Nationalsozialismus* (Hamburg: Hamburger Edition, 1996).

14. Compare Uwe Barrelmeyer, *Geschichtliche Wirklichkeit als Problem. Untersuchungen zu geschichtstheoretischen Begründungen historischen Wissens bei Johan Gustav Droysen, Georg Simmel und Max Weber* (Münster: Lit, 1997).

15. "Es ist und bleibt wahr, daß eine methodisch korrekte wissenschaftliche Beweisführung auf dem Gebiete der Sozialwissenschaften, wenn sie ihren Zweck erreicht haben will, auch von einem Chinesen als richtig anerkannt werden muß" (Max Weber, "Die 'Objektivität' sozialwissenschaftlicher und sozialpolitischer Erkenntnis," in *Gesammelte Aufsätze zur Wissenschaftslehre*, ed. Johannes Winckelmann [Tübingen: Mohr Siebeck, 1968], 46–214); (English translation in Max Weber, *The Methodology of the Social Sciences*, trans. and ed. Edward A. Shils and Henry A. Finch [New York: Free Press, 1949]; partly in Max

Weber, "'Objectivity' in Social Science," in *Sociological Writings* no. 1, 248–59, quotation Winckelmann, 155).

16. The title of Gadamer's essential book, *Wahrheit und Methode* (Hans-Georg Gadamer, *Wahrheit und Methode. Hermeneutik I: Grundzüge einer philosophischen Hermeneutik* [Tübingen: Mohr Siebeck, 1990]), points in this direction (corresponding to the tradition of methodology in the humanities); unfortunately, the whole book negates the *und* and is in favor of *oder.*

17. Compare Jörn Rüsen, *Rekonstruktion der Vergangenheit. Grundzüge einer Historik II: Die Prinzipien der historischen Forschung* (Göttingen: Vandenhöck und Ruprecht, 1986); and Chris Lorenz, *Konstruktion der Vergangenheit. Eine Einführung in die Geschichtstheorie* (Köln: Böhler, 1997).

An Ethically Responsive Hermeneutics of History

Rudolf A. Makkreel

The title of this volume, *The Ethics of History,* raises the issue of how ethical and historical interests intersect. Is there merely a conjunctive relation between them which would mean that we should speak of the ethical *and* the historical, or is there an inner connectedness that justifies the idea of an ethics *of* history? Since "history" can refer either to what has happened in the past or to how we represent these happenings, we may ask how ethics relates not only to the protagonists of history, but also to those who reflect on and interpret history, namely, historians and philosophers of history. Ethical questions pertaining to historical figures include, among others, the extent to which they are responsible for unintended consequences of their deeds. A possible ethical problem for historians is that the need to be selective in their narrative may lead them to present an unfair account of certain figures.

I would like in this essay to focus mostly on the ethical responsibilities of those who interpret history, and that is why I will add hermeneutics to this configuration of ethics and history. Adding a third discipline to the mix obviously complicates matters. However, reflection on the tasks of hermeneutics will show that it is intimately related to both ethics and history, which suggests that we need not settle for the mere conjunctive constellation of hermeneutics, ethics, and history. Hermeneutics as the theory of the limits of interpretation must necessarily undergo normative considerations in determining what parts of a phenomenon to focus on, select, or explicate, and it cannot avoid historical data in framing the overall context or whole within which to evaluate them. Exegesis may content itself with pure textual analysis; hermeneutics must also take into account the conditions that make interpretation possible, some of which are ethical, as we will see.

To lead up to the idea of an ethically responsive hermeneutics of history, I will begin by considering some more traditional philosophical discussions of the relation between ethics and history.

Reflective Interpretations
of the Moral Relevance of History

We often tend to think of the relation between ethics and history as a mere external one, where history is seen as the terrain of political and economic struggle, warfare, shifts of power, and ethics as the more exalted domain of philosophical discourse and theological speculation. Hegel mocked the schoolteacherly moralist who stands above the course of history to draw lessons from the foibles of past leaders. His own more communal ethical approach discerns an internal relation between historical conflict and the advancement of human freedom. Hegel's critique of Kantian moralists is precisely that they judge history and its agents by external standards. We must learn to move beyond an individualistic or pragmatic conception of history as the terrain of conflicting private interests to a philosophical conception of it as a sphere of universal public participation. This approach to history is more in the spirit of an immanent ethos of history.

Hegel's immanent interpretation of objective spirit paved the way for the Marxist materialist reading of history, where neither private morality nor public ethics have much relevance. History as the process where economic class conflicts work themselves out can be viewed in cold scientific terms. But scientific socialism had its background in the early, more humanistic writings of Marx which are informed by anthropological values such as human self-fulfillment.

Philosophers have divided between those who regard values as immanent to life itself and those who regard them as transcendent. Hegel and neo-Kantians such as Windelband and Rickert agree in regarding Kant as the prototype of a philosopher who judges history by transcendent and external moral standards. Yet there is more to be said about Kant. In his essay "Idea for a Universal History with a Cosmopolitan Purpose," he conceives of history as a process whereby it becomes possible for "all the natural capacities" in us "to be developed, completely and in conformity with their end."[1] From this perspective, history is a kind of unfolding of a natural plan. The paradox in this scheme is that among the capacities implanted in us by nature is a reason that can transcend nature. The transcendent demands of reason make it impossible for any human being to fully actualize the plan of nature. Only the human species as a whole can, and that is why history becomes so important for Kant.

Although reason has been implanted in us by nature, it differs from other implanted capacities such as the instincts, in that it doesn't just unfold naturally or by itself. Because nature "gave man reason, and freedom of will based upon reason," Kant argues that "man was not meant to be guided by instinct or equipped and instructed by innate knowledge; on the contrary, he was meant to produce everything out of himself."[2] It is as if nature places us humans on a certain path, but we must get to the end of the path by our own efforts.

Kant's interpretation of history seems to me to be both immanent and transcendent. Once we develop our reason we can go against nature, but that is not Kant's recommendation. He speaks of our rational enlightenment as instituting "a mode of thinking (*Denkungsart*) which can with time transform the primitive natural capacity for moral discrimination into definite practical principles."[3] It is not as if we invent or construct the categorical imperative out of nothing. Its justification may be a priori, but its genesis is based on an innately given natural capacity to make moral distinctions—a capacity which is then gradually refined. Our morality turns out to be rooted, if not grounded, in nature.

Of course, we cannot take moral credit for an action if a mere natural impulse or our schooling leads us to do it, but only if we also have determined it to be the rationally just thing to do. In the final analysis it is the latter determination that must take priority. It is important to recognize, however, that this priority need not have a transcendent source. It is a transcendental priority that we ourselves must establish.

In a later essay, "An Old Question Raised Again: Is the Human Race Constantly Progressing?" Kant explicitly opts for a natural, immanent interpretation of history and rejects a supernatural, transcendent interpretation. His approach to the question of moral progress is to look, not for prophetic supernatural signs about the future course of history, but for divinatory natural signs. One such "historical sign . . . demonstrating the tendency of the human race viewed in its entirety"[4] is the French Revolution. However, it is not the actual events involved in the French Revolution that Kant appeals to as a sign of moral progress. Rather, it is the experience of those like Kant himself who had witnessed the Revolution from a distance and sympathized with its republican ideals. Many of the direct participants had committed moral and legal crimes even if for supposedly good ends. The morality of even those agents who properly advanced the goals of equality and fraternity is difficult to judge. Can they themselves be sure from the Kantian perspective that they acted primarily out of respect for the moral law? The response of spectators is much easier to judge because they are not directly involved. The sympathy aroused in the spectators of the French Revolution may be in part aesthetic—displaying a pleasurable feeling of hope for historical progress—but its source is moral. As Kant writes, their "well-wishing participation . . . can have no other cause than a moral predisposition in the human race."[5] Hannah Arendt's thesis that this spectator response is aesthetically disinterested is not, however, borne out by the following passage where Kant speaks of a "universal yet unselfish participation (*uneigennützige Teilnehmung*) of players on one side against those on the other, even at the risk that their *partisanship* could become very disadvantageous for them if discovered."[6] Kant's sympathetic spectators are indirect participants in the French Revolution and their partisanship is rooted in a moral predisposition.

Once again we see Kant appealing to a "predisposition in the human race" for his interpretation of history. It may seem strange that Kant the transcendental philosopher is locating our moral predisposition in human nature. What needs to be remembered, however, is that Kant is here not speaking of what legitimates morality, but of what motivates it. In the *Critique of Judgment* Kant appeals to the idea of the supersensible to solve the antinomies of reason, but we can never hope to fully cognize this idea. It is for this reason that we cannot interpret the meaning of history and its direction in terms of supernatural signs. To the extent that Kant gives a moral interpretation of history, we should realize that it is not at all a traditional pragmatic interpretation judging the motives and actions of historical individuals. He is concerned with a much more general aim, namely, whether history is moving in the direction of law-governed states and their peaceful coexistence, which provide the optimal formal conditions for individual human beings to fulfill their moral destination. Kant's philosophy of history involves the rational belief that these political goals oriented towards our moral development are possible. But apart from this general orientation, we do not find Kant making moral judgments about individual agents from the standpoint of his philosophy of history. Indeed, we see Kant going so far as to claim in "Perpetual Peace" that "the problem of setting up a state can be solved even by a nation of devils (so long as they possess understanding)."[7] Again, in the "Idea for a Universal History with a Cosmopolitan Purpose," he writes that "nature should thus be thanked for fostering social incompatibility, enviously competitive vanity, and insatiable desires for possession or even power. Without these desires, all man's excellent natural capacities would never be roused to develop."[8] Kant is here adopting a kind of providential stance toward human history that cares more for the progress of civilization than for the moral worth of individuals. Along the same lines, he claims that "the sources of the very unsociableness and continual resistance which cause so many evils, at the same time encourage man towards new exertions of his powers. . . . They would thus seem to indicate the design of a wise creator."[9]

This interplay of the pragmatic and the providential can lead us to be deceived by appearances of moral worth in two ways. Actions that are in accordance with the moral law may nevertheless not be truly moral if they are not based on respect for the law. On the other hand, actions that are motivated by selfish interests may nevertheless produce good results for the human species as a whole. But obviously the conclusion that it is difficult to make moral judgments about individual historical agents does not mean that the philosophical interpretation of history has no moral content. What it does entail is that we are not in a position to make determinant moral judgments, but at best tentative judgments oriented to the ultimate moral goals of humanity. Notice the caution exhibited by Kant in the above passage concerning a design of a wise creator. In the essay "On the Failure of All Attempted Philosophical Theodicies" (1791), Kant warns that he cannot endorse a theodicy that transcends the limits of our cognitive capacities. But this is exactly what traditional *doctrinal* theodicies have done. They have made explanative claims about the future that exceed our capacities. Only an *authentic* moral theodicy that is rooted in our moral compass can orient us towards the future. Here we do not presume to know God's will, but seek to make as much sense of history as is needed to keep moral hope alive.

Taking note of the distinction between determinant and reflective judgments that Kant made in the *Critique of Judgment,* the year before the theodicy essay, a doctrinal theodicy might be called determinant and an authentic theodicy reflective. An authentic theodicy predelineates the trajectory of history by reflecting on the future in light of an exemplary present situation, such as the sympathetic response of spectators of the French Revolution. But it leaves much about the future indeterminate and open. This kind of interpretation is authentic because it is rooted in a natural ethical disposition—it is a rational response but not a purely intellectual one. Kant speaks of Job's response to his predicament as authentic because it manifested an "uprightness of the heart, not the prerogative of insight, the honesty to openly acknowledge one's doubts, and the shunning of feigned convictions."[10]

An authentic response to one's situation is a felt stance that may be theoretically indeterminate, but must be based on a determinate practical consciousness of the demands of the moral law. An authentic interpretation of the meaning of history is reflective insofar as it projects an outcome that cannot be fully known, but determinant in that it is rooted in the certainty about what is morally right. This moral certainty is inscribed in our heart as a natural disposition, according to Kant, and makes the philosophy of history inherently ethical. His interpretive approach to history discloses the intersection of two perspectives: the felt orientation toward a general outcome by reflective judgment (an aesthetics of hope) and the delimited grounding certainty of determinant judgment (an ethics of duty).

This dual dimension in Kant allows us to take a first step in distinguishing hermeneutics from mere interpretation or exegesis. Hermeneutics is not just a theory of interpretation, for there can be rules for interpretation in any discipline. Interpretation becomes necessary, for instance, in the natural sciences when the basis for inductive generalization is insufficient to determine the outcome. In his *Logic,* Kant considers a generalizing induction as one mode of reflective judgment, but there is another analogical mode of reflective judgment that has transcendental significance and orients both aesthetic and teleological judgment. It is through this analogical mode of reflective judgment that interpretation can become hermeneutical.[11] This is because it compares not just the items to be generalized, but also those who do the generalizing. An aesthetic, reflective judgment has transcendental significance, for in asserting an object to be beautiful I am not merely declaring my own pleasure in its formal qualities, but also the hope that the object will be pleasurable to the whole human community. The same conditions that underlie my judgment should make possible a consensus with the judgments of others. Kant's aesthetic judgment provides the basis for a hermeneutical relation of reciprocity in that here understanding strives at the same time to be communicative. This hermeneutical relation can be communicative in a projective sense, as in the case of aesthetic judgment, or in a regressive sense, as in the case of historical judgment, for in this case we attempt to make sense of something that already made sense in some earlier context. Together the aesthetic and historical dimensions of the hermeneutical relation delineate a public sphere of understanding.

We can thus stipulate that interpretation involves a reflective judgment in which a whole is characterized on the basis of partial evidence and is therefore subject to correction or modification. But an interpretation is hermeneutical only if it also involves the negotiation of perspectives among various judging subjects. Thus a historical interpretation is hermeneutical when it mediates the perspective of an interpreting subject with the perspective of some interpreted subject. When historians attempt to understand the significance of a past historical agent such as Robespierre, they should not ignore his original self-understanding, no matter however deficient it may have been. The structure of historical narrative is rooted in this asymmetry of retrospective and contemporary understanding. This asymmetry helps to articulate the very idea of historical development which gives historians an advantage over their historical subjects. From the hermeneutical perspective, this relation between the historian and the historical subject is itself an ethical one and requires the former to weigh how much present-day standards can be imposed on earlier generations.

The Ethical Roots of Hermeneutics

Recent discussions of hermeneutics have focused on the way it helps to preserve the continuity of a tradition by applying procedures that have stood the test of time to present-day problems. But if we go back to nineteenth-century reflections on hermeneutics still oriented by Kant's critical project, we can find the basis for a critical hermeneutics that is more explicitly ethical. This means taking note of the now oft-dismissed hermeneutics of Friedrich Schleiermacher and Wilhelm Dilthey. Schleiermacher expanded hermeneutics from its religious origins to apply it to the understanding of all texts; Dilthey went even further by extending it to all modes of historical objectification.

What accounts for the greatness of Schleiermacher's hermeneutics according to Dilthey is not just that he attempted to universalize its theoretical scope, but also that he grounded it in his practical philosophy. Friedrich Ast had already universalized hermeneutics by noting the circularity of human understanding and by offering a dialectical model for interpretation. According to Ast, the hermeneutical process involves three basic phases: first an anticipated general unity of meaning, then a plurality that relates constituent particulars to each other, and finally a totality in which unity and plurality are fused. However, this purely theoretical model for interpreting texts lacks the historical relevance of Schleiermacher's ethically rooted hermeneutics. For Schleiermacher the task of hermeneutics is not merely a contemplative one where one observes, analyzes, and defines some object or text, but the engaged practical project of discerning what is distinctive about another subject who is trying to communicate something. Two modes of interpretation are required to achieve this: (1) grammatical-historical interpretation that examines language as the medium not only of communication, but also of conceptual thought in general, and (2) psychological interpretation that brings out the distinctive creative and productive intuition that is being communicated. The overall task of this hermeneutical system is summarized by Dilthey as reconciling "the ideational or objective aspect of a given discourse, which belongs to language and analytical thought, and the ineffable individual aspect, which belongs to the realm of free synthesis."[12] Interpretation, according to Schleiermacher, involves a kind of divination that looks both for what is universally valid in the expressions of others and for what is original and distinctive about them. The term "divination" suggests that there is a religious aspect to interpretation, which acknowledges that hermeneutics was originally a religious discipline concerned with making obscure sacred writings accessible to ordinary human beings. That Schleiermacher bases his hermeneutics more broadly in ethics rather than solely in religion accounts for its universal scope. However, the universal ethical component of hermeneutics is complemented by a reverence for the distinctive originality of the individual, which is understood as the divine spark in the human. Dilthey is particularly sensitive to this reverence for the distinctive and aims to revive it in more secular experiential terms.

Dilthey's efforts to refer Schleiermacher's hermeneutics to Kant's ethical perspective on biblical interpretation are interesting because they resist the usual reductive accounts of the latter. Dilthey tries to show that when Kant uses the moral perspective as a critical standard to produce a coherent overall interpretation of the Bible, he is not merely ignoring or dismissing what does not fit. Instead, Kant is praised for acknowledging a symbolical "surplus" of meaning that is not explicable purely in terms of the moral law and that anticipates later views of "the Bible as mythology."[13] According to Dilthey, this mythical aspect of religion is to be understood in intuitive terms and places a limit on universal understanding.

If Dilthey is right in this evaluation of Kant's views on religious interpretation, we would be required to add a third dimension to Kant's conception of authentic interpretation. We already have analyzed the aesthetic reflective dimension of a projective hope and the ethically determinant stance of practical reason. The symbolical surplus of meaning found in religious texts is intuitive, not just in ways that can be shared aesthetically, but in ways that point to something incomparable. If Kant's aesthetics of hope reflects his theory of beauty, the symbolical dimension would seem to reflect his theory of the sublime. Whereas beauty points to what is exemplary for the taste of all, the sublime points to something distinctive, whether this be the ineffability of the religious experience or the originality of genius.

For Schleiermacher and Dilthey, however, it is not just the genius who is a distinctive individual. And if we follow this path, we can regard it as the task of hermeneutics to make possible the understanding that each individual is distinctive. The ethical responsibility of hermeneutics is to recognize that in negotiating the different perspectives of the interpreting subject and the interpreted subject, the integrity of neither may be compromised. This also becomes important in Dilthey's own reflections on hermeneutics in one of his early lectures. He seems in his own way to be articulating the tension between Schleiermacher's two hermeneutical principles of the identical and the distinctive when he opens this lecture with two apparently conflicting claims. He starts by asserting that in the moral world as distinct from the natural world, "I understand everything." But then he goes on to warn that "a person who can transpose himself into anything is not a moral person."[14] Although the moral world is in principle fully understandable, it would be a mistake for anyone to actualize such understanding by identifying with everything. To do so, one would have to give up his or her integrity as a real individual. Just as those successful actors who can transpose themselves into all kinds of characters are often said to have no character themselves, so there is a critical limit to the kinds of human situations we can identify with if we are not to lose our own distinctive inner core.

This limit becomes especially important if one conceives the understanding of others as a mode of congeniality. Reflecting on this Romantic theme of congeniality, Dilthey notes that Schleiermacher had claimed that "if sympathy is the basis of all understanding, then the highest understanding requires love."[15] But if to fully understand others is to be able to love them, then no historian would want to complete their understanding of a Hitler or a Stalin. It is thus necessary to place a moral limit on sympathetic understanding. As we will see later, historical interpretation must be as inclusive as possible in terms of what is to be made accessible, but this does not mean that critical evaluation can be dispensed with. Obviously, historians can not reflect on their subject matter without also making discriminations and disclosing where they themselves stand—reflection about others must eventually become reflexive or self-referential.

Reflexivity and the Need for Ethically Informed Interpretations of History

The reflexive moment of interpretation calls interpreters back to themselves, to where they stand not merely in terms of their place in the world, but also in terms of their stance toward the world. The latter is perhaps most boldly expressed in Luther's defiant cry: "I can do no other, here I stand."[16] If the reflexive is indexical and direct, what then is its relation to reflection, which seems to be indirect, that is, mediated by thought? There are two dangers here: the first is to regard the reflective and reflexive as unrelated, the second is to assume that the difference is merely one of a spelling preference.

I propose to relate the reflective and the reflexive as centrifugal and centripetal moments of awareness. The reflective operates on the level of judgment and compares possibilities of ever wider scope. The reflexive is not necessarily judgmental, but involves a sense of one's own standing in terms of one's actual place and distinctive stance. This polarity of the reflective-reflexive turns out to provide consciousness its ultimate bearings.

In light of this relation between the reflective and the reflexive, it is possible to simplify the formulation of the three moments of an authentic historical interpretation distinguished on the basis of Kant, namely: (1) the aesthetic moment of reflective orientation, (2) the ethical moment of universal grounding, and (3) the religious-symbolical moment of distinctive significance. Now we can redefine the three moments of the hermeneutical relation more simply as (1) reflective, (2) normative, and (3) reflexive. That is, interpretation is hermeneutical if what is understood requires (1) reflection on how we are related to others, (2) evaluation of what universal norms if any bind us, and (3) a reflexive sense of how this affects self-understanding.

Whereas reflection leads consciousness outside itself, the reflexive allows consciousness to relate to itself. According to Dilthey, all consciousness can potentially become an *Innewerden* whereby it becomes aware of itself. This self-givenness of consciousness is what I would call "reflexive awareness" as distinct from explicit self-consciousness. Reflexive awareness does not entail that we are always conscious of ourselves. We are often lost in consciousness and totally absorbed in what is being perceived. But at any moment it is possible to pause and apperceive what is being perceived. Then consciousness becomes reflexive awareness, the awareness that it is aware. This self-relatedness of awareness need not be grounded in any preexisting ego, and may be no more than a felt self-givenness. Yet it is an important condition for our hermeneutical orientation. Through it I register where I stand in understanding without necessarily fully recognizing this in any intellectual or conceptual way. This reflexive mode of characterizing distinctiveness allows us to augment transcendental and religious sources of hermeneutics with one that is immanent to life itself. The aesthetic reflective moment found in Kant could be said to prefigure what is *possible* for authentic interpretation, and the normative moment found in Schleiermacher in effect defines what is minimally *necessary*. The last reflexive moment in turn draws the balance for critical hermeneutics in an *assertorial* mode.

It is appropriate that an authentic hermeneutical interpretation should draw a reflexive balance because authenticity ultimately has to do with self-justification. Originally, authentic interpretations were religious interpretations that determined the meaning of this world in terms of what God actually intended it to be when creating it. Authenticity was initially measured by the authority of the Author's will. An authentic theodicy was one that justified the meaning of human life by seeing the course of history as confirming God's plan. Kant's ethical interpretation of the Bible led him to redefine authenticity from its original sense as a kind of divine pronouncement to a rationally justified human claim. Thus Kant argues that insofar as we humans conceive God rationally as a moral and wise being, it is *"through our reason* itself that God becomes the interpreter of his will as proclaimed in his creation."[17] This anticipates the Hegelian conception of divinity by claiming that it is through the medium of human practical reason that God authentically interprets his own will.

The original sense of authenticity stems from *philological criticism,* which is concerned to test whether a work is really the product of the author that it is reputed to be. Here authenticity literally means *being* an originary source. But for *philosophical critique,* authenticity must involve something more general, namely, *having* an appropriate relation to one's sources.[18] In this expanded sense of authenticity, an author need not be the sole authority. Authoritativeness thus becomes possible for someone who stands in a proper critical relation to his or her sources.

Whereas from a Kantian perspective, an interpretation is authentic if it can be justified by our participation in practical reason, from the existentialist standpoint there can be no such general grounding for authenticity. Although Sartre too derives authenticity from the will, there is no longer any authority associated with it. Authenticity is now purely individual and cannot be attained through a relation to a general source, whether ontological or normative. It involves a projective relation through which I reflect on what I will. Thus Sartre writes: "Pure, authentic reflection is a willing of what I will. It is the refusal to define myself by what I am (Ego) but instead by what I will (that is, by my very undertaking, not insofar as it appears to others—objective—but insofar as it turns its subjective face toward me)."[19] Through authentic reflection I will what I will and that is my self-justification. Directed against traditional ethical philosophers who think in terms of general duties and rights, Sartre writes: "I have no right whatsoever to will what I will, and what I will confers no right upon me, yet I am justified in willing it because I will to will what I will."[20]

Kant's authentic interpretation of history has been explicated as a transcendentally grounded ethical judgment on the course of history that makes room for reflective and reflexive considerations. For Sartre the constellation would have to be different in that he rejects all transcendental grounds. Moreover, the reflective and the reflexive tend to collapse into each other when the only recourse is self-justification. Although history and ethics are said to imply each other they are also shown to be constantly moving apart. Existential ethics is always demanding new beginnings even as history goes on and on. This has the effect of rendering history not just an objective totality, but what Sartre calls a "detotalized totality." Any reflective whole is subject to annihilation through a reflexive return to one's subjective starting point.

Sartre's perspective makes it more difficult to support a hermeneutics of the ethics of history. His existential ethics posits a kind of absolute freedom that constantly threatens to introduce discontinuities into the continuity of history. The goal of hermeneutics, by contrast, is to search for continuities whenever we come upon discontinuities without sacrificing the distinctiveness of individuals.

Another French challenge to hermeneutics can be found in the sociological take on reflexivity as found in the work of Pierre Bourdieu. Whereas Sartre's reflexivity involves a reflective doubling that literally doubles back onto itself and constantly pulls its own projects back to subjective consciousness, Bourdieu's reflexivity provides a "double reading"[21] of our social history so that we objectivize not only its subject matter, but also those who study it. Thus sociology must go on to "objectivize the objectivizing point of view of the sociologist."[22] This "reflexive return on the sociologist"[23] does not return to any subjective starting point, but goes behind the back of the sociologist, as it were. Bourdieu writes, "what must be objectivized is not (only) the individual who does the research in her biographical idiosyncrasy but the position she occupies in academic space and the biases implicated in the view she takes by virtue of being 'off-sides' or 'out of the game.' "[24] It is a reflexive objectivization that is being recommended, one which questions the firsthand objectivizations of the subject.

Whereas Dilthey's reflexivity was self-affirming, and Sartre's self-projecting, Bourdieu is proposing a mode of reflexivity that is self-negating by doubling the subject as an object. From the perspective of sociological reflexivity, Dilthey's and Sartre's conceptions of reflexivity seem too focused on individual subjects. Bourdieu's reflexivity refers individuals back to a "socialized subjectivity" that is to be understood through its *position* in a social field of forces (*habitat*) and by the *dispositions* imparted thereby (*habitus*).[25] Bourdieu assures us that this is not to be conceived fatalistically, for there is a two-way relation involved here: "On one side, it is a relation of *conditioning:* the field structures the habitus. . . . On the other side, it is a relation of knowledge or *cognitive construction*. Habitus contributes to constructing the field as a meaningful world, a world endowed with sense and value."[26]

At times Bourdieu speaks of the habitus as a "transcendental"[27] involving "durable and transposable systems of schemata of *perception, appreciation,* and *action*"[28] which would seem to parallel the contributions respectively of Kant's first, third, and second *Critiques*. But to the extent that our habitus is imparted by the social forces of the habitat our constructive contribution must remain derivative. It is not in any way constitutive and merely produces a "knowledge of a knowledge."[29] Our freedom lies in our capacity to recognize our situatedness so that we will not be surprised by what happens to us, but it seems incapable of initiating change. Addressing the question whether a reflexive sociology "comprises an ethic,"[30] Bourdieu responds affirmatively by saying that he wants to move beyond the "antinomy between the positive and the normative"[31] just as he has already moved beyond that of the subject and the object. But this is a very minimalist ethic. Reflexive sociology rejects any universal, transhistorical values and it provides "a way, not of justifying the world, but of learning to accept a lot of things that might otherwise be unacceptable."[32]

I have explicated Bourdieu's reflexive sociological program because it is meant as a challenge to hermeneutics that should be taken seriously. It is true that any hermeneutics of history must take into account how we are influenced by our social conditions and standing. But this social mode of reflexivity need not have the last word. It is also possible to reflect on these conditions, not merely to learn to accept them "without guilt or suffering,"[33] but to strive to transform them. Bourdieu has a deficient conception of hermeneutics when he dismisses it as pure theory divorced from research, as a "cult of the scriptures of the founding fathers."[34] The value of hermeneutics has always been to contextualize texts and to suggest the possibility of a true reciprocity between our habitat and our habitus. When we reflect on our situation we may be able to cultivate habits that not only conform to our habitat, but also serve to further our own interests. As impersonal as our social habitus may be, why deny that they have been shaped at least in part by the aspirations of past generations? Thus Dilthey and Sartre find it important to retain an idealistic Hegelian element when they understand our social milieu as at least in part an objectified mode of human spirit. The products of earlier generations have transformed our natural habitat and can influence us either blindly from behind or through hermeneutic reflection in a way that helps us to define our own choices in a more informed way. Hermeneutics in this enriched sense can help to frame our ethical tasks by means of reflection on historical possibilities and a reflexive taking stock of our distinctive position.

By asserting an ethical stance not only towards history, but towards hermeneutics as well, it becomes possible to expand the scope of more traditional accounts of history in which its trajectory moves from a state of nature to civilized societies conceived in terms of a variety of communal goods. Adi Ophir argues in "A Plea for a Hermeneutic Ethics" that traditional social theories have placed too much emphasis on how states can contribute to the realization of ideal positive goods and their just distribution.[35] It is even more imperative to be clear about the evils that the state must protect us from—unnecessary suffering, i.e., suffering that cannot be redistributed within a system but falls outside it altogether. There will always be misfits that a system will allow to fall through the cracks—the homeless, the unemployed, the alien, the sick, and the insane. This places a limit to Habermasian regulative procedures in conceiving historical progress. For such regulative procedures to function adequately, everyone must be a member of the community. According to Ophir, it is the task of a hermeneutic ethics to expand our social map to provide access to marginal modes of existence whose suffering has gone unrecognized. "Relying on the social theorists as well as the criminal, the poet as well as the journalist and pamphleteer, hermeneutic ethics should articulate evil in order to expose its conditions of possibility . . . it should deconstruct conceptual schemes that make one deaf to the outcry."[36]

Hermeneutic ethics can have a sensitizing function and thus question certain destructive commonplaces, such as the tendency of those who regulate socioeconomic systems of distribution to justify 4.5 percent unemployment as an acceptable hedge against inflation. By conceiving the main problem as one of preserving wealth, political economy has allowed the unemployed to be "exported"[37] from consideration. The task of a hermeneutic ethics is to extend our awareness beyond the parameters of social scientists. When we apply this idea of a hermeneutic ethics to our understanding of the past, we find that traditional historical accounts, no matter how much they thematized ethical conflicts between dominant agents, also manifested a certain ethical blindness by virtually ignoring the less dominant, the marginal, and the victims of history. The real ethical task of a hermeneutics of history is to be inclusive so that various perspectives can complement each other to bring about a better comprehension of the past. The ethical task of hermeneutics is to "problematize social categories and distinctions, like 'us' and 'them,' internal and external, crisis and everyday life."[38] Historians in the past often focused on those aspects of past civilizations that were most like themselves, but more recently they have begun to compensate for this one-sidedness. A hermeneutic ethics can be a guide to historians as they negotiate the need to select the most important factors in a situation and the duty not to overlook other contributing factors. Here we see constant adjustments being made, which means that such an ethics will be informal and nonjudgmental. It is when we move on to the evaluation of a historical movement as a theme for investigation that ethical considerations become more explicit, formal, and judgmental.

The idea of an ethics of the hermeneutics of history allows ethical concerns to govern both hermeneutics and history, although rather informally in the case of hermeneutics and more formally in the case of history. Another way to distinguish these two is to say that hermeneutics requires an ethics of responsiveness to one's subject matter, whereas history requires an ethics of responsibility. To be responsive is to be open to and reflect on our hermeneutical context even as we learn to reflexively accept our historical situation. To be historically responsible is to attempt to arrive at a more determinate judgment about what has happened in the past and to assess what still needs to be said or done in response.

Notes

1. Immanuel Kant, "Idea for a Universal History with a Cosmopolitan Purpose," trans. H. B. Nisbet, in *Kant's Political Writings,* ed. Hans Reiss (Cambridge: Cambridge University Press, 1991), 42.

2. Kant, "Idea for a Universal History," 43.

3. Ibid., 44–45 (translation altered).

4. Immanuel Kant, *Conflict of the Faculties,* trans. Mary J. Gregor (The Hague: Martinus Nijhoff, 1974), 151; Kant, *Kants gesammelte Schriften,* 29 vols., published by the Prussian Academy of Sciences of Berlin (Berlin: Walter de Gruyter, 1902–83), 7:84; hereafter cited as Ak.

5. Kant, *Conflict of the Faculties,* 153; Ak 7:85.

6. Kant, *Conflict of the Faculties,* 153; Ak 7:85 (emphasis added).

7. Immanuel Kant, "Perpetual Peace," in *Kant's Political Writings,* 112.

8. Kant, "Idea for a Universal History," 45.

9. Ibid.

10. Immanuel Kant, "On the Failure of All Attempted Philosophical Theodicies," in Ak 7:266–67 (my own translation).

11. An explication of the relation between reflective judgment and hermeneutics can be found in Rudolf Makkreel's *Imagination and Interpretation*

in Kant: The Hermeneutical Import of the "Critique of Judgment" (Chicago: University of Chicago Press, 1990), especially 51–66, 111–71.

12. Wilhelm Dilthey, *Hermeneutics and the Study of History,* vol. 4 of *Selected Works,* ed. Rudolf A. Makkreel and Frithjof Rodi (Princeton: Princeton University Press, 1996), 136–37.

13. Dilthey, *Hermeneutics and the Study of History,* 93.

14. Ibid., 229–30.

15. Ibid., 230.

16. Quoted in Robert Stupperich, *Die Reformation in Deutschland,* 3rd ed. (Gütersloh: Mohn, 1988), 178–79.

17. Kant, "Failure of All Attempted Philosophical Theodicies," in Ak 8:264 (emphasis added).

18. Here I apply a distinction made in a quite different context by Joel Rudinow in "Race, Ethnicity, Expressive Authenticity," *Journal of Aesthetics and Art Criticism* 52 (Winter 1994): 129.

19. Jean-Paul Sartre, *Notebooks for an Ethics,* trans. David Pellauer (Chicago: University of Chicago Press, 1992), 479.

20. Sartre, *Notebooks for an Ethics,* 482.

21. Pierre Bourdieu, *An Invitation to Reflexive Sociology* (Chicago: University of Chicago Press, 1992), 7.

22. Bourdieu, *Invitation to Reflexive Sociology,* 69.

23. Ibid., 68.

24. Ibid., 71–72.

25. See Bourdieu, *Invitation to Reflexive Sociology,* 26.

26. Ibid., 127.

27. Ibid., 189.

28. Ibid., 126–27 (emphases added).

29. Ibid., 127.

30. Ibid., 198.

31. Ibid.

32. Ibid., 199.

33. Ibid.

34. Ibid., 162.

35. Adi Ophir, "Beyond Good-Evil: A Plea for a Hermeneutic Ethics," *Philosophical Forum* 21 (Fall-Winter 1989–90): 94–121.

36. Ophir, "Beyond Good-Evil," 113.

37. Ibid., 117.

38. Ibid.

Committed History

Thomas R. Flynn

In the halcyon days of existentialism just after the Second World War, Sartre published a series of essays in his newly founded journal, *Les temps modernes*, in which he introduced the concept of "committed literature (*la littérature engagée*)."[1] To a public accustomed to formalist values and authors keeping a certain distance from their subject (perhaps the heritage of *l'art pour l'art* in the previous century),[2] he proclaimed that literature was a form of praxis, a kind of doing, not of being, and that the writer who did not speak up for the economically exploited and the socially oppressed of the day was a collaborator in such oppression and exploitation.

Specifically, it was prose that could and should be committed. In a distinction that would return to haunt him, Sartre distinguished prose from what he called "poetry" (which included music, sculpture, and painting) and argued that the latter was incapable of engagement beyond itself.[3] If poetry used words as things, prose dealt with the world via significations: "the empire of signs is prose" (*WL* 4). Prose, he insisted, "is in essence utilitarian" (*WL* 11).

And yet he left the door open through which a basic form of moral commitment could enter even "poetic" works when he described the relation between artist and spectator as one of "gift-appeal" between freedoms (*WL* 28 ff.). The artist invites the spectator to re-create the aesthetic object in accord with the directives set forth in the artwork. As elsewhere in Sartre's thought, the appreciation of an artwork is a synthesis of perception and imaginative creation on the part of the spectator and, of course, on the part of the artist as well.[4] Both subject and object are essential to this phenomenon. "The object is essential because it is strictly transcendent, because it imposes its own structures, and because one must wait for it and observe it." This is the "realist" dimension of Sartrean thought that will carry over into his philosophy of history. One must accommodate oneself to the given of a situation under whatever rubric Sartre may define it, whether as "facticity," "being-in-itself," or the "practico-inert." But, he continues, "the subject is also essential because it is required not only to disclose the object (that is, to make *there be* an object [in the phenomenological sense]) but also so that this object might *be* (that is, to produce it). In a word, the reader is conscious of disclosing in creating, of creating by disclosing" (*WL* 26). This dialectic of disclosure and creation, of the given and the taken, remains a feature of Sartrean ontology throughout his career. It dates at least from his admission in *Being and Nothingness* that "situation, the common product of the contingency of the in-itself and of freedom, is an ambiguous phenomenon in which it is impossible for the for-itself to distinguish the contribution of freedom from that of the brute existent."[5] The possibilities and limitations of such a dialectic of *creative disclosure* for a theory of historical writing will emerge as we continue.

Artist and public enter into a "pact" of mutual respect for the freedom of each: the freedom to disclose the world as value and the freedom to re-create that value by adopting the aesthetic attitude. "Though literature is one thing and morality another," Sartre admits, "at the heart of the aesthetic imperative we discern the moral imperative," namely an act of confidence in the freedom of both parties (*WL* 40). What might appear to be the merely formal condition of freedom respecting freedom assumes a substantive character when he concludes:

> The unique point of view from which the author can present the world to those freedoms whose concurrence he wishes to bring about is that of a world to be impregnated always with more freedom. It would be inconceivable that this unleashing of generosity provoked by the writer could be used to authorize an injustice, and that the reader could enjoy his freedom while reading a work which approves or accepts *or simply abstains from condemning* the subjection of man by man. (*WL* 40, emphasis added)

Essential to the concept of committed literature is the answer to the question, "For whom does one write?" In a manner suggestive of subsequent postmodern appeals to "difference," Sartre criticizes the eighteenth-century intellectual who, abstracting from such concrete differences among people as race, religion, or socioeconomic class, writes for "only universal readers" (*WL* 69). This appeal to concrete thinking , specifically to writing from out of and "for one's time" (much as Foucault would write a "history of the present"), Sartre describes here and elsewhere as "historialization."[6] He speaks of the demand of the art of writing conceived "as the particular and timely appeal which, by agreeing to historialize himself, a man launches in regard to all mankind to the men of his time" (*WL* 80; *S* 2:164, translation emended). It is a well-known principle of Sartrean existentialism that to be is to be "in situation." He repeats that maxim here: "Being situated is an essential and necessary characteristic of freedom" (*WL* 101). Accordingly, his criticism of abstract writers stems from their failure to appreciate the reality of "situation," their own and that of their audience. This accounts for their inability to grasp the phenomenon of concrete freedom.

And who was the writer's audience at that time? A generation whose traditional certitudes had been exploded by a world again at war: "Brutally reintegrated into history, we had no choice but to produce a literature of historicity" (*WL* 148). What he has called "historialization" approaches what he calls "commitment" (*l'engagement*) when he writes that "a writer is *engagé* when he tries to be as lucidly and as completely conscious of his involvement as possible; that is to say, when he raises engagement for himself and for others from the level of immediate spontaneity to the level of reflection" (*WL* 49; *S* 2:124). The committed agent like the "authentic" individual seeks the clearest possible understanding of his condition and situation and deliberately chooses in light of that insight. The truth of our ontological condition in Sartre's view is our "diasporic" status, the claim that each of us is not a self (substance) but a presence-to-self, as well as the famous thesis that "existence precedes essence." The truth of my specific situation is the sociohistorical and biographical facticity that defines and limits my possibilities here and now: the fact that Gustave Flaubert, for example, is born to a particular family in a specific region of France at a certain historical period and finds himself having made the previous choices that define his essence up to the point in question. The status of French literary society in Louis-Philippard France will modify the situation of the young Gustave in ways that leave his physician brother untouched. These constitute the "truth" of his situation which the historian attempts to articulate. The "committed" historian will not fail to assess Flaubert's manner of "transcending" his situation in terms of good and bad faith and may even extend those categories to the government and society of the time (as does Sartre in *The Family Idiot*). But, like an effective psychoanalyst, the historian must be as clear as possible about his own situation out of which this investigation is undertaken.

Above all, what history forced upon the writer and his/her public in the France of 1947 was the reality of *evil*—not the soft variety that could be atoned for "because man's heart is unfathomable," nor the kind sustained by the virtue of tolerance proclaimed by "republican humanism," nor even the collectivized evils of a dialectical materialism that makes "Good and Evil vanish conjointly" in historical necessity. What this generation experienced and what its writers were bound to address, Sartre insists, was the concrete synthesis of physical and moral evil in the daily fact of *torture:* "We heard whole blocks screaming and we understood that Evil, fruit of a free and sovereign will, is, like Good, absolute." It is the ontological and moral primacy of this "free and sovereign will" (which he will subsequently denote with the term "praxis") that makes the agent responsible and, in Sartre's hyperbolic discourse, "without excuse." And though another, subsequent age may look back and "see in this suffering and shame one of the paths which led to peace," Sartre insists, "we were not on the side of history already made. We were, as I said, *situated* in such a way that every lived minute seemed to us like something irreducible. Therefore, in spite of ourselves, we came to this conclusion, which will seem shocking to lofty souls, Evil cannot be redeemed" (*WL* 151). Parenthetically, it is not implausible to read the atheistic moralist Sartre's philosophy of history as a theodicy—a failed one, no doubt, but a theodicy nonetheless.

But the committed writer is not merely a negative critic. In fact, he contributes (in 1947) to the "invention" of the new man from the dehumanized creature of Nazi torture. For, Sartre claims, "we are all metaphysical writers." But in his usage, "metaphysics," he hastens to explain, means not "the sterile discussion about abstract notions that have nothing to do with experience," but "a living effort to embrace from within the human condition in its totality" (*WL* 153). That condition comprises both historical contingency and ontological necessity, that is, the de facto necessity of our being free-in-situation and the ambiguous contributions of facticity and transcendence, the given and the taken, to any existential situation. This translates into the following kinds of questions to be addressed by the writer in our time: "How can one make himself a man in, by, and for history? Is there a possible synthesis between our unique and irreducible consciousness and our relativity; that is, between a dogmatic humanism and a perspectivism? What is the relationship between morality and politics? How, considering our deeper intentions, are we to take up the objective consequences of our acts?" Such are the questions that "our age puts to us and which remain *our* questions" (*WL* 154).

Now Sartre hints at what will be his approach to history as a synthesis of the conceptual, the perceptual (perspectival), and the imaginative, when he adds: "We can rigorously attack these problems in the abstract by philosophical reflection. But if we want to live them, to support our thoughts by those fictive and concrete experiences which are what novels are," we must exchange the techniques of a previous generation geared toward a more stable world for existentialist methods that enable us to communicate the experience of contingency and forlornness. He allows that future historians may view us from a distance and illuminate our past by our future and the value of our undertakings by their outcome. "But if it occurred to us to meditate on our future writings, we were convinced that no art could really be ours if it did not restore to the event its brutal freshness, its ambiguity, its unforeseeability, if it did [not] restore to time its actual course, to the world its rich and threatening opacity, and to man his long patience" (*WL* 156). This, as we shall see, is what an existentialist theory of history proposes to achieve as well. It is, in fact, the goal of all "narrative" history, according to Raymond Aron: "What Sartre takes for the essence of the novel—the reader experiences the feeling that the characters are acting freely and, at the same time, that their acts are never arbitrary or haphazard (*quelconques*)—constitutes the final justification of the historical narrative as well."[7]

The concept of the *event* forms a bridge between the historical and the literary in Sartre's work. For it distills that ambiguity of the given/taken that pervades not only his work but, he claims, the human condition itself. "For us too," he admits, "the event appears only through subjectivities. But its transcendence comes from the fact that it exceeds them all because it extends through them and reveals to each person a different aspect of itself and of himself." Thus the technical problem that faces the novelist (and the historian, as we shall see) is "to find an orchestration of consciousnesses which may permit us to render the multidimensionality of the event" (*WL* 158 n). In so doing, he will have carried out his decision "to re-integrate the absolute [consciousness] into history" (*WL* 159). A history that discounts or ignores consciousness (and in Sartre's mind this means intentionality) is abstract and "dead." A living history will recount the experience at issue in any event: the risk and uncertainty, the chance and unpredictability, the emotion and the motivation, and, above all, the concomitant responsibility and all that goes with it of anguish, pride, shame, and the like.

What Sartre proposes is a "literature of praxis," of doing and producing changes, which he opposes to one of "hexis" or habit and consumption (*WL* 201). What such literature effects, above all, is changes in its readers: "We must *historialize* the reader's good will, that is, by the formal agency of our work, we must, if possible, provoke his intention of treating men, in every case, as an absolute end and, by the *subject* of our writing, direct his intention upon his neighbors, that is, upon the oppressed of the world. But we shall have accomplished nothing if, in addition, we do not show him . . . that it is quite impossible to treat concrete men as ends in contemporary society" (*WL* 190; *S* 2:297). Accordingly, Sartre hopes that this literature will be "moral—not moralizing: let it show simply that man is also a value and that the questions he raises are always moral" (*WL* 203). For it is by means of literature that "the collectivity passes to reflection and meditation [and that] it acquires an unhappy conscience, a lopsided image of itself which it constantly tries to modify and improve" (*WL* 205). We can expect that a theory of "committed" history will likewise be moral but not moralizing in character.

In his posthumously published *Notebooks for an Ethics,* written about the same time as *What Is Literature?* Sartre extends this concept of historialization to the situated historian and his era.[8] He speaks of an "antinomy" entailed by the fact that historical figures both express their epoch and transcend it:

> So before manifesting my epoch to itself, before changing it into itself and for itself, I am nothing other than its pure mediation. Except this mediation being consciousness (of) self [that is, implicit self-awareness] and assuming itself saves the epoch and makes it pass over to the absolute [of reflective consciousness]. This is what allows us to resolve the following antinomy: it is said that great men express their epoch and that they surpass it. The truth is: I can express my epoch only in surpassing it (to express is already to surpass the given—and furthermore expression is marginal. One expresses in a surpassing meant to change) but this surpassing is itself part of this epoch—through me my epoch surpasses itself and contains its own surpassing. For my epoch, being a detotalized totality of transcendences, is itself a transcendence. (*NE* 490)

There is no way that I can write from nowhere. To claim to do so, Sartre implies, would be to act in bad faith. Rather, he counsels that I embrace my epoch and give it voice by articulating the issues and concerns of my era "from *my* point of view" (*NE* 486). Far from being a disadvantage, he claims that "uncovering the *concrete* is done by claiming myself as *this* point of view" (*NE* 486; *CM* 503). This is his resolution of the problem of synthesizing "our unique and irreducible consciousness and our relativity" mentioned earlier.

History and Commitment

Although he never employed the expression "committed history," in a footnote to the text in which he introduces "committed literature" and in a manner that underscores the ambiguity of the existential situation, Sartre remarks:

Some day I am going to try to describe that strange reality, History, which is neither objective nor ever quite subjective, in which the dialectic is contested, penetrated, and corroded by a kind of antidialectic, but which is still a dialectic. (*WL* 10 n)

That promise was fulfilled with the *Critique of Dialectical Reason,* the first volume of which appeared thirteen years later (in 1960). In the process, he constructed a social ontology of praxis and the practico-inert (as dialectic and antidialectic respectively) that would allow him to articulate philosophically the convictions of his vintage existentialism, now broadened and "socialized" by his reading of Marx.[9]

Sartre shares with the pragmatists a rejection of knowing as a detached, "spectator's view" of an object. Ingredient in his theory is the refusal to distinguish sharply between theoretical and practical reason, theory and practice, a stance he shares famously with Marx. Already in *Being and Nothingness* (1943) he had insisted: "The viewpoint of pure knowledge is contradictory; there is only the viewpoint of *committed* knowledge. This amounts to saying that knowledge and action are only two abstract aspects of an original, concrete relation" (*BN* 308: EN 370). Our cognition reflects the perspective of our fundamental life-choice, our constitutive relation to the world. But in *Search for a Method,* which serves as the preface to the *Critique,* he insists: "Knowing (*connaissance*) is a moment of praxis, even of a most fundamental [praxis]; . . . it remains the captive of the action which it clarifies, and disappears along with it" (*SM* 92; *CRD* 64, trans. emended).[10] So, although he never worked this out, there will always be an evaluative dimension to human knowing, a link between what counts as knowledge and the life-orienting fundamental project of the existential subject. In this sense, Sartrean history could not fail to be "committed," that is, to be the expression of an existential project.

But "commitment" assumes a more specific meaning when it is attached to "history" just as it did in connection with "literature." And the meanings are not that distinct. Like the committed writer in general, the committed historian has sacrificed the impossible dream of an impartial picture for the (possible?) one of a disalienated society, that is, of History in an evaluative sense. Throughout the *Notebooks for an Ethics,* Sartre distinguishes History from the equivalent of Marx's "pre-history," namely, as an ideal state or goal for human endeavor synonymous with the "city of ends." Consider, for example, the following passage, remarkable in its openness to a plurality of facilitators of "History":

The more the historical agent chooses violence, lies, and Machiavellianism as his means, the more efficacious he is. But the more he contributes to division, the more he puts the accent on detotalization; the more he is himself an object in History and the more he defeats History (whose ideal existence would be in terms of totalization). The true historical agent is less efficacious; but by treating human beings as himself, he tries to make the Spirit exist as a unity, therefore [as] History. It is through him that a History is possible (through the writer, the philosopher, the saint, the prophet, the scholar). (*NE* 21–22; *CM* 27–28)

"History" with a Hegelian "H" is a Sartrean value that comprises the freedom for individuals to engage in "totalizing" praxis without subscribing to a fixed totality, as well as the sustaining respect for other freedoms as ends-in-themselves. He cannot accept Engels's "choice" of one History through a dialectic that appeals to "the viewpoint of totality— classless society," because Engels thereby "transforms a hypothetical determinism into an apodictic necessity" (*NE* 347). Note that the ideal toward which historical commitment strives is not that of an end-terminus to history wherein the conscious yearnings that define the human condition would all be fulfilled. That was the "viewpoint of totality" that he rejects. Rather, it is the nature of an ideal (the Kantian *als ob*) to be just that: an inspiration and a guide to constant striving, as well as a measure against which to assess the status quo. In Sartre's eyes, Engels's totality removes the essentially moral core from history, a criticism he will level against Marxist economism in *Search for a Method*. Rather, the sole "authentic" choice of a meaning-unity-totality for History is the moral one of the career of freedom-fraternity, which thereby furthers the advent of that value that directs the original choice.

At least three theses ingredient in Sartre's theory of committed literature as we have just explained it apply equally to written history as he conceives it. First, Sartre claims that freedom, of which literature is an expression, is both negative and constructive in its critique of unfreedom and alienation. "Our job is cut out for us," he warns. "Insofar as literature is negativity, it will challenge the alienation of work; insofar as it is a creation and an act of surpassing, it will present man as *creative action*. It will go along with him in his effort to pass beyond his present alienation toward a better situation. . . . [We should ask] What are the relationships between ends and means in a society based on violence? The works deriving from such preoccupations . . . will present a world not 'to see" but 'to change'" (*WL* 163–64). So committed literature performs the practical, "moral" function of bringing our alienated condition to critical awareness, while proposing the possibility of change.

The vehicle for this creatively disclosive function on the part of the historian is what Sartre calls "Dialectical Reason." It is a form of rationality that is holistic and processive; it reasons "in-situation." Dialectical reason incorporates the atomic facts and external relations of "analytic reason" as a stage in the larger picture. By introducing "totalizing praxis" as the creative action mentioned above and giving a primacy to individual organic praxis, Sartre underscores the moral stakes in the very choice of such rationality. "At a certain level of abstraction," Sartre writes in the *Critique,* "class conflict expresses itself as a conflict of rationalities" (*CRD* 1, 802). In the inaugural issue of *Les temps modernes,* Sartre explains: "One makes oneself bourgeois by once and for all choosing a certain analytic vision of the world which one tries to impose on all men and which excludes the perception of collective realities" (*S* 2:19). In other words, the issue extends from writing to our very perception of the world. So "at a certain level of abstraction," committed history entails the decision to think and write dialectically.

For a literature of praxis as distinct from one of *hexis* (habit), Sartre seems to believe that the recurrent problem of the subjective/objective and the historical/ethical is on its way to being resolved: "*Praxis* as action in history and on history; that is, as a synthesis of historical relativity and moral and metaphysical absolute, with this hostile and friendly, terrible and derisive world which it reveals to us. There is our subject. . . . It is not a matter of choosing one's age but of choosing oneself within it" (*WL* 165–66). We recognize here the call to "historialization" discussed above. The task of the committed historian is to articulate and respond to the "questions" that his or her age poses. Given the fact and nature of the human condition and our collective and individual situations, that question will always carry a moral tone; specifically, it will address the use and abuse of freedom.

We have observed this moral dimension determine the content of committed literature: the writer cannot ignore the sufferings of the present age. This obligation carries over to the committed historian qua writer. As I suggested, the problem of physical and moral evil belongs every bit as much to the theory of history as to the theory of literature, especially insofar as history *is* literature, the historian a kind of writer, and that literature "committed." The common source of this responsibility, in a Sartrean context, is the ontological freedom of all parties. Though we cannot undertake a rehearsal of his defense of that claim here, it is a basic Sartrean thesis and one that motivates his theory of committed history that no one can be free in a concrete sense unless all are free.[11] It follows that historical writing as a praxis of freedom, when committed, is also a liberating practice, one that addresses its public in the fashion of gift-appeal, that is, in a manner that respects *and fosters* the freedom of all.

If we accept this conceptual and professional overlap, we must explain the differences between history and imaginative literature, given the claim that both are, or, in Sartre's view, ought to be committed. How does literary commitment differ from historical commitment? This is another way of asking how history differs from literature *sans phrase*. The latter issue is one that I can treat only obliquely in responding to the former. So let me proceed by considering several objections to which the foregoing account will certainly give rise.

Incongruities

The concept of committed history, as I have reconstructed it from Sartre's writings, seems liable to at least three fundamental difficulties when faced with more traditional approaches to what Jörn Rüsen calls "metahistory." We might label them respectively epistemological, methodological, and moral.

History as Fiction as History

The epistemological difficulty arises from the proximity of committed history to literature, specifically, to imaginative literature. It is argued that one cannot create a historical narrative out of whole cloth and call it "history" as commonly understood. Historians, the argument continues, devote long hours to carefully examining the relevant documents and other sources in an effort to arrive at the most "likely" story in terms of the current state of scientific knowledge and the more general canons of sense-making in our day. One is free to hypothesize or fantasize as much as one wants, but to call the result "history" and not just fantasy is to ignore the difference between the imaginary and the real. The very criterion of "verisimilitude" attests to this distinction: the story or account must be "likely," that is, it must possess those features that we ascribe to reality and this includes a *link* with the space and time of our present experience. This is what philosophers of history mean by "datability." It is this last condition that disqualifies "histories" of the "once upon a time" variety, no matter how true-to-life their content and unfolding. This is the initial sense in which all history is history *in* the present (radiating from our here and now) as well as history *of* the present (the gap between our experiential time and the past being unbridgeable, as Michel de Certeau has insisted). This is the paradox of historical "knowing."[12]

One possible response to such an objection would be to push the postmodern envelope by appealing to Roland Barthes's concept of the "reality" effect in an attempt to keep the significative within the realm of the linguistic.[13] But Sartre, we have seen, will have none of that. His original conversion to phenomenology was motivated in large part by a desire to overcome idealism and reach the concrete. His disdain for philosophies that dissolve the reality of evil in the soft mucus of transcendental subjectivity, for example, attests to a realist rage that left even Husserl under suspicion early in Sartre's career.[14] As the spectator must accommodate to the objective demands of the artwork, so the historian must respect the exigencies of the historical event and fact. One could call this the "epistemic" moment in both aesthetic and historical experience. "If I say, 'the 18th Brumaire, Bonaparte carried out a coup d'état,' I create the eternal. It is true forever that Napoleon carried out a coup d'état on that day" (NE 108–9). But in both cases, the artwork and the historical event, the epistemic is to be met by a "creative" or "imaginative" moment—the moment where the "given" is modified by the "taken," the moment where the document is interpreted, the monument situated, the trace incorporated into a story line. As Sartre put it early in his career, the historian works at three levels: that of the for-itself (the existential level where the agent experiences the uncertainties of choice in the concrete historical context), that of the in-itself (or the historical fact as a brute given), and that of the for-others (the case under discussion) "where the pure event is recaptured, dated and surpassed by other consciousnesses as being 'of the world.' "[15] It is the ineluctable nature of brute facticality that keeps the story from being entirely imaginative. Phenomenological method, despite its associations with idealism and the occupational hazard of psychologism, affords Sartre the means to respect this hard evidence of the event and the unidirectional advance of time while not subscribing to a crude positivism of atomic facts. It is his early appeal to dialectical relations that shuttles him between object and subject, the given and the taken, in his account of historical situations.

Sartre savors the ambiguity of written history as neither entirely objective nor purely subjective when he describes his multivolume study of the life and times of Flaubert as "a novel that is true (un roman vrai)," the very expression by which Raymond Aron described historical narrative (l'histoire-narration).[16] Elsewhere he explains:

> I would like my study to be read as a novel because it really is the story of an apprenticeship that led to the failure of an entire life. At the same time, I would like it to be read with the idea in mind that it is true, that it

is a *true* novel. Throughout the book, Flaubert is presented the way I imagine him to have been, but since I used what I think were rigorous methods, this should also be Flaubert as he really is, as he really was. At each moment in this study I had to use my imagination.[17]

This is the model of the *creative disclosure* of the committed writer as the instrument of the existentialist historian.

Objectivity

The obvious objection to any theory of "committed" history is that it cannot be "objective," that it sacrifices value-free scientific investigation to partisanship, truth to ideology, history to propaganda. Is the difference between Sartre's study of the life and times of Gustave Flaubert (the five volumes of *The Family Idiot*) and a Fascist account of French history, then, merely a matter of degree?

The concept of objectivity has undergone a curious inversion from Descartes to Kant such that it is now compatible with a kind of relativism that Descartes and the Scholastics before him would have eschewed.[18] Setting aside the issue of the "scientific objectivity" of physical nature, the problem Sartre raises with his "committed" knowledge is that of our knowledge of cultural phenomena, the material of human history. And this is where his concept of situated knowing anticipates the claims of many contemporary authors. Writing from a feminist perspective, for example, Donna Haraway concludes: "So . . . objectivity turns out to be about particular and specific embodiment, and definitely not about the false vision promising transcendence of all limits and responsibility. The moral is simple: *only partial perspective promises objective vision*." In other words, the absolute "view from nowhere" is a mirage. Sounding like an existentialist, she continues: "This is an objective vision that initiates, rather than closes off, the problem of responsibility for the generativity of all visual practices. Partial perspective can be held accountable for both its promising and its destructive monsters. . . . In this way we might become answerable for what we learn how to see"—and, of course, for what we learn how not to see.[19]

The ambiguity of Sartrean "situation" leaves him equally ambivalent on the matter of objectivity. On the one hand, he seems willing to allow a kind of objectivity to the "absolutes" that are human consciousness and the historical event, Napoleon's 18th Brumaire, for example. And his understanding of analytic reason can accommodate a kind of Kantian objectivity (in the sense of intersubjective validity) with regard to the prescientific givens of human experience. On the other hand,

Sartre grows increasingly sensitive to the "interpretive" dimension of cultural phenomena (what I have been calling the dimension of the "taken"). This leads him to a dialectical understanding of the given/taken dichotomy, as when he argues:

> The only theory of knowledge which can be valid today is one which is founded on that truth of micro-physics: the experimenter is a part of the experimental system. This is the only position which allows us to get rid of all idealist illusion, the only one which shows the real man in the midst of the real world. But this realism necessarily implies a reflective point of departure; that is, the *revelation* of a situation is effected in and through the *praxis* which changes it. (*SM* 32n)

The knowing is a pragmatic, the disclosure, creative. But it is disclosure from "my point of view" that must be openly embraced in the praxis that is my way of transcending-revealing my epoch. It seems there is no other responsible choice. "What makes ["objective" historical] truth impossible," Sartre writes in 1948, "is that man makes history and that he makes it anew through the act of knowing it."[20]

Moral Relativism

The ethical objection arises from the question of moral measure. This has been a much-repeated criticism of Sartrean existentialism, namely, that it offers us more a style of acting than a standard for distinguishing good from bad consequences, right from wrong actions. The rather shopworn example is that of the "committed," that is, "authentic" Nazi. This issue is treated in *What Is Literature?* when Sartre categorically denies that one could write "a good novel in praise of anti-Semitism" and challenges anyone to offer a counterexample (see *WL* 41). The same could be said for "committed" history. In this case, it is not a matter of conjuring up events that did not occur or ascribing motives that were absent from an agent's mind. Rather, it comes down to the issues of selection and emphasis: choosing what issues are to be given the greatest attention and what standards of success or failure are to be adopted. And this, Sartre agrees with many theorists, involves judgments of value. To act as if such judgments were not operative or that the evidence "speaks for itself," Sartre implies, is to abdicate responsibility for the creative role the historian plays in voicing (or failing to voice) the cries of the exploited and the oppressed. The power of the historian like that of any writer engenders a corresponding responsibility that the "committed" writer must assume. The ground of this responsibility is the perceived social needs of the time. It would seem to follow that, as with art, there may be degrees of social "commitment" at work in various types of history (though the polemicist Sartre had little use for such nuances). For example, the mere chronological ordering of events, Sartre's second level of historical investigation, would be minimally evaluative but likewise minimally historical. As the sequence thickens into a story, as imagination and reason conspire to fill in the blanks in the "evidence," as we move to Sartre's first and third levels of historical investigation, the responsibility of the historian grows apace. One progresses from the "evident" to "evidence for" and that requires a shift in the question asked. And that shift is value-laden, first in terms of the point one is trying to make and more generally in terms of the issue under discussion (strategy and tactics of argument). That Brutus stabbed Caesar and not the converse seems beyond dispute. But that he thereby defended the Republic or even intended to do so (Sartre's third and first levels respectively) is far more value-laden and controversial. And that this account should be lodged in a larger story of the rise of Roman imperialism, the ambiguities of a slave economy, and the exploitation of the provinces is an imperative of the "committed" historian insofar as these issues are relevant to the "inventing of the human" in our day. In other words, it would be irresponsible to ignore such "lessons" from the past if they were relevant to the social issues of contemporary society.

Does that turn all history into social history the way Sartre graphically shuns "poetic" literature in favor of social service in the famous David Levine cartoon? Not necessarily. There may well be degrees of commitment in the one field as in the other, though Sartre seems bound to reject *historia historiae gratia* the way he rejects *ars artis gratia* and for the same reason: the demands of the victims of evil in our day cannot be responsibly ignored. There is something about the existence of social injustice and oppression that calls for rectification or at least for acknowledgment (if Sartre is correct to insist that "evil cannot be redeemed"). So the horizon of concern, it would seem, must include sensitivity to the social evils that present themselves in the field of investigation, even if those evils are not the sole or even the primary subject of the investigation itself.

What prevents "committed" history from lapsing into propaganda? I would argue on Sartrean terms that it is precisely what kept the anti-Semitic novel from being great literature: respect for the value of freedom on the part of the committed writer as contrasted with its obvious disregard by the others. In other words, "commitment," in Sartre's vocabulary, is not simply enthusiasm or blind loyalty to a cause. It has a content as well as a form. We find an illuminating parallel in another quarter. To quote Donna Haraway one last time, what Thomas Kuhn calls "'passionate detachment' requires more than acknowledged and self-critical partiality. We are also bound to seek perspective from those points of view, which can never be known in advance, which promise something quite extraordinary, that is, knowledge potent for constituting worlds less organized by axes of domination" (*SCW* 192). Such forms of "committed" history are open to counter-examples and contrary evidence precisely because they are not only in-situation but respect the freedom to transcend the givens of that situation toward new possibilities.

Is History a Thing of the Past?

It appears that history *à l'ancienne* is finished. This, at least, seems to be the voice echoing from the canyons of thinkers as disparate as existentialists, structuralists, post-structuralists, and Annales historians. But before we consign traditional history to its own dustbin, let us reflect on the hard recalcitrance of the "eternal" facts to which Sartre refers. The "given" in that dialectic of the given/taken cannot be ignored, the "real" cannot be subsumed in the ideal (not even in the linguistic or the textual ideal). Above all, the harsh blow of physical and moral *evil* has a way of shattering our conceptual and linguistic frameworks, leaving us to rummage through the ruins for meaningful shelter. Those elements of surprise, of chance, of unintended consequence, of injustice and of deliberate malevolence that are so much a part of our individual and collective self-understanding demand that we accommodate the "other" in our experience. There is still room for a mature but chastened history to gather and attempt to tame such phenomena in their very stubbornness. What the existentialist counsels is that the historian personally acknowledge in this undertaking both the possibilities and the limits of his or her "situation" and of ours.

Notes

1. Jean-Paul Sartre, *What Is Literature? and Other Essays* (Cambridge: Harvard University Press, 1998); hereafter cited in text as *WL*.
2. The paradigmatic exception, of course, being Emile Zola's *J'accuse*.
3. He would subsequently modify that claim, citing the commitment of black African poets as an example of using the language of the colonists against colonialism (see Jean-Paul Sartre, *Situations*, 10 vols. [Paris: Gallimard, 1947–76], 3:229–86; hereafter cited in text as *S*).

4. I have developed this thesis in my "The Role of the Image in Sartre's Aesthetic," *Journal of Aesthetics and Art Criticism* 33 (Summer 1975): 431–42.

5. Jean-Paul Sartre, *Being and Nothingness*, trans. Hazel E. Barnes (New York: Philosophical Library, 1956), 488; hereafter cited in text as *BN;* the original, *L'être et le néant* (Paris: Gallimard, 1943), is hereafter cited in text as *EN.*

6. I offer a length survey of his use of this term throughout his major works in my *Sartre, Foucault, and Historical Reason*, vol. 1 of *Toward an Existentialist Theory of History* (Chicago: University of Chicago Press, 1997), 81–87, 283–84n20, and 285nn25 and 27.

7. Raymond Aron, *Introduction to the Philosophy of History: An Essay on the Limits of Historical Objectivity*, 2d ed., rev. and trans. George J. Irwin (Boston: Beacon Press, 1961), 475.

8. Jean-Paul Sartre, *Notebooks for an Ethics*, trans. David Pellauer (Chicago: University of Chicago Press, 1992), hereafter cited in text as *NE;* the original, *Cahiers pour une morale* (Paris: Gallimard, 1983), is cited in text as *CM.*

9. Noting the similarities between Sartre and Julien Benda, whose *The Treason of the Intellectuals* anticipated in some ways Sartre's theory of commitment, Steven Ungar remarks: "The polyvalent affinities with Benda and Marx point to Sartre's problems in establishing *littérature engagée* as a program grounded in a fully articulated philosophy of history. Only later does he accept this polyvalence as a condition rather than a consequence of his notion of commitment" (introduction to Sartre, *What Is Literature?* 10). Although Sartre's interest in the philosophy of history dates back to the late 1930s and the "polyvalence" Ungar mentions is already evident in his concept of "situation" formulated in *Being and Nothingness* (1943), it is true that his theory of committed history served retroactively to ground his well-known theory of committed literature. And while inaugurated at roughly the same time as the literary theory, his corresponding historical theory received far greater elaboration in the succeeding years. As for the affinities with Benda, Sartre would probably qualify as one of Benda's "true 'clerks'"—at least he would were it not for Sartre's ideal of political engagement, pragmatist epistemology, and voluntarist tendencies that help account for the polyvalence of which Ungar speaks (see Julien Benda, *The Treason of the Intellectuals [Clerks]*, trans. Richard Aldington [New York: W. W. Norton, 1928], 159).

10. Jean-Paul Sartre, *Search for a Method*, trans. Hazel E. Barnes (New York: Random House, Vintage Books, 1968), 92; French edition *Critique de la raison dialectique* précédé de *Question de méthode* (Paris: Gallimard, 1960), 64, translation emended; hereafter cited in text as *SM* and *CRD,* respectively.

11. I call this Sartre's "universal freedom conditional" and reconstruct his defense of it in my *Sartre and Marxist Existentialism: The Test Case of Collective Responsibility* (Chicago: University of Chicago Press, 1984), 33–47.

12. Though history is not memory, if our time consciousness, as Husserl has argued, did not "extend" beyond the instant, if the temporal matrix of our experience were not what William James calls the "specious present," our understanding of the very meaning of "past" would be empty. Seeking the past would be like casting for fish by throwing out not only the line but the reel as well.

13. See Roland Barthes, "The Discourse of History" and "The Reality Effect" in his *The Rustle of Language,* trans. Richard Howard (Berkeley and Los Angeles: University of California Press, 1989), 127–48.

14. See Jean-Paul Sartre, "Intentionality: A Fundamental Idea of Husserl's Phenomenology," *Journal of the British Society for Phenomenology* 1, no. 2 (May 1970): 4–5. For his suspicion that Husserl has not overcome the "illusion of immanence" with regard to the nature of the image, see Jean-Paul Sartre, *The Psychology of Imagination,* trans. Bernard Frechtman (New York: Washington Square Press, 1966), 5 and 56.

15. Jean-Paul Sartre, *The War Diaries of Jean-Paul Sartre,* trans. Quintin Hoare (New York: Pantheon, 1984), 300; French edition *Les carnets de la drôle de guerre* (Paris: Gallimard, 1984), 364.

16. Jean-Paul Sartre, "The Itinerary of a Thought," in *Between Existentialism and Marxism* (New York: William Morrow, 1974), 49; also in Sartre, *Situations,* 10:94. On Aron's use, see *Introduction to the Philosophy of History,* 509; and *Magazine littéraire,* no. 198 (September 1983): 37.

17. Jean-Paul Sartre, "On the Idiot of the Family," in *Life/Situations* (New York: Pantheon Books, 1977), 112.

18. See Nicholas Rescher, *Objectivity: The Obligations of Impersonal Reason* (Notre Dame: University of Notre Dame Press, 1997), 215 n2. Consider, for example, Putnam's reference to John Dewey's "objective relativism," in Hillary Putnam, *Reason, Truth and History* (Cambridge: Cambridge University Press, 1981), 162. Of course, Kant would have been scandalized at the relativizing of the transcendental. It was the point of his Copernican revolution to short-circuit such relativizing moves.

19. Donna J. Haraway, *Simians, Cyborgs, and Women: The Reinvention of Nature* (London: Free Association Books, 1991), 190, emphasis mine; hereafter cited in text as *SCW.*

20. Jean-Paul Sartre, *Truth and Existence,* trans. Adrian van den Hoven (Chicago: University of Chicago Press, 1992), 77; French edition *Verité et existence* (Paris: Gallimard, 1989), 133.

History, Fiction, and Human Time: Historical Imagination and Historical Responsibility

David Carr

M ost people think that the historian has a responsibility to tell the truth about the past. This is one of the things that distinguishes the writer of history from the writer of fiction, who is free of this responsibility. But what if we could not in principle separate history from fiction? The historian's responsibility to tell the truth about the past could then in principle not be fulfilled.

How does it stand with the distinction between history and fiction? As literary genres, these are conventionally considered mutually exclusive: history relates events that really happened in the past, fiction portrays imaginary events, that is, things that never happened at all. But this distinction has lately been challenged by some literary theorists and philosophers of history. What reasons could there be for this challenge?

One can see why the distinction might begin to blur if we look first at works considered fictional. Recently some novelists (E. L. Doctorow and Don Delillo are good examples) have crossed conventional genres by attributing fictional activities to real historical characters. But even in quite traditional fiction, the imaginary events of novels (and plays and films) are often set in real places and against the background of real historical events. Thus many works classified as fiction contain elements of history. This is an uncontroversial observation with which few, including the novelists themselves, would disagree.

But it is much more controversial to claim, on the other side, that history unavoidably contains elements of fiction. With this most historians would probably not agree. Is this a justifiable claim? This is the question I want to take up in what follows. If true, this assertion might lead to the conclusion that the distinction between history and fiction could not be maintained, and that the historian's responsibility to tell the truth about the past could not be met. I think this would be a mistake. After examining this claim about history and fiction and placing it in its proper context, I want to show that while it is understandable, it rests on a number of confusions and is, in the end, untenable.

1. Questioning the Distinction between History and Fiction

The view I want to examine is usually associated with French post-structuralism, and is tied in with skeptical views about the capacity of language to refer beyond itself to the real world. But the relevant claims about history and fiction are in fact most fully expressed in recent work of Hayden White (who is not French) and Paul Ricoeur (who is not a post-structuralist). Its origins can be traced to certain theorists of the 1960s, and could be said to follow upon the discovery, or rediscovery, that history is indeed a literary genre.

In an essay on "Historical Discourse,"[1] Roland Barthes, one of the fathers of post-structuralism, evokes the conventional contrast between fictional and historical narrative and asks: "is there in fact any specific difference between factual and imaginary narrative, any linguistic feature by which we may distinguish on the one hand the mode appropriate to the relation of historical events . . . and on the other hand the mode appropriate to the epic, novel or drama?" ("HD" 145). He expresses his negative conclusion when he says that "by its structures alone, without recourse to its content, historical discourse is essentially a product of ideology, or rather of imagination" ("HD" 153).

Louis O. Mink, an American theorist of the same period whose work has influenced both Hayden White and Paul Ricoeur, came to similar conclusions. "Narrative form in history, as in fiction, is an artifice, the product of individual imagination." As such it "cannot defend its claim to truth by any accepted procedure of argument or authentication."[2] Hayden White, asking after "The Value of Narrativity in the Representation of Reality," comes to the conclusion that its value "arises out of a desire to have real events display the coherence, integrity, fullness and closure of an image of life that can only be imaginary."[3]

Paul Ricoeur, in *Time and Narrative,* though he does not try to break down the distinction between history and fiction, speaks of their "intersection" (*entrecroisement*) in the sense that each "avails itself" (*se sert*) of the other.[4] Under the heading of the "fictionalization of history," he argues that history draws on fiction to "refigure" or "restructure" time by introducing narrative contours into the non-narrative time of nature (*TR* 3:265). It is the act of imagining (*se figurer que . . .*) which effects the "reinscription of lived time (time with a present) into purely successive time (time without present)" (*TR* 3:268). Narrative opens us to the "realm of the 'as if'" (*TR* 1:101) through the "mediating role of the imaginary" (*TR* 3:269). This is the fictional element in history.

Besides *fiction* itself, the two other key concepts in these passages are *narrative* and *imagination* (or the imaginary). If we are to evaluate these views about the relation between history and fiction, it will be necessary to examine these concepts and their combination as they figure in the theories in question. It is clear that they stem in some way from an awareness of what we may call, in the broadest sense, the "literary" aspects of historical discourse.

Before we can appreciate the significance of this, however, we must begin by considering the background of these discussions in the philosophy of history. These authors are reacting to a positivistic conception of history that grew up in the nineteenth century and has persisted, in spite of many attacks, well into the twentieth. Prior to the late Enlightenment period, history was generally conceived as a literary genre more valued for the moral and practical lessons it could derive from past events than for its accuracy in portraying them. Only in the nineteenth century, first in Germany, did it acquire the dignity and trappings of an academic discipline or *Wissenschaft,* complete with critical methods for evaluating sources and justifying its assertions. The great Leopold von Ranke was explicitly repudiating the old topos of *historia magistra vitae* when he claimed that the task of history was simply to render the past *wie es eigentlich gewesen*—"as it really was."[5]

From the time it was firmly established in the academy, history has striven to maintain its respectability as a "scientific" discipline (at least in the German sense of *Wissenschaft)* and has played down the literary features of its discourse. With the rise of the so-called social sciences in the twentieth century (sociology, anthropology, economics, "political science"), many historians have coveted a place among them, borrowing quantitative methods and applying them to the past. Here the Annales school in France led the way, beginning in the 1930s. Meanwhile, in philosophy, neopositivism in the form of the "unity of science" movement tried to incorporate history by showing that its mode of explanation is—or rather could and therefore should be—assimilable to that of the natural sciences.[6]

But this attempt to make history into a science has never been very convincing. History has never in practice achieved the kind of "objectivity" and agreement which non-scientists attribute to and envy in the natural sciences. Nor is it completely assimilable to the social sciences, which themselves, in any case, have never quite lived up to their own scientific pretensions. Three interrelated features of historical discourse have been noted by those who disagree with the attempt to integrate history with the sciences: first, history is concerned with individual events and courses of events for their own sake, not in order to derive general laws from them (it is "ideographic" rather than "nomothetic"); second, to account for historical events is often to understand the subjective thoughts, feelings, and intentions of the persons involved rather than to relate external events to their external causes ("understanding" versus "explanation"); and third, to relate sequences of events in this way, with reference to the intentions of the persons involved, is to place them in narrative form, i.e., to tell stories about them.

For the positivists, it is precisely these features which history should suppress or overcome if it is to become genuinely scientific. And to some degree the Annales historians and their followers have tried to meet this demand: by shifting their focus from persons and their actions to deep-structure economic forces and long-term social changes, they produce a discourse which seems far removed from traditional history. But narrative history has never disappeared, and those who counter the positivist view claim that if social and economic history can dispense with traditional storytelling, they still need to be complemented by narrative accounts of conscious agents. Against the demand that history be assimilated to the social or even the natural sciences, many have argued that the narrative discourse of history is a cognitive form in its own right and a mode of explanation perfectly appropriate to our understanding of the human past. Indeed, beginning with Dilthey and the neo-Kantians at the end of the nineteenth century, a strong countercurrent to positivism has refused to accept natural science as the model for disciplines dealing with human events and actions, including even the social sciences, and has insisted on the autonomy and respectability in its own right of knowledge based on an understanding of conscious human agents which presents its results in narrative form.

How do Barthes, Mink, White, and Ricoeur fit into this picture? They arrive on the scene when the narrative form in general, and its role in history in particular, are being intensively discussed. It is this feature of history which is the primary focus of their attention, and White and Ricoeur, at least, believe that history is always essentially narrative even when it tries to divest itself of its storytelling features.[7] At the same time, they still think of history as asserting its capacity to "represent" the past "as it really was," i.e., as claiming "scientific" status for its results. Their view is that this latter claim cannot be upheld in view of the narrative character of historical discourse. Why?

The passages quoted above indicate that for these writers, narrative, as the act of storytelling, is not appropriate to the rendering of real events. A story weaves together human acts and experiences into a coherent whole with (as Aristotle said) a beginning, a middle, and an end. Its criteria are aesthetic, not scientific. It is an imaginative act of creation, not the representation of something already given. Thus narrative is properly at home in fiction, which makes no pretense of portraying the real world. When narrative is employed in a discipline which purports to depict the real it comes under suspicion. If, like history, it deals with a reality which is no longer available—the past—it is doubly suspect. It is suspected of representing things not as they really happened but as they ought to have happened—according to what is thought to make a good story.

Worse still, history may be obeying not aesthetic but political or ideological rules. We all know the uses to which history has been put by authoritarian regimes. In our society, even where it still speaks in the traditional narrative voice, history often clothes itself in the authority of an academic discipline claiming to tell us the truth about the past, to be not fiction but fact. But as narrative, according to these authors, it can no longer uphold this claim. History must, at the very least, be recognized as a mixture of fiction and fact. Indeed, it seems that the whole distinction between fiction and nonfiction must be questioned.

2. A Response

We have outlined the challenge to the distinction between history and fiction. It is time to respond to it.

The first thing to be noted about this challenge is that it places its advocates, perhaps unwittingly, in league with the positivists. Barthes, Mink, et al. emphasize those features of historical discourse which differentiate it from scientific explanation, but instead of defending history as a legitimate cognitive enterprise in its own right, they challenge its cognitive pretensions. For the positivists, history could become a respectable form of knowledge only if it cast off its "literary" garb and replaced storytelling with causal explanations. For the authors we are examining, too, it is the literary form of history which seems to prevent it from making claims to knowledge.

Agreeing with the positivists is not necessarily wrong, as if a theory could be proven guilty by association. The fact is, however, that this agreement derives from some tacit assumptions that these theories share—again, unwittingly—with the positivists, assumptions which can be shown to be dubious at best. These assumptions concern the three basic concepts we found combined in the challenge to the distinction between history and fiction, namely *narrative, imagination,* and *fiction* itself. They could also be described as assumptions about reality, about knowledge, and about what fiction is.

The first assumption concerns the alleged contrast between narrative and the reality it is supposed to depict. Stories portray events which are framed by beginning, middle, and end, which exhibit plot structures, intentions and unintended consequences, reversals of fortune, happy or unhappy endings, and a general coherence in which everything has a place. Reality, we are told, is not like that. In the real world things just happen, one after the other, in ways which may seem random to us but are in fact strictly determined by causal laws. Of course such a reality bears no resemblance to narrative form, and so narrative seems completely inappropriate to it. Storytelling seems to impose on reality a totally alien form. Conceived in this way, purely in terms of its structure, narrative seems necessarily to distort reality.

The second tacit assumption of this view, it seems to me, involves a strong opposition between knowledge and imagination. Knowledge is a passive mirroring of reality. Imagination, by contrast, is active and creative, and if imagination gets involved in the process of knowing, and actively creates something in the process, then the result can no longer qualify as knowledge.

The third assumption is that there is really no difference between fiction and falsehood or falsification. What history, and other humanities too, are being accused of doing is wittingly or unwittingly presenting a false rather than a true picture of the world. This is what is meant by calling them fictional or claiming that they contain fictional elements.

I propose now to examine these three assumptions in reverse order.

1. Fiction and Falsehood

First, the use of the term "fiction" to mean falsehood creates a conceptual confusion which needs to be straightened out before we can decide whether a valid point is being made here. Falsehood can occur as the deliberate assertion of untruth—lying—or simply as error. Fiction, as we usually use that term, is neither, since it makes no claim to represent reality. Novels, plays, and films principally portray persons who never existed and actions and events that never occurred. What is more, this is understood by author and audience alike. What is truly remarkable is that in spite of this knowledge we can get emotionally caught up in the lives of fictitious persons. But no untruth is being told here, at least not in the sense that someone is making a mistake, deceiving or being deceived. In a sense, in fiction the question of truth or falsity simply doesn't arise.

Of course, the question of truth in fiction can be raised on other levels: fiction can be more or less true to life, i.e., lifelike or plausible. If fiction is true in this sense we mean that it portrays things *as they might have been,* even though we know (or assume) that they were not so. At a higher level, fiction can be truthful in the sense that it conveys—perhaps indirectly—truths about the human condition, or about art, or nature, in general. And if fiction can be true in both of these senses, it can be false as well. But neither of these senses of truth and falsity concerns the reality of the persons and events portrayed.

Must we not say that fictional statements are literally false? Some statements *in* fiction, as already noted, are not. (For example, "London is usually foggy in the late fall.") But even an explicitly fictional statement—e.g., "On a Friday afternoon in the late fall of 1887 a tall man crossed London bridge, deeply immersed in his own thoughts"—could, by coincidence, be true. The statement, in that context, would still be fictional. Why? How do we distinguish between fiction and nonfiction? Writing on "The Logical Status of Fictional Discourse," John Searle, after comparing a journalist's account with a novel, concludes that "there is no textual property, syntactical or semantic, that will identify a text as a work of fiction."[8] Instead, the identifying criterion "must of necessity lie in the illocutionary intentions of the author," that is, in what the author is trying to do by writing this text. These intentions are usually indicated outside the text, e.g., by labeling it "a novel," as opposed, for example, to a memoir, an autobiography, or a history. These terms tell the reader how to take the statements made in the text—including whether the question of their truth should arise or not. Searle's point should be compared with that of Roland Barthes, cited on p. 248: when he asks whether there is any "linguistic" feature distinguishing historical from fictional discourse, he is referring to what Searle calls its "syntactical or semantic" properties. Searle agrees with him that there is none. But in typically structuralist fashion, Barthes overlooks those extra-textual features, such as the author's intentions and the whole conventional setting of the text, which for Searle constitute the difference.

The criterion for distinguishing fiction from nonfiction is thus not that the former consists largely of statements that are untrue; rather, it is that these statements are *intended* by the author not to be true, and not to be *taken* as true, and are in fact not so taken by the audience as well. If the character in a novel resembles an actual person, and is even portrayed as doing some things that person did, we might say the novel was "based on a true story," or even that the resemblance was an amazing coincidence. But we wouldn't reclassify it as nonfiction. To take a contrasting case: in a recent historical account of the empress Hsu Tsi of China, the author describes previous accounts of his subject as getting things so wrong, even to the point of attributing to the empress the actions of another person altogether, that we would have to conclude that there *was* no one person at all who did the things described.[9] Would we then move these accounts to the fiction section of the library? Of course not: they remain history, even if it is extremely bad history.

When the claim is made that history contains fiction, or elements of fiction, or more broadly that it calls into question the boundary between history and fiction, surely this does not mean that historians are making statements they and their audience *know* to be about things that never happened, or whose truth or falsity are not important. Historians certainly intend and claim to speak of real persons and events and to tell us true things about them. If the first assumption is even to make sense, the point must be that, knowingly or unknowingly, historians are doing something like what fiction writers do—imagining things *as they might have been*, perhaps, rather than representing them as they were—and that because of this the truth of what they say is somehow questionable. The claim is not just that their results *are* untrue—something that would have to be shown in each case—but that they *must* be untrue or that their truth or falsity is in principle undecidable, apparently because of whatever the historian shares with the novelist.

2. Knowledge and Imagination

And what is that? Presumably the capacity to imagine. Thus if our interpretation of the first assumption is correct, it makes sense only if the second assumption is true. The capacity to imagine is opposed to knowledge as if they were mutually exclusive. Knowledge as "representation" is thought to be the passive reflection of the real, simply registering or reporting what is there. But this is a naive and simplistic conception of knowledge which ignores some of the best insights of modern philosophy. Since Kant we have recognized that knowledge is anything but passive, its result not merely a copy of external reality. Rather, it is an activity which calls into play many "faculties," including sense, judgment, reason, and, very importantly, the capacity to conceive of things being other than they actually are. It may be thought that anything that is the object of the *imagination* must be *imaginary* in the sense of nonexistent. But this is only part of what we mean by imagination. In the broadest sense, imagination is best described as the capacity to envision what is not directly present to the senses. In this sense we can imagine things that *were,* or *will be,* or *exist elsewhere,* as well as things that don't exist at all.[10]

Is fiction a product of the imagination? It certainly is. But so, it could be said, is physics; and so is history—though none of these is a product of the imagination *only.* If the historian draws on the imagination, it is in order to speak about how things *were,* not to conjure up something imaginary. The difference between knowledge and fiction is not that the one uses imagination and the other doesn't. It is rather that in one case imagination, in combination with other capacities, is marshaled in the service of producing assertions, theories, predictions, and in some cases narratives, about how the world really is, or will be, or was; and in the other case it is used to produce stories about characters, events, actions, and even worlds that never were.

Thus the second assumption, like the first, dissolves upon closer examination. Historians use their imagination—along with other capacities, of course, like sense, judgment, and reason—not to produce fiction but to make claims about the real world—in particular, to produce narrative accounts of how things really happened. So what is it about these accounts that renders them "fictional," in the sense of being untrue, i.e., that prevents them from counting as genuine knowledge? This brings us to the third assumption, which is that narrative can *never* give us an account of how things really happened, because "the way things really happen" is utterly at odds with the narrative form.

3. Narrative and Reality

This view seems to me an expression of the one of the deepest assumptions our authors share with the positivists. This is the idea that in order to qualify as real the world must be utterly devoid of those intentional, meaningful, and narrative features we attribute to it when we tell stories about it. Reality must be a meaningless sequence of external events, and time must be nothing but a series of nows, and anything else we attribute to it is at best mere fantasy or wishful thinking, at worst imposition or distortion. What is somehow forgotten is that history is not about the physical but about the human world. That is, it is principally about persons—and groups of persons—and about their actions. But if these are to be understood they must be related to the intentions, hopes, fears, expectations, plans, successes, and failures of those who act.

It can be argued (and I have argued at length elsewhere)[11] that the human world manifests a concrete version of the narrative form in the very structure of action itself. The means-end structure of action is a prototype of the beginning-middle-end structure of narrative, and it can be said that human beings live their lives by formulating and acting out stories that they implicitly tell both to themselves and others. Indeed, in this realm time itself is human, narratively shaped by beings who live their lives, not from moment to moment, but by remembering what was and projecting what will be. Although it is assuredly embedded in the physical world and is datable, human time is not that of the numbered sequence (t_1, t_2, etc.) or even the time of before and after, earlier and later, but the time of past and future as experienced from the vantage point of the present by conscious, intentional agents.

If this is so, then the narrative form inheres not only in the telling of history but also in what is told about. Those who argue against this view often point out that life is often messy and disorganized, that it does not have the "coherence, integrity, fullness and closure" (Hayden White) of fictional stories: things go wrong, randomness intrudes, actions have unintended consequences, etc. But they overlook two things: one is that this is the very reality the best fictional stories are about; only the worst detective stories and Harlequin romances have the kind of boringly predictable "closure" White has in mind. Second, life can be messy and disorganized *because* we live it according to plans, projects, and "stories" that often go wrong—that is, because it has, overall, the narrative and temporal structure I have tried to describe.

But the real opposition to the view I have outlined stems, I believe, from the belief that the only true "reality" is physical reality. This is, as I have said, the basis of positivist metaphysics, but it is also one of the deeply rooted prejudices of our age. Somehow the world of physical objects in space and time, the world of what is externally observable, describable, and explainable in terms of mechanical pushes and pulls, and predictable by means of general laws, counts as reality in the primary sense. Everything else—human experience, social relations, cultural and aesthetic entities—is secondary, epiphenomenal, and "merely subjective"; and the only true explanation of it is going to trace it back to the physical world.

Now there may be a good metaphysical argument for the primacy of physical reality and even for the primacy of physical explanation—though I have never seen either. But such arguments would not be relevant to the point I am trying to make. As conscious human beings acting in the world, the intentions, meanings, cultural structures, and values, not only of ourselves but also of others, are as real as anything we know. They are real in a sense that can never be touched by metaphysical speculations: that is, they *matter.* Even the physical world enters into this picture, but not as a merely objective realm. It is the constant background and theater of operations for human actions, and it comes laden with economic, cultural, and aesthetic value for the persons and communities that live in it. This is nature not "in itself," but nature as experienced, inhabited, cultivated, explored, and exploited by human beings and societies.

Whether it is real or unreal, more real or less real in some abstract metaphysical sense, it is this *humanly real* world that history, and other forms of truth-telling or nonfictional narrative, like biography and autobiography, are about. Narrative is appropriate to it because the structures of narrative are already inherent in human reality. The historian does not have to "reinscribe" lived time into natural time by the act of narration, as Ricoeur says; lived time is already there before the historian comes along. To tell stories about the human past is not to impose an alien structure on it but is continuous with the very activity that makes up the human past.

This is not to say that every historical narrative is true, or that some narratives are not better than others. It is simply to deny that narratives are incapable of being true *just because* they are narratives. Likewise, when we spoke of the role of imagination, we were not claiming that every use of the imagination in history is legitimate; only that not everything produced by the imagination need be merely imaginary. I will not try to answer in a definitive way the question of how we evaluate narrative accounts in history and how we distinguish the better from the worse. But we shall see that it involves more than just checking sources.

3. An Example

It may be helpful at this point to test some of the things we have been saying by considering an example of historical discourse. I choose quite deliberately a passage that some historians may regard as an extreme case. In his recently published *Landscape and Memory,* Simon Schama describes Sir Walter Ralegh planning his Guiana expedition in Durham House, London:

> From his lofty vantage point on the north bank, where the Thames made a snaking, southern bend, Ralegh could survey the progress of empire: the dipping oars of the queen's state barge as it made its way from Greenwich to Sheen; bunched masts of pinnaces and carracks swaying at their berths; broad-sterned Dutch fly boats bouncing on the dock-tide; wherries taking passengers to the Southwark theaters; the whole humming

business of the black river. But through the miry soup of refuse that slapped at his walls, Ralegh could see the waters of the Orinoco, as seductively nacreous as the pearl he wore on his ear.[12]

There are several things we must note about this passage: the first is that it is obviously not fictional in any conventional sense of the word. It is presented *as* part of a historical account which is clearly marked as such in all the conventional ways. What this indicates to us is that the author intends in this particular passage to portray something that really happened, not some imaginary scene.

Second, there are core features of this passage that can obviously be backed up by historical evidence: Ralegh's presence in Durham House during the planning of his expedition; the view of the Thames available from that place; the boats that could be seen on the Thames at that time, together with their descriptions; even the pearl in Ralegh's ear. (I have no idea whether there actually *is* evidence for any of these things, or for that matter against them; it is just that they are susceptible of confirmation by reference to sources.)

Third, the imagination of the author is clearly at work here, not in producing an imaginary scene, but in bringing together these various elements to portray something real. Schama doesn't even say Ralegh *did* but only that he *could* survey the "whole humming business of the black river" visible from his vantage point. Of course, as a sailor Ralegh would hardly have overlooked it. Schama goes further, though, when he says that what Ralegh could see in this busy scene was "the progress of empire." At the very least this tells us that the actual scene *did* symbolize the progress of empire, whether Ralegh saw it that way or not.

Of course, Schama is suggesting that he *did* see it that way; and further, in the climax of the passage, that Ralegh not only could but *did* see, "through the miry soup" of the Thames before him, the waters of the Orinoco. What has Schama done here? He has described Ralegh's view of things, his state of mind, *as it may have been* during a particular time. Earlier we described "true to life" fiction as portraying events *as they might have been*. Is Schama not doing something close to that? Perhaps, but again Schama's intention as a historian is to portray the real; and what is more, the whole passage could be seen as *building a case* for saying Ralegh actually did see things this way. It is not a conclusive case, needless to say, but it does give us reasons for accepting Schama's descriptions as veridical. It provides a form of evidence, if you will—different from reference to sources, but evidence still—for believing his account.

The persuasiveness of this passage has another source, and that is the larger narrative of which it is a part. The passage itself describes only Ralegh's activity at Durham House. But what he is doing there is planning an expedition, so it is understandable that his thoughts should be on his goal. Here Ralegh is presented as a human being in the human world. His physical surroundings are not just impinging on him causally; they have significance for him, a significance which is derived from their relation to a long-term project in which he is engaged. In this sense they are embedded in a story which Ralegh is projecting before himself and which he will proceed to act out. This is the primary narrative which shapes the human time of Ralegh's own past, present, and future. It is this first-order narrative that Schama's second-order narrative is about.

4. Conclusion

I hope the foregoing reflections support the conclusion that the distinction between fiction and history, in its commonsense form, is a valid one and must be maintained. I have tried to show that current attempts to fudge this distinction rest on a number of confusions and untenable tacit assumptions concerning the nature of fiction, the role of imagination in knowledge, and the relation between narrative and historical reality. These confusions and assumptions derive, we have seen, from a consideration of the "literary" character of historical discourse and from certain dubious metaphysical doctrines, ultimately derived from or shared with positivism, about the nature of reality.

Of course, history is a literary genre, and as such it shares many features with fiction, notably the narrative form. Furthermore, like writers of fiction, historians use their imagination. But it does not follow from this that history merges with fiction or that these elements *eo ipso* introduce falsehood into historical knowledge or make it impossible to distinguish the true from the false. Historians avail themselves of these elements precisely *in order* to tell the truth about human events in the past. Whether they actually succeed in doing so in any particular case is another matter, to be decided by appeal to evidence, to considerations of coherence, to psychological insight or theory, and many other things. But their capacity for success cannot be ruled out simply on the grounds that their inquiry makes use of imagination and narrative form. Far from standing in the way of historical truth, these are appropriate means for achieving it. The reason for this, I have tried to argue here, is that they derive from the very structure of historical reality and from the nature of human time.[13]

Notes

1. Roland Barthes, "Historical Discourse" in *Introduction to Structuralism,* ed. Michael Lane (New York: Basic Books, 1970), 145–55; hereafter cited in text as "HD."

2. Louis O. Mink, "Narrative Form as a Cognitive Instrument," in his posthumous collection *Historical Understanding,* ed. B. Fay, E. Golob, and R. Vann (Ithaca: Cornell University Press, 1987), 199.

3. Hayden White, "The Value of Narrativity in the Representation of Reality," in *The Content of the Form* (Baltimore: Johns Hopkins University Press, 1987), 24.

4. Because of Ricoeur's choice of words, I am quoting from the original French with my own translations: Paul Ricoeur, *Temps et récit,* vols. 1–3 (Paris: Seuil, 1983–85).

5. On the growth of the "historical school" in Germany, see Reinhard Kosellek, "Historia Magistra Vitae" (pp. 31–32) and other essays in *Futures Past: On the Semantics of Historical Time,* trans. K. Tribe (Cambridge: MIT Press, 1985); also Jörn Rüsen, *Konfigurationen des Historismus* (Frankfurt am Main: Suhrkamp, 1993).

6. The locus classicus is Carl G. Hempel's "The Function of General Laws in History," in *The Journal of Philosophy* 39 (1942).

7. In *Time and Narrative* (1:290 ff.) Ricoeur attempts to show the implicit narrative elements of what is often considered the masterpiece of Annales non-narrative history, Fernand Braudel's *The Mediterranean and the Mediterranean World in the Age of Philip II.*

8. John Searle, "The Logical Status of Fictional Discourse," in *Expression and Meaning: Studies in the Theory of Speech Acts* (Cambridge: Cambridge University Press, 1979), 65.

9. Sterling Seagrave, *Dragon Lady: The Life and Legend of the Last Empress of China* (New York: Vintage Books, 1992), 11–17.

10. See Jean-Paul Sartre, *The Psychology of Imagination* (New York: Citadel Press, 1963), 16.

11. See my *Time, Narrative and History* (Bloomington: Indiana University Press, 1986), especially chapters 1–3.

12. Simon Schama, *Landscape and Memory* (New York: Alfred A. Knopf, 1995), 311. My attention was first called to this passage by Keith Thomas's review, "The Big Cake," *New York Review of Books* 42, no. 14 (September 21, 1995): 8.

13. A shorter, earlier version of this paper appeared under the title "History, Fiction, and the Limits of Understanding," in *Grenzen des Verstehens: Philosophie und humanwissenschaftliche Perspektiven,* ed. G. Kuehne-Bertram and G. Scholtz (Göttingen: Vandenhoeck und Ruprecht, 2002), 247–55.

Notes on Contributors

F. R. Ankersmit is professor of intellectual history and historical theory at Groningen University (The Netherlands). He has published widely in the fields of historical theory and political philosophy, and his books include *Narrative Logic; History and Tropology; Aesthetic Politics;* and *Historical Representation.* His new book, entitled *Historical Experience,* will be published by Stanford University Press.

John D. Caputo is Thomas J. Watson Professor of Religion and Humanities at Syracuse University and David R. Cook Professor Emeritus of Philosophy at Villanova University, where he taught for 36 years until 2004. His most recent books are *On Religion* and *More Radical Hermeneutics: On Not Knowing Who We Are.* He is also the editor of *Blackwell Readings in Continental Philosophy: The Religious,* coeditor of *Questioning God* and *God, the Gift and Postmodernism,* and the author of *Deconstruction in a Nutshell: A Conversation with Jacques Derrida* and *The Prayers and Tears of Jacques Derrida: Religion without Religion.* He is currently preparing a book entitled *Sacred Anarchy: Deconstruction and the Kingdom of God.*

David Carr is Charles Howard Candler Professor of Philosophy at Emory University. He has translated and edited Husserl's *The Crisis of European Sciences and Transcendental Phenomenology* and is the author of *Phenomenology and the Problem of History: A Study of Husserl's Transcendental Philosophy; Time, Narrative, and History; Interpreting Husserl: Comparative and Critical Studies;* and *The Paradox of Subjectivity: The Self in the Transcendental Tradition.*

Joan Copjec is the author of *Imagine There's No Woman: Ethics and Sublimation* and *Read My Desire: Lacan Against the Historicists,* as well as the editor of several books, including *Supposing the Subject; Radical Evil;* and *Giving Ground: The Politics of Propinquity.* She teaches in the English, Comparative Literature, and Media Study departments at the University at Buffalo, where she is also director of the Center for the Study of Psychoanalysis and Culture.

Arthur C. Danto is Johnsonian Professor Emeritus of Philosophy at Columbia University, as well as art critic of *The Nation*. He is the author of *Analytical Philosophy of History* and other works in analytical philosophy; and *The Transfiguration of the Commonplace; After the End of Art;* and *The Abuse of Beauty* in the philosophy of art. He has also won numerous prizes for his art criticism and his writings on photography.

Thomas R. Flynn is Samuel Candler Dobbs Professor of Philosophy at Emory University. He is the author of *Sartre and Marxist Existentialism: The Test Case of Collective Responsibility* and *Sartre, Foucault, and Historical Reason*, vol. 1, *Toward an Existentialist Theory of History*, and vol. 2, *A Post-Structuralist Mapping of History*. He is also coeditor with Dalia Judovitz of *Dialectic and Narrative*.

Jean-François Lyotard until his death in 1998 was one of the leading "Continental" philosophers of his day. Among his numerous books, the best known in English translation are *The Libidinal Economy; Just Gaming* (with J. L. Thebaud); *The Postmodern Condition; The Differend: Phrases in Dispute; Heidegger and "the jews";* and *Inhuman: Reflections on Time*. A terminal illness prevented his attending the conference at which his contribution was presented.

Rudolf A. Makkreel is Charles Howard Candler Professor and Chair of Philosophy at Emory University. He is the author of *Dilthey: Philosopher of the Human Studies* and *Imagination and Interpretation in Kant: The Hermeneutical Import of the "Critique of Judgment."* He is the coeditor of Dilthey's *Selected Works* (vol. 1, *Introduction to the Human Sciences;* vol. 3, *The Formation of the Historical World in the Human Sciences;* vol. 4, *Hermeneutics and the Study of History;* vol. 5, *Poetry and Experience*). He was also the editor of the *Journal of the History of Philosophy* from 1983 to 1998.

Joseph Margolis is Laura H. Carnell Professor of Philosophy at Temple University. He is the author of more than thirty books, including *The Flux of History and the Flux of Science; Interpretation Radical but Not Unruly: The New Puzzle of the Arts and History; Historied Thought, Constructed World: A Conceptual Primer for the Turn of the Millennium; Selves and Other Texts: The Case for Cultural Realism;* and *Reinventing Pragmatism: American Philosophy at the End of the Twentieth Century*.

Allan Megill is professor of history at the University of Virginia. He is a historian of ideas with a particular interest in modern European thought and in the philosophy of history. He is the author of *Prophets of Extremity: Nietzsche, Heidegger, Foucault, Derrida* and *Karl Marx: The Burden of Reason*. He is the coeditor (with John S. Nelson and Donald N. McCloskey) of *The Rhetoric of the Human Sciences: Language and Argument* *in Scholarship and Public Affairs* and editor of *Rethinking Objectivity*. He is currently working on the theme "historical thinking."

Jörn Rüsen is president of the Institute for Advanced Study in the Humanities in Essen (Germany) and professor of general history and historical culture at the University of Witten/Herdecke. Among his many books are *Historische Vernunft; Zeit und Sinn; Studies in Metahistory; Geschichte im Kulturprozeß;* and *Kann Gestern besser Werden? Essays über das Bedenken der Geschichte.*

Edith Wyschogrod is J. Newton Rayzor Professor of Philosophy emerita at Rice University. Her books include *An Ethics of Remembering: History, Heterology, and the Nameless Others; Saints and Postmodernism: Revisioning Moral Philosophy;* and *Spirit in Ashes: Hegel, Heidegger, and Man-Made Mass Death.* She has written extensively on the philosophy of Emmanuel Levinas and is currently working on theories of altruism.